HELPING THE RETARDED CHILD

HELPING THE RETARDED CHILD

Sol Nichtern, M.D.

GROSSET & DUNLAP
Publishers New York

PUBLISHED SIMULTANEOUSLY IN CANADA

LIBRARY OF CONGRESS CATALOG NUMBER: 73-11395
ISBN 0-448-01305-3

FIRST PRINTING

PRINTED IN THE UNITED STATES OF AMERICA

To the fulfillment of life through
conception, childbearing, and child-rearing

Contents

Foreword

Dr. Nichtern is clearly among those of us who consider ourselves advocates of children. In this book, he has demonstrated his deep concern for *all* children while focusing on one of the most important human problems — retardation. There is an extensive body of literature available to the professional and the lay reader concerning retardation, but, until now, nothing has been written that approaches the problem with such a practical yet scholarly orientation. Dr. Nichtern presents a distillation of this vast body of information concerning factors causing retardation and very sound and innovative ideas about the management of the sequelae of the problem. Throughout the book one will notice that Dr. Nichtern never refers to "mental retardation," but uses the term "retardation" alone. He believes that the term "mental retardation" is irrelevant to the proper care of the retarded. He regards retardation as a variant of normal human development.

Many professionals in the mental health field tend to sidestep the area of retardation, feeling that there is little to be done about it other than offer custodial care to the retarded. Dr. Nichtern's presentation of the problem would change that view for anyone who reads this book. He presents a realistic yet positive approach that can not only alter traditional methods of dealing with the retarded, but can change social attitudes sufficiently to provide greater emotional fulfillment in the lives of the patients and their families.

It is clearly understandable why Dr. Nichtern presents his ideas in such a careful and scholarly manner; his experience as a pediatrician and child psychiatrist provides for this capacity. He writes for the professional as well as the lay person interested in a comprehensive body of knowledge from which he can make his own judgments and decisions toward helping the retarded child. While presenting his unique approach to the care and treatment of the retarded, Dr. Nichtern provides a clear description of normal behavioral development from the earliest through the later stages. This gives the reader a longitudinal view of normal development simultaneously with developmental and social problems of the retarded.

His recognition of the magnitude of the problem allows him to include information ranging over a broad spectrum. Dr. Nichtern's path leads from government actions on aid to retarded children to a discussion of the ways families can seek help for their problems outside the family. Perhaps one of the most thought-provoking ideas is Dr. Nichtern's advocacy of families and communities as the most effective and appropriate custodians and teachers of the retarded. Important social developments, from changing life-styles of families to the economic realities of institutional care, can affect the retarded.

This idea also relates to the nature of family and institutional problems as they exist in general.

Dr. Nichtern makes the very significant point that care for the retarded often serves the interests of the institutions rather than the needs of the retarded.

His discussion of the concept of retardation and the diagnostic methods available is challenging to those who prefer to see retardation as specific and the methods for its diagnosis as absolute.

Dr. Nichtern shares my interest in the prevention of mental disturbances. He points to many factors discovered in recent years that contribute to developmental abnormalities: poor nutrition, excessive use of pharmacological products, radiation etc., during pregnancy. The presentation of the ideas in this book are similar to a well-woven fabric. Keeping in mind his greatest concern — helping the retarded child — he demonstrates the interaction of such significant biological and sociological facts as the effects of the emancipation of women on childbearing age and its influence on the possible risk of retardation. Reflected in Dr. Nichtern's words is a humanness essential for helping the retarded child: "Very young infants . . . are best off with . . . familiar and loving responses to their impulses. Institutions introduce multiple and varying nurturing. The familiar gives way to the impersonal. The impersonal makes loving difficult."

As a mental health professional engaged in diagnosis, treatment, teaching, and research, I am constantly asked a multitude of questions concerning various aspects of the retarded child. If it's not a distraught parent searching for someone to offer another diagnostic study, it may be a parent who has realistically accepted the problem but is now concerned with some of the sexual difficulties of his retarded teenage son; it may be a nurse eager to understand more of the metabolic or endocrine variables associated with retardation; or possibly a medical student asking about community resources for the retarded or their legal rights. In all cases, I can direct them to this book — a source which offers a broad yet comprehensive perspective on the problem, written by a man whose respect for all humanity penetrates his ideas, which are expressed with warmth and compassion for the retarded.

Lee Salk, Ph.D.
Director, Division of Pediatric Psychology
The New York Hospital — Cornell Medical Center
New York City
April 1974

HELPING THE RETARDED CHILD

CHAPTER I

The Anguish of Retardation

Children are a wonderment. They deify and involve us with the ultimate creativity—the initiation of life (conception), the production of life (childbearing), and the molding of life (child-rearing). They reinforce our awareness of the energy and potential of all living things. They provide us with the enriching identity of parent and the excitement of this ever-changing role linked to their development. This challenging process stimulates and recruits our imagination. It permits us to approach our own pasts within the current dimensions of our existence as parents. It provides us with highly personal hopes for the future. It extends the dimensions of our living and gives us a sense of immortality by an ongoing identification with youth. It encourages us to preserve our most cherished ambitions by our ability to project them onto our children.

There are few who fail to invest their dreams and aspirations in thoughts of family and children and many who search for their maturity through procreation. This links fertility forever with the coming of age and demonstrates its progeny as proof of the achievement. This union of potency and pregnancy unleashes fantasies of strength, virility, and accomplishments, binding them to the fulfillment of self. A defective product of this coupling assaults this image and tests the real mettle of who and what we are by the demand for acceptance of imperfection—our own as reflected in our children. The reality of their imperfections becomes ours. We become impatient with their lack of progress as if it were our own. Their failures are ours and we become victimized by the discrepancies between our imagination and their developmental realities. The inadequacies of our children are painful to us and the recognition of them is the pain of retardation. This pain causes many different reactions—denial, guilt, anger, despair, withdrawal, under- or overinvolvement, dependency, abandonment, devotion, love, hate—the entire gamut of human emotions. It challenges our fabric and our ability to tolerate pain. The recognition of defect becomes an unavoidable stimulus. What is it? Why did it occur? What will it mean to me or mine? What can be done about it? Is there hope? Why did it have to happen? Why me? The awareness demands a response often far more complex than the defect.

The birth of a child with defect and potential for retardation is accompanied by many different reactions by parents and professionals. These reactions are rooted in the individuality of each. Some are predictable and others not. Pregnancy is a nine-month expectation filled with dreams of the future. The advent of a recognizable defect destroys most of these dreams and replaces them with our grief and the shadows of our anxieties. The period of mourning may last as long or longer than the pregnancy that bred the dreams. But then the demands of the living thrust themselves upon this reaction. Care must be given and planning must take place. Sometimes the motivation for the care and planning is in response to the grief rather than the child. Such reactions tend to accentuate the pain of retardation by distorting the reality of the needs of the child and parents. Separation is recommended and sometimes consummated without proper recognition given to the basis or appropriateness of the decision. This creates a home divided between dreams and need. It provides the seeds for future uncertainties that perpetuate frustrations, anxieties, and pain. Parents exist with a sense of inadequacy while professionals emerge as capable of problem-solving. Both these assumptions may be far from the truth. Parents need to resolve their grief by being parents. They must be helped to make decisions relative to the needs of their children. Professionals need to help relieve the pain generated by the defects and participate in the preservation of both child and parents. There is no way to avoid this initial pain, but it can be ameliorated by sensitive responses from all concerned.

Sometimes the profoundly as well as the lesser retarded require special care that cannot be provided within their family or particular community. In such instances, the necessity for placement unleashes other forces that can be as painful as the initial discovery of defect. The thought of separation activates not only our concern for them but also our own reservoir of anxieties concerning events of loss in our pasts. This merging of unrelated realities and feelings can intensify the painfulness of the responsibilities and disturb the needed judgments. It is also capable of resurrecting the sorrow of the unfulfilled memories and dreams.

This combination becomes the Pandora's box of retardation. It is capable of releasing our thoughts and actions tainted by our pain, grief, and anxiety. It may account for the endowment of so many of our fears upon the retarded—our fears of helplessness, of incompetence, of loss of control, of stupidity, of deficiency, of unattractiveness, of failure, and even of insanity. It may explain our collective need to identify the retarded, give them invisibility within institutions, and turn away from the responsibilities of their care. They remind us of our imperfections. They destroy our fantasies of omnipotence. They keep us from the magic of eternal life and knowledge. We are no longer godlike, but only molded in the image of God with the imperfections of humans that may be seen among those identified as retarded.

The growth of our children not only moves them away from us and out of the family but brings them to the public marketplace as products as well as consumers before they may be ready. Their identification as something special—retarded—makes them both a special product and a special consumer. This movement and classification can be most expensive. The human values involved should be recognized in order to appreciate fully the nature of the expense. The provision of special programs always requires large numbers of people, each of whom must become invested in the particular problems of each child. The large numbers result not only in varied approaches to the same problems but in variable responses to particular needs. These variations often surround the child and parents with conflict. What is best for my child? Am I doing all that is possible? Have I been neglectful? And so the conflicts of uncertainty become added to the pain of retardation. Simultaneously, the continuing need of the immature for consistent and uniform relationships may be responded to in various ways. The resulting confusion may stimulate conflict within the child and disturb the search for the constancy the child so urgently needs. To whom do I belong? What is important for me to experience and learn? Which value system is significant? Who shall be my model? And so confusion becomes an added burden of retardation.

The special program for the special child adds yet another dimension. Often the participating individual acquires the identity of the program. This is true for child, family, and professional alike. Once given the identity of "retarded" or any other similar designation, this classification tends to track the individual. Encapsulation within special programs may create a new kind of special isolation. It permits identification for any purpose—exclusion as well as inclusion; less as well as extra; deprivation as well as enrichment; separateness as well as involvement. This potential for segregation can accentuate the loneliness of one's grief, the intensity of one's anxiety, and the breadth of one's conflicts. It helps make identification a broken promise of dreams never to be achieved and goals never to be fulfilled.

It has long been debated whether man makes history or history makes the man, and the concept of retardation does little to resolve this argument. The concepts of *less* and *greater* derive from our earliest thought organization and life experiences. There has always been and there will always be a significant number of lesser individuals among us by the nature of our judgments. An examination of the historical perspectives of retardation serves to define better many of our own characteristics while making the anguish of retardation a universal experience. An understanding rooted in a knowledge of this history may help us live a little more easily with the problems and to show greater compassion for those whom we designate as retarded.

Many of our attitudes toward retardation stem from preoccupations with our origins, with who and what we are, with how we live with each other, and with what will become of us. These concerns determine many of our thoughts and activities. They exist within the fabric of our religion, history, scientific inquiry, and social organization. They help shape the images of ourselves and others. They give rise to a never-ending interest in nature and nurture. Many of these concerns with ourselves become exposed as we attempt to deal with retardation or disturbance. Is it caused by defects of structure, function, heredity, or environment—by one or the other or all? Why has it happened? Who bears the responsibility? What can be done about it and by whom? These are the questions that preoccupy us all and consume some. They affect every individual, family, and society in some manner.

At some time in our lives, we are all plagued by our nature, by our incompleteness, or by our defects: as infants and toddlers by our sense of helplessness; as young children by thoughts of our size and strength; as older children by uncertainty about our capacity to learn; as adolescents by anxiety about our emerging sexuality and sociality; and as adults by apprehension of our ability to perform and compete. Each of us develops a real or imagined awareness of our strengths and weaknesses. We make all kinds of adaptations to these perceptions, including the involvement and often requiring the acceptance of those with whom we live and, particularly, those to whom we give life. And so our nature becomes our nurture, forever intertwined, inseparable, and the source of many of our conflicts and anxieties.

Every family experiences the impact of these conflicts and anxieties through natural concern for itself and its progeny. Conception gives birth to the idea of possible defect. The actual birth of an infant introduces both reality and fantasy to the possibility. The progression of development supplies ever-changing ingredients to the events and adds the challenge and excitement of this change to the family experience. Defects of development, whatever they are, wherever they may come from, and however painful they may be, intensify the awareness and extend the dimensions of life of the family. Retardation and other developmental anomalies become part of the wonder of life by bringing new and different qualities to family interactions. They cannot and should not be judged by the ordinary values of everyday experiences. Each retarded child brings an uncharted course of living to the family members. As with all ventures into the unknown, there are the excitement and the rewards of the accomplishment of the unexpected joined by some fear of what might be. There are, of course, the accompanying concerns with helplessness, weakness, capacity to learn, and ability to perform. These concerns, however, must be separated from the tasks of child-rearing, and the strengths and resources of each member of the family recruited for the demands of this unknown.

Society's response to the presence of its retarded and disturbed has varied with the needs of the social structure as much as with the needs of the individuals concerned, but the duality of response, both social and personal, has always been present. It is the role of society to provide common modes of existence. The retarded, however, do not respond easily or well to generalized goals. They become vulnerable and are at the mercy of the broader aims of society. This is a principal reason why the retarded become an irritant when in public view. They defy organized structure by their need for individualization. They cannot be recruited easily for broad social objectives. They challenge the very nature of these objectives by their noncompliance and their difference. These characteristics place the retarded in the unusual role of protagonist without portfolio within every social system in history. As such, their treatment becomes a glaring indictment of society's weaknesses. This may account for many of the contradictory attitudes and controversies surrounding the management and treatment of the retarded. It may explain our ambivalent devotion to their humanity, for many of our procedures serve only to dehumanize them. It may be why we invest in their identification to exclude them or hide them away. The history of the care of the retarded remains a stirring documentation of the social and moral values of any given society.

The achievement of a balanced response to individual and social needs is one of the objectives of life. The retarded tend to defy this objective, and the resulting dilemma serves to define a primary goal of their management and care. They must be helped to achieve to the optimum of their potential while maintaining the balance between their individual and social needs. They must be helped to sustain this complex interrelationship within each stage of their life as developmental progression alters the circumstances of their existence. Recognizing that retardation is the consequence of arrest or disturbance of this developmental progression, the key to helping the retarded is contained within an understanding of human development—its components, sequences, pathways, and the stages and their characteristics. Such an understanding permits appropriate responses to needs as they arise. Retardation should be viewed also as a temporal disturbance. The accompanying developmental arrests result in functions and skills failing to appear at expected times or persisting into stages where they should have been replaced by new ones.

Another aspect of the temporal disturbance of retardation can be seen within the merging and integration of physical, emotional, and social experiences. The discordancy among these vital areas of growth experiences can be great. The results may be behavior, thoughts, emotions, and responses that appear inappropriate to time and place. Examined and judged against the perspective of developmental achievements of the retarded individual, these responses are no longer inappropriate but merely the product of a particular combination of experiences. Regretfully, this individuality of response has come to be identified as a significant manifestation of retardation and recognized as disturbance. This entire process has been accelerated by the general social movement toward standardization and conformity. The number of individuals identified as retarded or disturbed is growing with this movement. Thus the balance between social and individual needs may play a significant role in the production of those identified and treated as retarded.

A developmental approach to the subject of retardation demands that recognition be given to our children as individuals from the moment of their conception and that this individuality be preserved throughout their existence. The special quality of the retarded provides them with a singular role in society and marks their distinctive contribution to the common good. Their developmental defiance of conformity does much to preserve the rights of all of us to our own individuality. This special contribution can be considered as significant as those of the tillers of the soil, the builders of bridges, or the writers of books.

The impact of children on a family is always great. The immaturity of children requires parents and perhaps other members of the family to assume responsibility for their physical, intellectual, and social experiences. Ordinarily, this demand is limited to the developmental periods characterized by dependency and is viewed as one of the rewards of family life. The very nature of the retarded extends and alters the parameters of this demand. It tests the fiber and mettle of each member of the family. It stresses the fabric of family interaction by increasing the period of dependency and altering the nature of the demands. These alterations stimulate many different reactions. They may draw upon the imagination and ingenuity of family members, as well as fragmenting and consuming the delicate harmonies. The retarded have the capacity to bring unusual and rewarding experiences within the resolution of their problems. Their problems should never be permitted, however, to exhaust the resources of the family. It is to the achievement and maintenance of this balance that the efforts of others must be devoted.

The need for support of the retarded and their families is ever-present within every society. Each responds in its own way—with involvement or neglect; with sophistication or ignorance; with kindness or cruelty. The results can be seen through the determination of social attitudes, the organization of significant institutions and practices, and the establishment of value systems. Thus this need leads to demand and contribution. It becomes part of the nature of the retarded. They and those associated with their cause must be respected and helped in every way possible.

The information contained in this book is offered first to the parents who must help their children grow. It is also our hope that this book may be found useful by physicians who must give succor and counsel to the retarded and their families; by nurses and childcare personnel who must minister to their needs; by social workers who must advise and direct; by educators who must teach and train; by policemen who must control; by judges who must order; by religious leaders who must guide; by politicians who must plan; and by all of us devoted to the common cause of survival and the quality of life with each other.

CHAPTER II

Historical Perspectives

The history of retardation suggests that it is as much a record of society's needs and organization at any moment as it is of the existence of the retarded. There are almost no available references to the care of the retarded before the ninteenth century. It is as if they did not exist before this time. A few direct references can be found in the residual literature of some of the past civilizations and in the Talmud, the Bible, and the Koran. They are meager and offer little information other than remonstrations that the feebleminded should be cared for gently.

Even the origins of some of the words in current usage to describe retardation appear unrelated to the past. The words *fatuous* and *fatuity* can be traced back to the same root as *infatuation*. The word *idiot* is derived from a Greek term denoting a private person. It evolved to mean the common man, then the unsophisticated layman, and then the ignorant, ill-informed individual. It was not until long after the complete mutation of its Greek origin that it received the current meaning of "mental defect." The word *imbecile* demonstrates a similar evolution. *Imbecillus* meant "weak" and denoted any form of debility to our early Roman scribes. It was not until long after the fall of the Roman Empire that this word became attached to weaknesses of the mind. The word *moron* comes from the Greek word *moros*, meaning "dull," which, in its ancient past, had served as the prototype of the Latin derivative *morosus*, meaning "fretful." Thus some of the major words associated currently with the concepts of retardation offer little evidence of any relationship with retardation in the past. Even the more ample records of the Middle Ages, replete with their references to dunces, fools, and jesters, appear devoid of meaningful comments about retarded individuals. For the most part they were regarded as "infants of the good Lord" and were allowed to roam unmolested. Some became victims of the prevailing religious fervor of the times and the accompanying demonism. Martin Luther made reference to the feebleminded as godless. "The Devil sits in such changelings where their soul should have been!"

The casualties of conception, pregnancy, birth, disease, and injury produce a significant presence of retarded individuals at all times. It is safe to assume that their numbers should have been even greater in the past because of the lack of advantages provided by modern science and technology. How then can this "absence" be accounted for? The circumstances suggest that the retarded were present but were looked upon and treated differently while their existence was determined by other aspects of the social structure than they are today. Some of the answers can be found in a historical examination of the structure, mores, and customs of family life.

During the earliest nomadic existence of man, only the

strongest and most adaptable of the young survived. This provided a natural system of biological selection, resulting in a continuous process of family pruning. Under such conditions the immature, the weak, and the damaged were eliminated early from the family unit and were never permitted to become a matter of ongoing concern. As man moved toward an agrarian existence, new forms of selection for survival had to emerge. The limited resources of early families required the adoption of a form of social judgment that continued the process of family pruning. The fathers of these early families were given the right of life and death over family members. This right included the responsibility of examining newborns to judge whether to give them the privilege of survival or abandon them in the wilderness. The criteria for this kind of selection would become invested naturally in fitness and judgments based on the needs of the family. This kind of selectivity would have again eliminated the immature, the weak, and the damaged so that they would not become a drain on limited resources.

The early agrarian family quickly became rooted to the land and had to develop rules of conduct relative to neighbors as well as themselves. Many of the established attitudes within the family served as the basis for the emerging patterns of social interactions and became incorporated within the religious and political structure of the tribes. The right and responsibility of judgment for survival was transmitted to the elders and priests, bringing new forms of selection and elimination into existence. Children were offered in sacrifice to the gods. It may be more than coincidence that firstborns were chosen most frequently for sacrifice. It is now known that the highest incidence of developmental deviations occurs within first pregnancies of young females. The elders of our early tribes may have had their ancient forms of computerized research. Some of the religious and political patterns of selection by early civilizations suggest a correlation with natural systems for survival.

This emerging pattern of selection by judgment reached its heights among the Spartans. The rearing as well as the production of children were determined by the state instead of being left to the caprice of individuals. Women were trained by physical exercises for health and the duties of motherhood. Marriage was permitted only in the prime of life. Men who did not marry were subject to social criticism. The newborns were submitted to inspection by elders of their tribe. If strong and well-formed, they were reared. If not, they were allowed to die. This careful selection of the stock was followed by appropriate training. Children were conditioned early to endure darkness and solitude without fear and to cure themselves of peevishness and crying. At the age of seven, the boys were taken away from the care of their parents and placed under the supervision of a public official. Nothing was omitted to make them efficient members of the state. Family life was obliterated by public activity. It was a society of soldier-citizens in which the immature, the weak, and the damaged were eliminated purposefully. And yet this dominant group did not endure, suggesting that still other factors were involved in the survival of a society, and that these exist even among the immature, the weak, and the damaged.

The strong demand the existence of the weak so that they may remain strong. Slavery came into being as a productive social system. The survival of slaves as a class was linked to their ability to be productive in manner and form determined by others. Dependency became a way of life. Immaturity was fostered. Even defect was valued. In ancient Rome it was not uncommon for the wealthy to keep a "fool" or "jester" for the amusement of the household and its guests. The Roman Seneca related the following to his friend Lucillius:

> You know that Herpaste, my wife's fool, was left on my hands as a hereditary charge, for I have a natural aversion to these monsters;

> and if I have a mind to laugh at a fool, I need not seek him far, I can laugh at myself. This fool has suddenly lost her sight. I am telling you a strange but true story. She is not aware that she is blind and constantly urges her keeper to take her out because she says my house is dark.

Interaction between classes makes the immature desirable, the weak productive, the damaged insightful, and the retarded acceptable within an organized social structure. This pattern of interaction between social classes persisted through many centuries, providing a haven for the retarded within society. It served repeatedly to put to rest the myth of the supremacy of selective breeding as seen among the Spartans. Selective breeding has survived only for special purposes, such as breeding racehorses whose achievements in life are marked by their ability to run around a circle very rapidly; and for special causes, such as the myth of Aryan supremacy of Hitler's Germany.

However, the emergence of social classes generated conflict within the established family structure, again determining some of the attitudes toward the retarded and their fate. The feudal system of the Middle Ages saw the social, economic, and political power locked into the family and transmitted by hereditary rights from one generation to another. This filial devotion of feudal society ensured the preservation of property and the means of existence, and the protection of both against external aggression, thus providing the weaker individuals with security for their existence within their families. These circumstances brought a natural protective and accepting attitude toward the retarded, so that they were preserved as part of the society and no special provisions were needed for their care. Not only were fools and jesters part of court life but the less fortunate were permitted to wander and be protected as children of God. The devotion to inheritance was so great that the history of this period is replete with descriptions of retarded and disturbed monarchs preserved in their titular roles by elaborate family arrangements.

Another historical aspect of feudal society that must have had a significant impact upon the existence and numbers of retarded was the great epidemic of plagues of the Middle Ages. The new mobility of people generated by trade and commerce, the great Crusades, and the many wars of conquest served to expose large populations to new and virulent forms of disease. The immature, the weak, and the damaged would have been more than vulnerable to this exposure, and then, even more than now, they would have fallen easy prey to this form of biological extinction. All of these circumstances provide some explanation for the paucity of references to the existence of the retarded during this period and the lack of investment of these past societies in their care and management.

Suddenly, interest in the retarded spread rapidly throughout Europe and the United States at the end of the eighteenth and the beginning of the nineteenth century. This interest was stimulated by several different sets of circumstances. The number of individuals recognized as retarded appeared to be increasing, or else they were becoming more visible. The medical community, reacting to the enlightened, romantic intellectualism of the times, discovered the retarded as a lost frontier. In France, Jacob Pereire responded to the educational challenge of neglected deaf-mutes; Jean Itard attempted the conversion of the Wild Boy of Aveyron from a primitive savage to a civilized being; and Edouard Seguin began his experimentation in educating idiots. In the United States, Samuel Gridley Howe introduced his concepts of training the feebleminded. But it appears that the Industrial Revolution of the period may have served as the important stimulus to this recent interest. New methods of production demanded competence, speed, departure from the simple to reliance on the complex, the introduction of standardization, and the abandonment of individualization. The accompanying shift of attitudes revealed suddenly a growing number of people who could be judged as incompetent, slow, and simple. As the Industrial Revolution spread and increased the number of such individuals, it also provided the stimulus for approaches to them. It lent its practices of standardization to intelligence tests and classifications; its principles of production, to the organization of the retarded into special groups for care, education, and training; its designs of factories, to the construction of institutions for housing; and its ability to mass-produce, to the destruction of the individualism of the retarded as well as the rest of us.

This changing social organization accompanying the Industrial Revolution set the stage for a new concept of group care of children, as well as stimulating a sense of public responsibility for it. The ideas and practices of institutional training of groups of children gained public acceptance and support. Facilities for the retarded appeared in nearly all of the countries of Western civilization by the middle of the nineteenth century. Institutional training of groups of retarded children with combined emphasis on medical care and education originated with Johann Guggenbühl and his facility for cretins at Abendberg, Switzerland. This institution became the center of great controversy but served as the prototype for most of the residential programs of the nineteenth century, many of which are in operation to this day.

The first attempt at residential care for retarded children in the United States occurred in the state of Connecticut in 1818 when provisions were made for the care of a limited number of such children at the Asylum for the Deaf and Dumb in Hartford. The idea of special residential schools for the feebleminded had its origins in the state of Massachusetts, where Hervey Wilbur took a group of defective children into his home at Barre in 1848. In the same year, Samuel Gridley

Howe convinced the Massachusetts state legislature that the training and education of the feebleminded was a public responsibility. He made the following statement in his report to the state legislature:

> Massachusetts admits the right of all her citizens to a share in the blessings of education. . . .The benefits to be derived from the establishment of a school for this class of persons ("the poor idiots—the most wretched of all who are brought to her"), upon humane and scientific principles would be very great. Not only would all the idiots who should be received into it be improved in their bodily and mental condition, but all the others in the State and the country would be indirectly benefited. The school, if conducted by persons of skill and ability, would be a model for others. Valuable information would be disseminated through the country; it would be demonstrated that no idiot need be confined or restrained by force; but they can be redeemed from odious and filthy habits, and there is not one of them of any age who may not be made more of a man and less of a brute by patience and kindness directed by energy and skill.

An era of rapid expansion in the use of institutions took place. This was in response to the recognition of need for the care and training of the retarded as well as the search for more efficient and economical methods of protecting and housing their growing numbers. During this period of institutional growth, residential training and education gave way to the practice of custodial care. Medical concepts changed from "cure" to amelioration. Permanent retention became popular and the number of retarded individuals within institutions began to grow rapidly. By the early part of the twentieth century committing the mentally retarded to institutional care for life had become a common practice. Soon many of these institutions became detention units for the retarded who were being judged as undesirable elements in society. Custodial care with limited training and education was the sole help offered in many places.

This evolution coincided with the growing acceptance of compulsory education for all, so that programs for the retarded began to appear in the public schools at about this time. The first special classes in public schools were established in Germany during the last half of the nineteenth century and rapidly spread to other schools across the European continent. In the United States the first class for retarded children was started in Providence, Rhode Island, in 1896 and was followed in rapid succession by classes set up by cities and states across the country. All of these efforts preceded major educational changes initiated by Binet and Simon, whose introduction of mental testing inaugurated a new era of educational instruction based on testing the ability of each pupil. Regretfully, it also inaugurated classification by numbers—the intelligence quotient. The quest for instruments for measuring intelligence stemmed from the growing practice of establishing general criteria and systems of mass instruction, which were then adapted to the needs of individual children. It had become evident that intellectual functioning, or lack of functioning, was not an absolute value and that there were degrees of intelligence and retardation. Such words as *idiot*, *imbecile*, and *moron* were recruited to denote the range. A duality emerged in the management of the retarded. The more severely impaired gravitated toward the residential institution. The less handicapped were programmed within the public school system.

In the beginning of the twentieth century the eugenic scare influenced attitudes strongly. Richard Louis Dugdale had published his genealogical survey of the Juke family in 1877, under the title *The Jukes, A Study in Crime, Pauperism, Disease and Heredity.* The major implications of this report were to link crime and pauperism to the hereditary transmission of mental deficiency. The accuracy of this work was exceeded only by its passion, and it heralded a growing attempt to link the retarded with many of the worst aspects of society. In 1888 the Reverend O. C. McCuloch offered his description of the "Tribe of Ishmael," which attempted to describe a family with a history of pauperism of several generations. McCuloch made reference to them as "decaying stock" and "festering mass" and implied the link to mental deficiency. In 1905 J. Jorger described a family of vagrants whom he called Zeros and offered them as a sample of hereditary transmission of retardation. In 1911 Charles Davenport declared: "Two mentally defective parents will produce only mentally defective offspring. This is the first law of inheritance of mental ability. . . . The second law of heredity of mentality is that, aside from 'mongolians,' probably no imbecile is born except of parents who, if not mentally defective themselves, both carry mental defect in their germ plasm." In 1912 Henry Herbert Goddard added the fictitious family name of the Kallikaks to the growing number of descriptions of tainted families. The Jukes and the Kallikaks were quickly joined by the Nams and the Hill Folk, the family of Sam Sixty, the dwellers in the vale of Sidden, and dozens of others in a flood of reports. The doom of the human race through its genetic, deviant population was forecast. This led to the popularization of such ideas as euthanasia, restrictive marriage laws, eugenic education, scientific breeding, birth control, colonization, and sterilization. The retarded had succeeded, by their mere presence, in making a remarkably broad and rich contribution to our intellectual and cultural heritage of ideas.

The pall of the eugenic scare began to lift as more modern techniques of scientific investigation began to tear away the pseudoscientific attitudes that cloaked so much of this work. The big breakthrough came in 1934 when Fölling identified one form of retardation with a metabolic disturbance of one of the chemicals in the body and called it imbecillitas phenylpyruvica. This discovery served to introduce a new dimension paralleling Binet and Simon's elimination of the all-or-none concept of retardation by their psychological measurements of human intelligence. The new era introduced by Fölling led to search for causation, with its possibilities of specific remedial interventions. Many of the hardened attitudes on management of the retarded crumbled under the impact of this search. Programs became varied and more hopeful. They began to extend across the entire range of man's knowledge—genetics, biochemistry, psychopharmacology, psychology, social work, psychiatry, and education. They introduced the idea of a multidetermined process affecting the course and outcome of human development. These programs began to invest in the concept of intervention based upon the identification of cause and effect. They helped to reestablish our recognition of the retarded as individuals in need and dissipated their isolation in category and classification, which set them apart from the rest of us while making them less than human.

Sir Aubrey Lewis in the first Adolf Meyer research lecture, given in 1960, had offered the following insightful statement reflecting on what had then begun to take place.

> Defect is not a biological entity, or indeed a psychological or pathological entity, but rather a congeries of morbid conditions. Its prevalence is not an absolute, but a conditional estimate. The cultural values and attitudes of a society have much to do with its recognition and may determine how heavy will be the economic and social burden it creates. More, here kindness may be cruel, and efficient provisions a hardship; for in a wealthy, humane, highly organized society, people who are poorly endowed may be set aside and debarred from living a normal life, so that they cannot contribute their self-respecting mite to the common stock or fulfill their side of the social contract, whereas in a ruder, less exacting society they might be integrated into the life of the community and be indistinguishable from the common run of its members.

The recognition of defect as something other than a specific entity emerged slowly from the growing body of knowledge on causation. Fölling's identification of the enzyme defect found in phenylketonuria opened up a new Pandora's box. Many biochemical disorders became identified with retardation. Then many kinds of infections and injuries were found to have causal relationships, as were poor maternal and infant nutrition, emotional and social deprivation, chromosomal abnormalities, and others. What slowly emerged from this extensive investigatory activity was the complex, multidetermined nature of retardation and the simple truth that almost anything capable of arresting or disturbing the early course of human development might produce retardation. However, our ability to demonstrate the numerous causes led also to the myth of the specific cure. The recent history of the subject of retardation in the United States is replete with as many claims of special cures as there were causes. Specificity bred specificity. If cause could be identified so well, why not cure? Claim after claim tumbled across the pages of the journals on retardation. Glandular and tissue extracts, hormonal replacement therapies, mineral and chemical additives, vitamin supplements, surgical procedures, teaching machines, muscle exercises, and even exorcisms came to be recruited, while we failed to see that the wealth, humaneness, and high degree of organization of our society were setting aside and debarring our poorly endowed from living a normal life. Special program followed special program. All served to provide some of the needed services while contributing as much to the further segregation of the retarded from the mainstream of life.

It was the growing awareness of the effects of this segregation, the limitations of existing programs, and the inability to cope with seeming increases in the numbers of the retarded that led finally to a critical reappraisal of the efforts being made in their behalf. During the early part of the 1960s in the United States, many government-sponsored and national meetings took place, with the essence of their considerations summed up within the history-making message by the late President John F. Kennedy to the Congress of the United States on February 5, 1963:

> We, as a Nation, have long neglected the mentally ill and the mentally retarded. This neglect must end, if our Nation is to live up to its own standards of compassion and dignity and achieve the maximum use of its manpower.
>
> This tradition of neglect must be replaced by forceful and far-reaching programs carried out at all levels of government, by private individuals and by State and local agencies in every part of the Union.
>
> We must act —
>
> to bestow the full benefits of our society on those who suffer from mental disabilities;
>
> to prevent the occurrence of mental illness and mental retardation wherever and whenever possible;
>
> to provide for early diagnosis and continuous and comprehensive care, in the community, of those suffering from these disorders;
>
> to stimulate improvements in the levels of care given the mentally disabled in our State and private institutions, and to reorient those programs to a community-centered approach;
>
> to reduce, over a number of years, and by hundreds of thousands, the persons confined to these institutions;
>
> to retain in a return to the community the mentally ill and mentally retarded, and there to restore and revitalize their lives through better health programs and strengthened educational and rehabilitation services; and
>
> to re-introduce the will and capacity of our communities to meet these problems, in order that the communities, in turn, can reinforce the will and capacity of individuals and individual families.
>
> We must promote—to the best of our ability and by all possible and appropriate means—the mental and physical health of all our citizens.

President Kennedy signed a bill, HR 3386, into law just a month before his death. This bill was designed to amend the Social Security Act, "with the objective of assisting States and communities in preventing and combatting mental retardation, through expansion and improvement of the maternal and child health and crippled children's programs, through provision of prenatal maternity and infant care for individuals with conditions associated with childbearing which may lead to mental retardation, and for other purposes." This legislation was characterized by two important features that revealed the growing awareness of the importance of the social aspects of retardation. One was the emphasis placed on preventative measures through an extension of health services to mothers and children at the point of risk. This carried the admission that retardation was connected closely with adverse social conditions. The other was the provision of means for stimulating services at a local level but on a nationwide scale through federal grants. By doing this the legislation placed the problem within a national context by combining local and federal responsibility.

This major piece of legislation was followed by a second, which was called The Construction of Research Centers and Facilities for the Mental Retarded. This provided funds for building construction and placed great emphasis on the centers' responsibility for training professionals in the field of care of the retarded. However, it had built into it the shibboleth of research being used to attract people to the field. It succeeded in attracting people to research more than to meeting the basic needs of those already identified as retarded. Also, it may have partially accounted for the dramatic increase in the cost of care of the retarded that has taken place by its emphasis on research over service.

The mid-1960s can be viewed as a period of expansion by legislative fiat. There was another amendment to the Social

Security Act, The Mental Retardation Facilities and Community Mental Health Centers Construction Act Amendment, the Elementary and Secondary Education Act and its Vocational Rehabilitation Amendment, and the Economic Opportunity Act. All of these included comprehensive measures directed at combating social deprivation, as well as more specialized measures by which they attempted to provide the means for the early detection of possible retardation in children. Their efforts to counteract the destructive influences of poverty included supportive day care, preschool facilities, remedial reading, family supplements, and other programs focused on cultural and social stimulation. Increased community involvement was predicated on the growing awareness that a significant number of families did not have the resources within themselves to provide adequate stimulation. It is necessary to give some thought now to the impact of these and other such efforts on the American family. This is particularly important in view of the prolonged states of immaturity and dependency of the retarded and the greater costs in human effort and emotion when they are cared for outside of the family.

There is little question that the family has been undergoing a dramatic evolution within our present-day industrial society. This evolution has not only changed the relationships between generations. It has altered the nature of family life to such a degree that many families are no longer able to assume sole responsibility for care of their dependent members—and particularly their retarded offspring. Economic, social, and emotional needs have resulted in more than 60 percent of our adult women working outside of the family. Who then remains within the family to assume responsibility for its dependent members? In 1971 there were over a million divorces in the United States, compared with about 700,000 the year before. The same increase has taken place in many other countries as well. The rapid change has resulted in a fragmentation of family life, which again poses major problems in the care of dependent members. This divorce rate and the increasing number of children being born out of wedlock has caused more than 40 percent of the children in the United States to be reared with only one or none of their biological parents available to them. This breakdown of biological kinship impinges dramatically on all intrafamily relationships. However, with the retarded and their prolonged dependency and greater needs, this breakdown leads more readily to greater demands on the responsible, child-rearing parents, and to greater stresses, turmoil, exhaustion, and the possibility of ultimate abandonment of each other.

Many other factors in contemporary life affect a family's ability to care for its dependent members. The migration from rural to urban sectors has placed 93 percent of the population of the United States crowded together in our cities—visible to each other and interacting to a degree never before experienced. Under such circumstances, a retarded member becomes a heavy burden to other family members who find themselves obligated to compensate for some of his difficulties within the community. Also, there is a greater sensitivity of all to the presence of the retarded, both within the family and the community. The new mobility of our society has further complicated matters. No longer is there a stabilized community where established relationships among individuals and families provide the security of the known. American families move about at an ever-increasing rate and over much greater distances. This movement has caused a significant breakdown in boundaries of time and place that brings greater complexities to the existence of the retarded within the community as well as the ability to offer them supportive services.

Some of the efforts of the government to provide cultural and social stimulation to the young have hastened the changes of family life. Day care, preschool facilities, Head Start programs, and other programs have accelerated the movement of the child out of the family, reduced the period of dependency within the child-parent relationship, and introduced variations of care into the young child's life when many of his early needs must be satisfied within a dependent, constant, and limited relationship. Sometimes this premature movement of the child out of the family reduces the commitment to child-rearing by the family and hastens its change of values. The responsibility for corrective intervention had been a primary role of family for many centuries. Now this has been delegated to the remedial expert, with a further erosion of parental responsibility.

Another curious dimension of government action on behalf of children can be found within the Social Security system. A principal section of this system is Aid to Dependent Children, where efforts are directed at preserving dependent children within their family in recognition of the contribution of family life to the welfare of the young. In New York more than 70 percent of welfare funds are distributed through this Aid to Dependent Children. A closer examination of this distribution reveals that little of the funds actually go toward preserving any meaningful family constellation. Many of the children are born out of wedlock. The patterns of reimbursement place a premium on keeping a man or potential father out of the house, since his presence might lead to the cutoff of aid. The premium for this "no family" is even greater for the handicapped or retarded, since other government subsidies become more readily available under these circumstances. This contradiction has served to accelerate the change of many families' life-styles, as well as contributing to the movement of individuals out of family—adults as well as children. It is evident that we are increasingly making it economically impractical to exist as a biological family unit. Many of our practices are depriving young children of their rights to dependency. All of this exaggerates the plight of the retarded with their prolonged state of dependence and more complex needs.

The Joint Commission on Mental Health of Children evolved from a growing concern for the unavailability of sufficient children's services. This national commission undertook a three-year endeavor to study and identify some of the current needs of children in the United States. Its members recognized that health, mental health, and environmental influences were interwoven, particularly in the earliest years of life. They portrayed crises of our society that precipitated many kinds of childhood malfunctioning and gave rise to the need for many kinds of intervention. They gave equal priority to prevention and remediation. They reported their findings and recommendations to Congress and the many government officials in June, 1969. It is interesting to note that they suggested: "It is clear that if we are to dedicate ourselves to meeting the needs of our children and youth the required services and programs in child-rearing, which is our largest 'industry,' should be one of the largest in optimal manpower utilization and therefore costs." Thus our children were decreed finally to be children of industry in a society in which they are as much the commodity as the consumer.

This transition has been inexorable. It has affected them, their families, and their relationships to everyone and everything. It has led to the mass production of their problems and to our attempts to solve them by using mass production techniques. It has robbed our children of their individuality, although they are neither reproducible nor replaceable. It has led us to generalize about them while we specialize in them. It has made those with immaturity, weakness, or damaged potential rejects from the family and second-class citizens of the community. It has served to set many of the retarded apart from the mainstream of life—in institutions where they exist unremarked and poorly cared for.

This steady transition has led over and over again to society's need to reaffirm its commitment to all of its children and to their rights as stated in the final report of the Joint Commission on Mental Health of Children:

- the right to be wanted
- the right to be born healthy
- the right to live in a healthy environment
- the right to satisfaction of basic needs
- the right to continuous loving care
- the right to acquire the intellectual and emotional skills necessary to achieve individual aspirations and to cope effectively in our society
- the right to receive care and treatment through facilities which are appropriate to their needs and which keep them as closely as possible within their normal social setting.

It is within this historical perspective of child, family, and community that we must come to deal with the special problems of the retarded.

CHAPTER III

Concepts of Retardation

Not until the middle of the nineteenth century did the professional community attempt to define and identify the characteristics of mental retardation. The problems emerged as primarily physical, psychological, educational, or social, depending on the special points of view. The physician saw retardation as a series of symptoms derived from organic disturbances resulting in physical and mental defects of varying severity. The psychologist saw retardation as disturbance of function primarily in the areas of cognition and motor behavior. The educator recognized retardation as a disorder of learning. The socially oriented identified retardation as the inability to meet social standards, with a possible infringement upon the social code. The timing of this emerging interest and the varying points of view suggest the concept of retardation to be more dependent on man's interpretation and prejudice than an entity unto itself. If this is so, how can it be defined? Why does it exist? What purpose does it serve? What is it?

These historical perspectives suggest that mental retardation may be as much or more part of a social process than it is a clinical entity. It serves to bind people together into two groups—the retarded and the nonretarded. This makes the retarded a distinct subgroup of society. They become a kind of social class subject to special regulations governing their interaction with society as a whole. The judgment of the professional identifying an individual as retarded almost always relegates that person to particular attitudes, special management, and segregation within family and community. A child with a congenital heart defect may be limited as severely in his capacity to perform, adapt to life's demands, and meet life's stresses. Yet such a child will never be considered for exclusion from the family because of his congenital defect. He will be programmed in the same school as other children. He will be considered for a place in society to the limits of his defect and ability.

This is not so for persons who have been labeled as retarded. They are shunted into special programs and schools. They are considered as candidates for institutional care because of their retardation and not because of specific defect in need of remediation or rehabilitation. They are not considered for a place in society to the limits of defect and ability. Their only escape is to somehow lose the identification of retarded. And, fortunately, many do as they move toward their physical maturity and find niches in society that permit them to hide from the identity given to them by others. Recent surveys have demonstrated that 89 percent of all persons identified in this manner are mildly retarded. The remaining 11 percent are severely handicapped by defects accompanied by retardation and require care for their defects more than they do for their retardation.

These simple facts suggest the concept of retardation to be something other than a diagnostic category or classification of people. Yet its universal application over the past hundred and fifty years offers it as a well-defined instrument and institution of our contemporary society. On closer examination, it has served as an instrument for identification, grouping, packaging, and distributing. It has even served to produce an increasing number of individuals recognized as retarded. It must, therefore, be seen for what it is: part of the institutional structure and practice of our industrial society. It has no more relation to the individual than does a job description. It does provide a system for identifying individuals as adequate or inadequate to the tasks of the society, and for judgment of their capacity to function, to be recruited, and to be used. We have designed and staffed an elaborate apparatus to this purpose. We have constructed an expensive plant for its operation. One of the big questions facing us is whether all of this can be converted to the benefit of the individuals who fall prey to this social institution known as mental retardation.

All of this is not to deny the existence of a significant group of individuals who fit the definition of the American Association on Mental Deficiency and others. This definition states: "Mental retardation refers to subaverage general intellectual functioning which originates during the developmental period and is associated with impairment in adaptive behavior." "Subaverage" has been further defined as a score of more than one standard deviation below the mean of the general population on a standardized test. Other definitions have been proposed that include additional requirements. The words "significantly subaverage" have been offered as one modification. The Group for the Advancement of Psychiatry has suggested the recognition of mental retardation as a chronic condition. They have offered the following definition: "Mental retardation is a chronic condition present from birth or early childhood and characterized by impaired intellectual functioning as measured by standardized tests. It manifests itself in impaired adaptation to the daily demands of the individual's own social environment. Commonly these patients show a slow rate of maturation, physical and/or psychological, together with impaired learning capacity." Some of the earlier definitions stressed a biological or constitutional base as well.

These definitions, however, as specific as they attempt to be, refer to incomplete standardizations and changing value systems. Measures of adaptive behavior are poorly developed, and the few in general use apply primarily to young children (for example, the Gesell Developmental Scale) or to the severely and profoundly retarded (for example, Vineland Social Maturity Scale). Then again, there has been no attempt to reach nor may there be much possibility of reaching an agreement on criteria for measuring adaptive behavior. Adaptation to what? To the rapidly changing social system, which now affects even the very young as they are pulled and pushed out of the family into an ever more affluent society? To the internal developmental needs of living with one's own defects? Or to the need to equal the expectation of others as rated against their performance? Yet the capacity for adaptation can be easily recognized as one of the results of maturation, development, and growth, with maturation representing the internal process of change, development representing this change in relation to time, and growth representing this change in relation to environment. However, we are different unto ourselves and each other (genetic, constitutional characteristics). We develop at different rates (physical and mental characteristics). And we have different growth experiences (emotional and social characteristics). To be able to standardize by measure this complex interweaving of life's dimensions lies beyond man's everchanging creative abilities, whose productivity becomes the symbol of his adaptive behavior.

An important aspect of this adaptive capacity rests with social change. This change promotes an evolution of society leading constantly to different and more complex organization, just as maturation, development, and growth do for the individual. The resulting complexities demand different and changing levels of adaptive behavior. The ancient hunter-warrior needed swiftness, stamina, perseverance, and the ability to tolerate hardship. He did not have to know how to read, write, or do arithmetic. Modern man needs different skills than did the hunter-warrior. Thus a changing selectivity becomes part of adaptation and further complicates our attempts to standardize the criteria for judgment of those who depart from the median. A shift to a technological society with its urbanization has altered existence dramatically. It has introduced population density, industrial pollution, urban decay, recurrent unemployment, poverty amid plenty, a changing family life, mobility, and so on. All of these phenomena are more generalized and involve more people than ever before. The number of individuals with impaired adaptive behavior has increased tremendously under these circumstances. Should they too be viewed as potentially retarded?

These dilemmas about adaptive behavior have led everyone to rely more on standardized measures of intellectual functioning—the other major criterion for identifying mental retardation. This standardization is far more attractive. It is concrete, definite, highly structured, representable by a numerical system, easily communicated, and therefore easily applied and highly visible. These characteristics have recruited us all to its application as a universal instrument for identifying and cataloging the retarded individual, as well as ourselves. The classification of intelligence is an inference made from the function, behavior, and communication of any particular person relative to others. By its very nature, it becomes a grouping process and produces best, better, average, poor, and worst. It attempts to identify the average and then scales all performance against this average. This locks the concept of retardation into the concept of average representing normalcy. It helps to define retardation as an abnormality instead of as variations of human function, behavior, and communication. It permits the numerical scoring known as the intelligence quotient (IQ) with a competitive grading system of 100 representing the average. It provides a method by which any variation from the average can be given a numerical representation and subgroups developed. This type of classification, applying the revised Stanford-Binet test of intelligence to the retarded, has resulted in five subgroups for them.

1. Borderline intelligence. IQ range, 83–68. One standard deviation from the mean.
2. Mild retardation. IQ range, 67–52. Two standard deviations from the mean.
3. Moderate retardation. IQ range, 51–36. Three standard deviations from the mean.
4. Severe retardation. IQ range, 35–20. Four standard deviations from the mean.
5. Profound retardation. IQ range, below 20. Five standard deviations from the mean.

This method of classifying intelligence allows for the construction of many different tests provided they are standardized properly and administered carefully. They provide a measure of a person's present ability to perform a series of tasks that are identified as requiring intelligence for successful completion. They are scored by comparing individual performance with the relevant norms for the particular age group of the general population. A good intelligence test will correlate with those activities in life that are commonly recognized as depending on intelligence. Items are selected for inclusion by statistical methods and standardization trials on population samples.

This kind of construction of intelligence tests permits their use on similar groups with the same cultural and social heritage. Their accuracy is reduced or breaks down with departure from similarity. Deviancy or disturbance resulting in modifications in responses to the tasks within the test alter the score further and tend to represent failure. In most instances, this lowers the possible score. There are other limitations to intelligence tests. These include such problems as reliability of measurements, errors in test construction, variability of administration, and cultural and social factors. It is impossible to explore these limitations in any depth without departing from the problems of the retarded. It seems more appropriate to identify some of these general limitations of intelligence tests so that their results are used with discretion and caution.

The broadest agreement within the many considerations on the concepts of retardation is the significance of the early developmental periods of life. It is during these periods that changes occur rapidly, at varying rates, and with different interactions. The fluctuations in the rate of change determine the mixture of developmental ingredients, how fast or slow maturity comes, or whether maturity comes at all. Retardation emerges as one of the many developmental pathways within which progression becomes altered and slowed by physical, emotional, or social events with possible lasting effects on the life-style. An understanding of retardation is linked more to the awareness of what takes place within the process of development and its possible outcome than to knowledge of measures of intelligence. This awareness breeds an appreciation for the adaptive resources within the retarded and demonstrates much of their function, behavior, and communication to be part of the way they adapt to life's stresses. Retardation must be respected like all other forms of human adaptations as a system of survival. If we wish to help the retarded, we must direct our efforts to providing the best possible combinations for each stage of their life—the early stages where nature and nurture blend to give the possibilities for infinite variations to their existence in their conception, pregnancy, birth, infancy, childhood, and adolescence, and the later stages where by our nature and nurturing we provide the resources and climate for the achievement of their potential, whatever it may be.

CHAPTER IV

Early Stages of Human Development

Life begins with conception. The various elements of maturation, development, and growth come into existence with it and become organized into identifiable patterns. These patterns determine the course and outcome of life and can be seen within the achievements of each stage of development. They are contained within all of the functions, behavior, and communication of the growing child. These patterns affect the rate of change while preserving the special traits that identify each of us to ourselves, to our biological origins within the family, and to our roots within our environment.

There are special qualities to these patterns. The most important is the capacity for change. Many things exist within nature with highly determined and fixed boundaries. They are unchanging and predictable. However, human development is dynamic. It evolves constantly into new patterns of organized function. The organization of human functions is predictable only to a certain degree. This quality of change permits the second most important characteristic to emerge: progression. This progression can be identified through observable behavior. It may be stable or unstable. It may become arrested and, in some instances, regressive. It is alterable to the limits of the genetic and constitutional characteristics of the individual and, to a limited degree, by the efforts directed at encouraging growth to take place.

The progressive change of development has its own distinctive qualities. It moves from the undifferentiated state to the differentiated. Simple organization is replaced by more complicated organization. Poor function gives way to more integrated and synthesized responses. The undetermined is replaced by a discriminating selectivity. Formerly diffuse patterns of functioning become associated with predictable, behavioral responses to self and environment. Communication emerges from this interaction.

CONCEPTION

The human counterpart of this developmental sequence starts with conception. An egg is fertilized by a sperm. These two small cells unite. They bring together their separate chromosomal codes of inherited characteristics, as well as a multitude of biochemical messages that start the maturation of the fertilized ovum. One cell divides into two, two into four, four into eight, and so on. It has been estimated that forty-four cell divisions are necessary to bring into being the number of cells present at birth and fewer than sixteen more cell divisions are needed to bring the newborn to adult size. In the nine months from conception to birth, there is an increase in body weight of almost two thousand million times. From birth to adulthood, the body weight increases only about twenty times. These differences in rate of change prior to and following birth are like the speed of light compared with the speed of the tortoise. It makes gestation, the stage of life from conception to birth, a most significant stage.

THE PERIOD OF THE OVUM

The cellular division of the fertilized ovum starts before there is any binding agreement made for its survival. It occurs as this forming human being is moving toward its first home —the uterus of its mother. The continuing cellular division results first in an undifferentiated, globular mass of cells all of which appear to be almost the same. Then an amazing and complex process of differentiation begins, which coincides with the implantation of the ovum into the wall of the uterus. This union becomes a contract for the perpetuation and determination of life. If it is not consummated, the fertilized ovum is cut off from the nurturing flow of biochemical instructions, molecular food, and the stabilizing, protective shelter of the maternal womb. Its existence is terminated quickly and dramatically by nature's rush to prepare the setting for another creation. In two short weeks, decisions are made forever affecting the entire course of human life, initiated by conception, but determined by the quality of the ovum, the sperm, and the readiness of the maternal uterus to house the fertilized ovum. It is within this period of the ovum that hereditary disturbances leading toward some forms of retardation are established.

But even here nature has some kind of selectivity whose secrets have yet to be unraveled. The ovary of the mature female contains approximately a half million unshed ova. As few as four hundred of these will pass into the Fallopian tube and be available for fertilization during a lifetime. Two hundred and fifty million spermatozoa are produced with each ejaculation of the male, and yet only one of these will be involved with the direct fertilization of an ovum. The nature of the selection within this fertilization process remains unknown. Yet the survival of the human race over many thousands and thousands of years confirms a process of natural selection suggesting that some design assures the best possible combinations. The existence of this safeguard of genetic selection is confirmed over and over again by the relatively small numbers of genetically deviant individuals to whom we must give our attention. There is perhaps one in ten thousand for any particular type of genetic defect altering and retarding human development.

There are many other dimensions to this creative moment. The complex problems of fertility play an important role in setting the stage for this genetic selection. Current infertility rates among married couples approach 10 percent. Infertility of the female is associated with the inability to ovulate, the inadequacy of ovulation, or unavailability of the ovum for fertilization by the sperm. Infertility of the male is associated with insufficient quantity or inadequate mobility of spermatozoa. There must be a minimum of eighty million mobile spermatozoa for fertilization to occur. Conception, as with so many other parts of life, including the care of the retarded, requires the devotion of the many to the few.

The products of conception may themselves determine some of the accompanying circumstances. Almost 120 males are conceived for every 100 females. The casualties of gestation result in a reduction of the ratio to 106 male live births to every 100 female live births. Thereafter, males die more frequently than females in every stage. This vulnerability of the males to become biological and social casualties is also seen vividly in the different rates of defects of male and female. The number of males with defects leading to retardation of development is more than double the number of females. Also, the more severe defects and forms of retardation occur among the male population, suggesting a natural biological supremacy of the female.

THE PERIOD OF THE EMBRYO

The embryonic period is characterized by rapid changes and differentiation. Principal systems, organs, and general features of body form are established. This period extends from the end of the second week through the eighth week of gestation. The solid mass of cells becomes hollow and then turns in on itself so that a tube comes into being that forever determines a beginning and end, an in and out, and a top and bottom to the embryo as further differentiation takes place. The creation of this access to the body is accompanied by a rudimentary blueprint of the organs, systems, and parts of the body. The rapidity with which this takes place makes the embryo particularly vulnerable to any disturbance either of its own internal harmony or to the womb. This vulnerability may have two results—spontaneous termination of intrauterine existence or massive congenital defect involving total or systemic abnormalities. The embryonic period is distinguished by the initial development of the nervous system. Generalized defects are more than likely, therefore, to be accompanied by defects of this system with severe developmental retardation.

In recent years these developmental abnormalities have been linked with the presence of many different extra- and intrauterine pollutants, besides anatomical and physiological disturbances. Poor nutrition, excessive use of pharmacological products and drugs, smoking, radiation, and many other agents of our modern civilization have assaulted and breached the protective barriers of the uterus. The possibilities for deviancy or retardation are increased by the exposure early in a pregnancy to these different elements. It is difficult to measure accurately the consequences of this assault. Its impact, however, has been documented over and over again and suggests that caution must be exercised. Fortunately the biological governor of this early period of embryonic existence inspects and judges fitness for existence. Most of those judged as unfit are cast out into the cold world before they have differentiated to a level of development capable of survival. Spontaneous abortions occurring early in pregnancy, although sometimes a sad event, should be viewed as one of nature's devices for tending to the quality of its stock.

THE PERIOD OF THE FETUS

Once the occupancy, form, and structure of the tenant embryo have been firmly accepted by the progressive changes of the maternal womb, the period of fetal development begins to unfold. This period is characterized by rapid increase in size and further definition of structure. Changes occur as a result of differences in rates of development of the various parts, organs, and systems of the body. The top (upper or rostral) end and front undergo a more rapid rate of transition than those of bottom (lower or caudal) end and back. This pattern of rostral and frontal dominance is repeated over and over again in the unfolding of subsequent developmental events and emerges as another special quality of maturation. Its significance is seen in the persistence of the dominance of rostrally determined functions over all others and in the more dramatic fetal abnormalities affecting the upper portions of the body. The head part not only contains the controlling organ of the body, the brain, but also harbors some of the most essential functions related to the preservation of life—breathing, eating, hearing, and seeing. This rostral dominance is repeated during the initial interactions between child and parent both during nursing and with the exchange of affect by sounds and smiles. It occurs again at the emergence of the growing child's awareness of self with the earlier, more elaborate preoccupation with head and upper parts of the body. It is repeated and preserved in nearly all of our cultural patterns with our continuing concern with head and face. So many of our anxieties as well as our fashions and arts appear to be determined by this rostral dominance. Our hair and face have been always personal and universal points of reference.

Fetal development is characterized by rapid differentiation. All tissues and organs have their own rate of maturation crucial to their nature. This timing introduces critical moments within developmental sequences. Certain things must occur at the proper interval if normality is to be achieved. Slowing or hastening the rate of change may alter the outcome significantly. A most dramatic representation of this has been the recent experiences with thalidomide-induced disturbances of fetal development. Pregnant women using a thalidomide derivative as a sedative unknowingly altered the rate of maturation of parts of their unborn infants' bodies. This resulted in a number of fetal abnormalities, the most visible of which were primitive upper limbs. This disorder appears to coincide with a period of rapid differentiation of the fetal limb buds during the fourth month of pregnancy. Exposure to thalidomide derivatives before or after this developmental moment does not result in this kind of abnormality.

A similar time-related disturbance of fetal development is seen among women who contract rubella (German measles) during their first trimester of pregnancy. This relatively minor viral infection causes the developmental havoc of congenital deafness and general retardation—but only before the end of the third month of the pregnancy. The probability of occurrence of this and other associated defects has prompted the medical practice of justifiably terminating pregnancies that are complicated by rubella.

A growing awareness of these and other possible fetal hazards demands a greater attention by all to their existence, their potential effects on the outcome of life, and their impact on some of our practices and mores. Indiscriminate distribution and use of many of the newer chemical products has become as dangerous a form of industrial pollution as the smoke in the air from our factory chimneys and their waste products in our streams.

Our knowledge of circumstances leading to fetal damage requires greater efforts directed at prevention and also at intervention. We appear to be devoting so much of our energies now toward selectively controlling the forces of nature; perhaps we should divert some of this human effort toward selectively controlling our own nature. The issue of elective abortion has many moral, ethical, and social implications. It cannot be viewed adequately without due consideration given to the developmental realities of the fetal period. Technical advances permit us to create and preserve many more of the fetally damaged than ever before. Their preservation, in face of this potential for their greater production, raises serious questions about the resulting disturbances of human ecology. The historical perspectives of man's approaches to his own ecological balance offer possible ways of recruiting modern scientific techniques for controlling the numbers of fetally damaged births. It should be recognized, however, that such decisions are social rather than medical. Until our society is able and willing to face the problems of selective determination, our responsibility to prevent fetal damage grows. It is equally true that those born with fetal damage will have more difficulties in survival as our society becomes more specialized, and we will have a greater responsibility to them for their care and management.

Critical developmental periods vary in duration with rate of change and stage of development. The earlier stages are brief and the later ones have longer time intervals. As demonstrated by animal research, these periods during fetal life vary in duration from a few minutes to a few weeks, depending upon the tissues and organs involved. Their characteristics are determined mostly by genetic and constitutional factors. These periods continue with birth and extrauterine life but are determined more by the circumstances of environment and are of much longer duration. Prevention and intervention are most successful when directed at influencing the critical moments within development.

Just as good maternal nutrition during pregnancy goes far toward offering the fetus the much-needed constitutional equipment for developmental adequacy, so does good infant nutrition offer the circumstances for achieving this adequacy. Recent research on causation reveals that both inadequate maternal and infant nutrition are significant to general retardation. Malnutrition during pregnancy has more profound and lasting effects. Malnutrition during infancy must be more protracted in order to be as profound. This ratio of time to change is true for all of the nurturing ingredients of life, both physical and emotional. It makes those interventions of early life most significant. The developing fetus needs good maternal nutrition. The hungry, crying infant needs both food for his hunger and an emotional response to the crying. The hungry, crying child needs food for his hunger, emotional response to his crying, and instruction on how to satisfy his own hunger. The essence of this transition is contained in the nature and nurture of the individual as seen within each developmental period.

Disturbances of the fetus are numerous because of the rapid physical changes taking place. Fortunately many of these early-determined fetal abnormalities cause negligible or minimal malfunction that become apparent only with the stresses of later life. A slight anomaly of an organ may go unnoticed and become a more serious disorder only under conditions of infection or injury. Thus a mild developmental defect of the central nervous system can remain quiescent until a generalized infection with high fever triggers off an underlying vulnerability to convulsions. One study of six thousand live births revealed some minimal defect in as many as 7 percent of these infants by the end of their first year. Less than half of these defects were even suspected at birth. The percentage of recognizable defects in this same group increased slightly as they grew older. Neither the significant prenatal defects nor their contribution to later disturbance can be appreciated fully because of the difficulties in making direct correlation between cause and effect. Some correlations, however, are felt to exist.

Estimates of the number of infants born in the United States each year with significant fetal defects range to over a quarter of a million. Approximately half of these infants are retarded in later life, and considerably more than half are male. These figures, compared with the numbers of severely and profoundly retarded, indicate that the disabilities of the majority of these children are determined prior to birth. Less than 10 percent of the total number of these fetal defects are the result of genetic disturbances. This suggests that as many as 90 percent of fetal defects may be prevented or modified by efforts made during the period of gestation. Some understanding of the climate of the gestational period will help achieve these goals.

THE ENVIRONMENT OF THE UTERUS

The onset of the fetal period coincides with the firm implantation of the embryo into the uterine wall and the appearance of the placenta. This placenta grows and develops rapidly within the uterus. It serves as the organ of physiological exchange between the mother and the fetus. It transmits the necessary supplies for sustaining the life of the fetus and for encouraging its development and growth. The placenta, however, is known to have many more functions besides transmission. It acts as a protective barrier by preventing material harmful to the fetus from crossing over to it. It serves as a biochemical factory by producing needed hormones and enzymes. It provides food and storage space. It is essential for the sustenance of life, development, and ultimate growth of the fetus. Known disturbances of the placenta are accompanied by a higher incidence of fetal defects.

THE ENVIRONMENT OF THE MOTHER

The fate of the uterus, placenta, and fetus are related to each other during the entire period of gestation. This makes the nature of the maternal existence one of the most important facets of gestation. The nutrition and health of the developing fetus become linked totally to the mother by the interdependence of this period. The intimacy of this relationship is never broken, once established. It is modified only by the passage of time and the different stages of development. During the period of the fetus, the mother recruits, processes, and produces nearly all the requirements of the fetus. These include both the necessary food and antibodies, hormones, and other essential ingredients for the protection and stimulation of growth. The general state of maternal health and function becomes paramount to fetal survival and capacity for development.

This relationship makes maternal nutrition one of the most important prenatal influences. The period of gestation places many physiological demands on the mother. Any established maternal deficiencies are exaggerated by the needs of the fetus and may influence the harmony of their joint existence. For example, many young women are known to have nutritional deficiencies because of their poor eating habits. The nutritional demands of the fetus may then become a contributing reason to the high maternal mortality rate of 6 percent during pregnancy and childbirth among girls under nineteen years of age. All maternal nutrition must be adjusted to compensate for the demands of pregnancy if ideal conditions are desired for mother and fetus. Inadequate maternal diets have been associated with poor fetal development, unsatisfactory conditions during labor, prolonged labor, and difficult afterbirths. The infants born in such conditions have a greater incidence of prematurity and higher morbidity and mortality rates. There have been recorded declines in female fertility and infant birth weights during war periods, when malnutrition is more likely to be present. All of this stands as evidence of the need for adequate nutrition during pregnancy for the prevention of fetal defects with their accompanying developmental retardation.

There are so many descriptions of fetal abnormalities and retardation with alterations of the biochemistry of the mother that mention of only a few serves to highlight the nature of some of these disturbances. Vitamin deficiencies have been identified with many types of fetal abnormalities. Such deficiencies within the mother have a high predilection for causing possible defects within the central nervous system of the fetus. Sometimes the lack of essential elements within the maternal diet has been known to produce developmental aberrations such as those seen in cretinism. The physical and mental retardation of cretinism has been traced to the lack of iodine intake by the mother during pregnancy. All of these biochemical disturbances are preventable, with the exception of the genetically transmitted whose incidence is limited and may be limited further by genetic counseling. However, all become preventable only through our willingness to invest in adequate prenatal care.

There are many maternal dysfunctions capable of altering the circumstances of gestation. Diabetes can change the rate and nature of fetal development. Disturbances of the thyroid gland may affect both the process and product of gestation. Fetal abnormalities have been related to hormonal imbalances of the maternal adrenal, pituitary, and parathyroid glands. Increased rates of fetal damage and wastage have been associated with blood disturbances and immunological incompatibility between mother and fetus. A common type of blood-group incompatibility that may be harmful to the fetus and that carries with it the potential for fetal damage and retardation is known as erythroblastosis fetalis. One out of every twelve pregnancies involves this incompatibility of mothers with Rh-negative blood carrying fetuses with Rh-positive blood. Fortunately, not all such combinations lead to damage. However, the resulting destruction of the red blood cells of the fetus may cause a jaundice severe enough to damage the brain and liver of the newborn in as many as one out of every two hundred pregnancies. The accompanying hydrops fetalis results in the death of the fetus if the jaundice is severe. This jaundice (also known as kernicterus), if occurring to a lesser degree, causes varying kinds of neurological damage with retardation. Other states involving maternal-fetal incompatibilities, sensitizations, and allergies may plague the harmony of coexistence. Most of these are identifiable early enough to be helped in ways that protect the well-being of the mother and the outcome of fetal development.

THE ENVIRONMENT FOR THE MOTHER

There are many variables present within the environment of the mother altering the conditions of gestation and its outcome. Maternal infections pose some real dangers. Such diseases as syphilis and smallpox have left their mark on the progeny of man and woman throughout recorded history. Many other infectious diseases also cause fetal damage. These congenitally transmitted conditions are diffuse in nature and introduce many physical and functional disturbances. Some of the bacterial diseases not only damage but often destroy. The current widespread use of antibacterial agents has improved our ability to preserve fetal existence, but infections occurring at so early a stage of development still cause considerable damage. Also, viral infections may affect the outcome of pregnancies while increasing the possibilities of congenital maldevelopment. In addition to rubella, other viral diseases capable of changing fetal survival rates include regular measles, mumps, chicken pox, poliomyelitis, and viral hepatitis.

General technical advances have produced new hazards for fetal existence. The environment has become filled with all types of chemical agents. The range of substances influencing the developing fetus grows at an alarming rate. Many of these substances may become noxious agents to vulnerable tissues still undergoing development. This has particular significance for the central nervous system, whose prolonged immaturity minimizes its capacity to resist damage. This newly developing threat extends through infancy and childhood as well. Chemical poisoning has become one of the major disasters of early life. Availability of chemical agents should be considered as one form of our contemporary pollution danger.

Special mention should be made of the hazards of radiation. This new hazard in our modern civilization has been documented by the existence of a small but growing number of developmental defects and deviant individuals whose origins can be traced to excessive radiation exposure of mother or fetus. It should be noted that radiation may not only disturb the equilibrium between the mother and fetus but affect both mother and fetus at the same time. Of particular concern is radiation's potential for increasing genetically determined mutations and abnormalities. No genetic counseling can alter this hazard. Only careful attention paid to avoiding unnecessary exposure, and national agreements preventing the contamination of our atmosphere with atomic by-products, will limit this danger. And a great danger it is. The slightest increase of potential for genetic mutation within the general population is capable of producing a dramatic increase in deviancy. All of us fall prey to this danger—not only those who may harbor some recessive genetic trait that may or may not produce developmental defect among our progeny.

Social and cultural forces play yet other important roles in establishing attitudes of life-style affecting conception, gestation, and birth. A good example of this interweaving of socially determined attitudes with these biological happenings is the age of the mother at the time of the events. A woman's childbearing period ranges over thirty years of her life. The highest incidence of casualties of conception, gestation, and birth occur at either end of this age spectrum. The incidence of Down's syndrome (mongolism) is directly associated with maternal age and occurs with highest frequency among the very young and the very mature. Many other disturbances affecting the integrity of the fetus show similar correlations to the maternal age. Conditions altering pregnancy such as toxemia, eclampsia, prolonged labor, premature births, miscarriages, stillbirths, and malformations all fall into this category. Thus the patterns of childbearing as determined by attitudes toward the family may affect the incidence of occurrence of fetal damage. Our sexual revolution has been accompanied by a significant increase of pregnancies in very young girls, with many of these births taking place out of wedlock. Such circumstances are not conducive to good prenatal care and, biologically, carry a higher risk for maternal and fetal damage. At the same time, the emancipation of women with their movement out of the home and into the labor market has spread childbearing toward the upper maternal age limits, which also carries a higher risk of maternal and fetal damage. Such combinations have subtle but significant impact on the incidence of retardation. There is a definite increase in all types of retardation among the children born to older females, just as there is a higher risk of damage to life among very young females.

These biological truisms have been well documented. The incidence of developmental abnormalities of the central nervous system of the fetus correlates directly with maternal age. The incidence is twice as great in forty-year-old mothers as in twenty-year-old mothers. Prematurity demonstrates a similar pattern of causation, as do most of the other physical hazards of maternal life. These physical elements, however, appear to blend inseparably with the environmental influences on the mother. This correlation has been demonstrated by the linking of maternal age to social process. This can be extended even further to the emotional climate of the mother, which is more completely the product of her interaction with her environment. There is considerable evidence to support the assumption that maternal emotions affect gestation through alterations of nutritional state, chemical equilibrium, and hormonal balance. The evidence suggests that emotional stresses can cause disturbances ranging from infertility to false pregnancy (pseudocyesis). These may be viewed as effects of direct maternal reactions. Indirect effects must play a similar role in establishing the adequacy or inadequacy of the pregnancy. There may be a lack of effort to secure adequate prenatal care or a good nutritional state.

There are also other physiological disturbances with strong psychological components known to modify the course of gestation. Diabetes is a good example. It is a metabolic disease of the mother capable of altering the rate and nature of the growth of the fetus. There is a known danger to the safety of the mother and fetus in all such metabolic disturbances. There is also an emotional liability accompanying most of these difficulties. This blending stands as evidence of the inseparability of the environment of the mother and the developing fetus.

THE BIRTH PROCESS

The physical and emotional state of the mother continues to be important to the outcome of the gestation up to the moment of birth. The period of labor and birth are events of dramatic proportions. Once started, a dynamic interaction unfolds that leaves its imprint upon mother, child, and family forever by its successes or failures. The circumstances of the birth process are physical, chemical, emotional, and social. They involve the mother, child, family, and community. They occur rapidly and often dramatically. With so much and many involved, the possibilities of variations, casualties, or disturbances are great. Mother and fetus must come to the occasion well prepared for the rapid changes and sequence of events, which require a unity of purpose from both. The well-established equilibrium of the intrauterine fetal life must be replaced by a new kind of existence leading toward the first stage of independent functioning for each in relation to the other. The physical ties binding mother and fetus together need to be severed without loss to either so that new ties can be forged between mother and infant more suitable to independent existences for both. This quality of destruction of the old to achieve the construction of the new is yet another pattern of maturation. Birth makes this pattern a natural part of all subsequent parent-child relationships.

The act of labor is initiated by the inability or unwillingness of the uterus to continue housing the fetus. With increasingly violent contractions, it begins the process of severing its connections with the fetus. The act of labor becomes a demand upon the fetus to begin an independent existence. This stimulus and response known as birth is one of the miracles of life. It establishes the fetus as an infant with the ability to respond for its own survival and existence.

The rapidity of events requires many synchronized changes

to take place. The completely formed fetal respiratory and circulatory systems must undergo simple but major anatomical transitions to achieve separate functioning. The survival of the infant is dependent on these changes taking place at the right moment within the sequence of the birth process. It is to the credit of the design and their lengthy period of fetal functioning that both of these systems make the transition with only an occasional developmental abnormality disturbing their subsequent roles.

The real vulnerability of the fetal infant during this transitional period exists within the central nervous system. Unlike all the other major organ systems, which achieve considerable developmental maturity by the time of birth, the central nervous system remains immature, vulnerable in its immaturity, and susceptible to the stresses of the events of labor and birth. The particular nature of the susceptibility is linked to the need for a constant supply of oxygen by the tissue cells of the nervous system. Any sustained alteration of this supply may affect the integrity of the nervous system by the injury of essential cells. It is not the system itself that is harmed but rather the components of the system, so that the quality of its function becomes altered. This kind of subtle brain injury may or may not be accompanied by more generalized impairment of functioning leading to retardation.

Regretfully, the circumstances of labor and birth temporarily increase the possibilities for poor oxygen supply (anoxia) to the fetal infant. The uterine contractions and the process of expelling the fetal infant from the uterus can be responsible, as can the switchover of the fetal infant's respiratory and circulatory systems, the many disturbances of labor and birth, or some of the interventions required for delivery of the infant. It is usually the combination of all four that results in circumstances leading to injury of the infant or the infant's central nervous system. The best possible care should be given during the delivery of the newborn because of this complexity. Yet the incidence of preventable casualties of birth remains alarmingly high even in countries with advanced systems for delivery of health services. Here is another major area for both prevention and intervention to reduce the number of potentially damaged and retarded individuals.

The nature of damage at birth to the fetal infant's nervous system will vary from the damage that may occur at the beginning of the period of fetal existence. The nervous system is immature at both stages. However, the degree of differentiation of structure and function is considerable at birth. This degree serves to limit and localize the impact of damage from any prolonged period of poor oxygen supply. This difference serves to protect the life of the fetal infant by making vital functions of the central nervous system less vulnerable to potential injury. But the more sophisticated parts devoted to the functions of perception and motor response are not well developed as yet and therefore are the parts remaining more vulnerable to damage and disturbance. This variation accounts for the different type of defects seen as a result of birth injuries. There may be mechanical impairment of parts or functional disturbances reflecting interference with ability. Thus birth injuries are more likely to be accompanied by continued development and disturbed function, while fetal damage is more likely to be accompanied by impaired development and the lack of function. The early fetal damage is more likely to be accompanied by severe, diffuse disability and retardation. Birth injury is more likely to be accompanied by mild, specific disability and retardation. All children with brain damage from birth injury are not necessarily retarded, but many such children do demonstrate specific impairments early in life with sensory motor dysfunction, or later in life with disruption of learning skills.

Some comments need to be made on the emotional aspects of birth. Our history, religion, literature, customs, and family life reflect adult perceptions and emotional involvement with this momentous occasion. Does the fetal infant also record the event as a significant emotional experience? Some have viewed the birth process in this way and have suggested it to be the initial source of emotional trauma and stress of life. Sigmund Freud referred to the birth process as a "concatenation of painful feelings, of discharges of excitation, and of bodily sensations, as to have become a prototype for all occasions on which life is endangered, ever after to be reproduced again in us as the dread or 'anxiety' condition."

He offered further:

> The enormous increase in stimulation effected by the interruption of the renewal of blood (the internal respiration) was the cause of the anxiety experience at birth—the first anxiety therefore was toxically induced. The name *Angst* (anxiety)—angustiae, Engee, a narrow place, a strait —accentuates the characteristic tightening in the breathing which was then the consequence of a real situation and is subsequently repeated almost invariably with an affect. It is very suggestive too that the first anxiety state arose on the occasion of the separation from the mother.

Otto Rank made reference to the sense of security being associated with the life in the womb and constituting a blissful state that birth interrupts and destroys. He suggested that birth became the primal separation and made separation the cause of prime anxiety associated with feelings of helplessness. Phyllis Greenacre suggested the existence of pre-anxiety reactions in fetal life without any psychic content and birth as the stress predisposing the infant to anxiety. She suggested birth to be the experience producing the organization and patterning of bodily components that then served as the physiological base for anxiety. These components formed the somatic patterns of anxiety responses later in life, accounting for why some of us get headaches and others stomachaches under stress.

These several comments reinforce an awareness of the dimensions of birth as a total experience for our fetal infants as well as ourselves. Occurrences during this period leave their imprint on every aspect of human development. Damage or disturbance of the birth process may affect the emerging patterns of interaction between the infant and his environment so as to impair or alter reactive capacities. Any extensive impairment will be manifest as a functional retardation, while alterations of the reactive capacities of the infant will be viewed as disturbed behavior. This division is more a product of the adult perception of a single process than it is a true separation of disturbances affecting developmental progression. Thus some of the casualties of conception, gestation, and birth come to be viewed as damaged, others as disturbed, and yet others as retarded. All of them are, however, the product of a life period taking place in very rapid sequence while hidden from view in the maternal womb. Our own orientation to time, space, and place makes this period of life one of darkness and mystery. But, if we are to help those whom we call retarded (or disturbed), we must invade this darkness and destroy the mystery by appropriate preventative measures and interventions designed to permit these critical stages of human development—conception, gestation, and birth—to unfold in the full glory of a healthy newborn infant. And if this unfolding reveals one of the casualties of this eventful period of life, we must then free our imagination and all the resources at our command to continue the nurturing process that permits all of us to achieve to our best potential.

CHAPTER V

Infantile Development

The patterns of maturation, as of birth, do much to determine the nature of subsequent human development and endow their special characteristics (constitutional) upon later functions, behavior, and communication. These capacities for change, the progressions, the selections, the dominances, the critical stages, and the destruction of the old for the new can be identified within all subsequent phases of postnatal life. Simple organization gives way to more complex and better integrated ones. Reflexes become part of reactive states. Perception and response become directed at environmental changes as well as self. Functions become discernible within behavior. Behavior causes interaction and the need for communication. Communication recruits function and behavior for relationships that become paramount. The infant is born.

The best way to define infancy is through the concept of relationship. An infant is someone's infant. It never exists by itself. An infant is dependent on someone other than itself. An infant is helpless and vulnerable to the vicissitudes of its environment, making the relationship with this environment its nuclear existence. Being related becomes the essence of this stage of life. This relatedness dominates the nature of the changes taking place. Progression through infancy becomes molded by the ability of the infant to relate to itself and then to significant human beings upon whom it is dependent. Much, therefore, of the emerging character depends upon this interaction. The needs of the infant and those of the caring parent both play a role in selecting the stimulus to be responded to, the order of priority, and the nature of the interval between stimuli and responses. The old biological determinism of prenatal life gives way to a new social determinism.

The resulting kinship of parent and child emerges as the critical force in shaping events and outcome. The infant's reflexive responses to itself become recruited for reactive responses with its parent. Hunger reflexes become linked to crying reflexes, become linked to sucking reflexes, become linked to parental responses of holding, feeding, and emotions. Thus the relatively simple organization of the isolated reflex becomes tied together into highly complex, integrated patterns of behavior between parent and child. The perceptions and responses of the infant become redirected into a more complex awareness of self and environment. These perceptions and responses are repeated and become as much a product of the interactions as the original reflexes. Now the hunger contraction of the stomach evokes behavior directed at achieving a response from the environment. The hunger cry changes to motivated communication rather than remaining random, self-determining activity. Communication, learning, and teaching are born from these events, converting the simplest of biological reflexes into complex social interaction.

Interruptions or variations of this transition result in arrests or disturbances of the progression of infant development. An understanding of this progression within infancy, and what may happen to it, offers many clues to useful procedures that can be recruited for prevention, intervention, and rehabilitation for those individuals who are retarded by genetic or constitutional events and their early life experiences.

THE PERIOD OF SENSORY-MOTOR ORGANIZATION: THE REFLEX PHASE

The newborn infant is already a highly complex organism with many functioning organ systems that are vital to its biological existence, i.e., the circulatory system, the digestive system, and so on. Each of these systems is organized relative to itself and the others by messages called impulses and through reflexes, which are recognized as conditioned or unconditioned responses to the impulses. The conditioned responses remain the same once they are established, so that varying stimuli within a particular range evoke the same response. These conditioned reflexes assure the basic pattern of functioning of each organ system and their relationship to each other. There would be biological anarchy if they were not present, since all responses would be variable and unpredictable. It is this predictability which gives each organ system its identifiable role and relationship to the total design of bodily functions.

The nervous system serves as the principal conveyor of messages among the various systems of the body. It provides many complex message centers within the central nervous system for processing the impulses of perceptions and responses, and a complex distributing pathway within the peripheral nervous system for conducting the impulses of perception and responses, and messages among the various organ systems of the body. The nervous system is reasonably able to integrate and synchronize the internal impulses and messages as a result of its period of fetal development. But birth introduces a new set of circumstances. The protective barrier of the maternal womb is lost forever. This barrier served to limit and control the kinds, the number, and the nature of stimuli reaching the fetus. The loss of this barrier exposes the fetal infant to the infinite variation of life. Stimuli become different, innumerable, and of unlimited variations.

The newborn must recruit all that it had already learned from its period of fetal development in order to organize its perceptions of the infinite number of stimuli to which it becomes exposed after birth. It begins a new process of selection based on some of the old priorities. It organizes and integrates in a manner designed to assure its developmental progression and the dominance of those perceptions which are critical to its survival and nature within a now ever-changing world. This early period of sensory-motor organization can be identified as necessary for the determination of a new hierarchy of perceptions and responses. Which environmental stimuli are important? Which reflexes from fetal existence serve best to respond to infant needs? What new combination of reflexes can be developed? Which responses are most appropriate and effective? Do they represent a biologically economical utilization of established reflex patterns? Do new reflex patterns need to be developed?

This reflex phase of early sensory-motor organization represents the initial interaction of the infant with its new environment. It is dependent on genetically and constitutionally determined reflex equipment recruited for processing impulses from an ever-changing world. It makes this phase impulse-related. It becomes the moment of living where impulse reigns supreme, uncluttered by any social rule or order. Stimulus evokes response. Impulse is gratified by immediate reaction.

There is no delay other than the biological order of things. The stomach contraction evokes the cry of hunger and the demand of impulse for instant gratification. No quarter is given. The hunger contractions must be satisfied by feeding, or an increasing tension results, with more frequent stomach contractions and more persistent hunger cries. If still not satisfied, the entire reflex response system breaks down by exhaustion. Hunger no longer evokes stomach contractions. Stomach contractions fail to evoke crying. The order of the internal reflexes gives way to the disorder of haphazard responses or none at all. Unpredictability of response becomes the nature of reactions.

The key to the stabilization of impulse and reflex during this early phase can be found within the interaction of infant with nurturing parent. Appropriate timing of response by the parent to cues emanating from the infant results in a reinforcement of significant impulses and reflex response systems, with relaxation of tension. The mechanism and timing of the biological clock becomes synchronized and ordered by parental efforts and leads to new, patterned functions and behavior. Without this necessary reinforcement, the combinations of variable stimuli and responses result in poor patterning of essential functions and unpredictable outcome. The order and progression of developmental events become variable. The accompanying uncertainty slows down the emergence of expected sequences, so that retardation emerges as a potential end point of inadequate nurturing of the very young infant.

It should be stressed that the adequacy of this early nurturing is dependent on several factors. Genetically established defects introduce the presence or absence of chemical and enzymatic substances that alter the biological impulses, so that reflex responses are changed or absent. When possible, these alterations must be compensated for by medical interventions as well as protective nurturing. Fortunately, these genetic defects are rare and are being helped gradually by research devoted to their early identification, and by attempts to correct their chemical imbalances. Constitutionally established defects are more numerous and introduce many different kinds of developmental lags that alter the internal systems, so that reflex responses are highly individualized. Where possible, these alterations must be compensated for by early identification and specialized nurturing.

The adequacy of nurturing our young is subject to so many pitfalls that its widespread achievement stands as a monument to human imagination and creativity. The infant born with defect is a constant stimulus to this creativity. But some of the pitfalls must be recognized if the continuation or introduction of developmental retardation is to be avoided. Each newborn is already a highly distinctive individual with its own reflex patterns. Lack of sensitivity to these patterns introduces the lack of constancy in response and the possibility of failure of needed reinforcement. Very young infants require consistent, knowing handling. They are best off with constant, familiar, and loving responses to their impulses. They are less well off with just consistent and familiar responses. They are least well off with only consistent responses. And they are worst off with inconsistent handling of their impulses. It is easy to see how the kinship of parent and child becomes one of the essential ingredients of all child-rearing. It should be just as easy to see how institutional care of infants and children destroys this essential ingredient, no matter how well motivated the institution and its personnel may be. The institution introduces multiple and varying nurturing. The familiar gives way to the impersonal. The impersonal makes loving difficult.

These early universal human needs become the basic requirements of most retarded individuals through much of their life. The defects and developmental lags of retardation demand an extra investment of time, as well as consistency, familiarity, and response to needs. Consistency breeds familiarity for the retarded. Familiarity permits them to respond. And then their responses approach our needs. Time and interaction permit the retarded to learn and those of us devoted to their care to teach. These essentials of the pathway to communication with the retarded must be part of every program for them, within family and within community.

Nearly all disturbances of this early period of infant sensory-motor organization, as well as those that have preceded it, will cause some significant degree of developmental retardation unless attenuated or corrected by the nurturing care. The principal characteristics of these disturbances are found within the manner in which impulses are organized and handled. Since the patterning of impulses is poor, the same stimulus may evoke variable responses. A pinprick may cause a cry of pain or no cry. It may stimulate a motoric withdrawal of the part or none. It may elicit a response of movement of an unrelated part of the body. This unpredictability becomes a major pitfall of nurturing. Attempts to identify needs of the infant meet with a higher incidence of failure. Variability of infant responses introduces an uncertainty that may then lead to inconsistencies. Lack of response introduces frustration to the relationship of nurturing parent to infant. Frustration provides a poor climate for kinship and love. It is this sequence that plagues the relationships with all retarded persons, young and old. Until their special needs and individualized responses come to be recognized for what they are, it is difficult to respond appropriately to them.

Another aspect of the problem of the retarded can be seen in the early infantile efforts to relate and cope with impulse. Developmental progression leads toward the organization of impulses into reflex responses, which then become incorporated into reactive behavioral responses to environmental cues.

Reflex responses are recruited when reactive responses fail to develop. An unpleasant situation causes a reaction of aversion in most of us. The failure to develop this behavioral capacity for aversion may result in the substitution of a reflexive response such as a head-jerking, neck-twisting tic that simulates aversion by recruitment of a primitive tonic-neck-reflex response. Subsequently, all unpleasant, tension-producing situations may trigger this tic. The persistence of such reflex in place of reactive behavioral responses serves impulse but not relationship. This is but a single example from many disturbances of impulse that are commonly seen among the retarded.

Yet another form of infantile coping with impulse can be seen in the enlistment of rhythmical and repetitive activity. Such behavior directs many impulses into simple and familiar patterns. It releases tension by attaching impulse to familiar motor activities with predetermined outcome. All rhythmical activity should be viewed as tension-reducing behavior because it recruits and organizes impulse, makes it purposeful, satisfies the need for response, and provides boundaries for the accompanying behavior. The common occurrence of masturbatory activity among the young and the retarded represents a fine example of this process. Both have excessive, undifferentiated impulses with poorly defined goals and boundaries. Both have yet to achieve to their gratification and fulfillment from their environment. Both have a need to find behavior that satisfies their impulses unto themselves. Masturbatory activity provides the opportunity for all of these, as do thumb-sucking, body-rocking, and other forms of rhythmical behavior seen so commonly among the retarded.

An awareness of the persistence of this impulse-coping system among the retarded does much to improve our sensitivity to their tensions, frustrations, and lack of fulfillment. For it provides us with visible behavioral manifestations of their difficulties. All that need be done is to respond appropriately. They must be helped with their tension-producing frustrations.

They must be directed into activities that give them fulfillment to their potential and not to our ambitions or society's goals. They must be redirected into productive activity that recruits impulse in simple, repetitive, and rhythmical manners that bring them into positive relationships with others. There are many such goal-oriented tasks available for all age groups. It is in the design of these tasks and life experiences that our imagination comes to be stimulated by the immature and the retarded. This interaction can lead to a creativity and relationship that is meaningful for all.

The recognition of retardation as a developmental anomaly serves to explain other forms of impulse disturbances that may be related to this reflex phase of infantile sensory-motor organization. Developmental progression has its own characteristics, which affect the outcome of impulse organization. Many of these have been described. They now need to be applied to an understanding of retardation of impulse organization. The capacity to change impulse patterns is slowed. Progression takes place, but at a different rate. This alters the selection of impulse pathways, the preference of some over others, and the dominance of earlier determined patterns. Some behavioral responses are undifferentiated. Others are reflexive and not reactive. Many show rostral preference with a priority for infantile oral gratification through such behavior as excessive touching, mouthing, or smelling of objects, compulsive eating, experimentation with vocalizations, and compulsive talking. In their stage-by-stage evolution, functions lose their distinctive features and merge with each other so that an undifferentiated quality permeates the more sophisticated behavior. This is sometimes described as the amorphous quality of the retarded. The old is not destroyed for the sake of the new but lives on, so that no clear developmental transition is evident. Real maturity escapes the retarded by the persistence of some of these early-determined impulse-related patterns of behavior.

Severe disturbances of this early reflex phase of sensory-motor organization are always accompanied by some significant degree of retardation and by disorders of behavior and communication. The more genetically and constitutionally deviant demonstrate serious impulse disorders dominated by the persistence of early reflex patterns and the inability to relate impulse appropriately to themselves, to other objects of their environment, and to people. Their behavior remains primitive, poorly determined, and unrelated. Their ability to communicate is impaired to such a degree that expressive language is badly disturbed and speech is limited or even absent. Those subjected to circumstances that interfere or prevent impulses from becoming properly integrated or related present a similar degree of retardation and disturbed behavior. The severely brain-damaged and autistic young fall into this category. The existence of all such individuals stands as mute evidence of the significance of impulse-related existence.

THE PERIOD OF SENSORY-MOTOR ORGANIZATION: THE INHIBITORY PHASE

The constant interaction with a changing environment generates the need for some kind of stability, permitting significant experiences to be repeated. Survival rests in such selective ability. There is no way that an infant can stabilize its external environment or develop self-control without being dependent on repeated parental reinforcements. Both serve to bring new and vital dimensions to the existence of the infant. Impulse has to give way now to rule and order. Not only does impulse evoke response but it must evoke the same response if it is to become part of a gratifying experience. The need for this kind of selective ability introduces a demand to control impulse by choice, by delay, by tolerance of tension, and by the help of the caring parent. All of these serve to make the inhibition of impulse critical to developmental progressions.

This recruitment of inhibition marks the first active expression by the infant toward self-determination. It makes inhibition the significant controlling force of the emerging self. It establishes the dominance of inhibition over excitation within the order of maturation. It makes inhibition the earliest and one of the most important of infantile acts. It gives inhibition a high priority within the functional order of maturation, and because it appears so early, it becomes a generalized phenomenon affecting all subsequent behavior. This may account for the presence of depression (a generalized reactive state of inhibition) as a universal human experience. It does account for depression as an infantile and childhood experience, when recognized not as a mood but by the active inhibition of essential functions. Such infantile depressions may have serious repercussions within development. They may make the inhibition of function the dominant response to future stresses. Their prolonged existence within infancy by extensive physical or emotional deprivation may result in growth failure, emotional stunting, and generalized retardation. These effects may be of lifetime duration if corrective efforts are not made during infancy to assure an adequate physical and emotional environment. This adequacy must be sought for all of our young through good infant and child care programs, excellent infant nutrition, and the providing of consistent, loving care.

It must be sought particularly for those who enter infancy with defect, for they are more vulnerable and their vulnerability exposes them to the possibility of their recruitment of inhibition as a preferred style of response. So many of the retarded seem to turn off their latent abilities and turn away from demands to perform. And those who pursue the retarded with demands for performance fail to understand the deep-rooted and early origins of this pattern of response. They fail to recognize that with the demand must come an acceptance and an emotional climate that does not evoke this early-determined inhibition of functions.

One of the most significant aspects of this inhibitory phase of sensory-motor organization is the emergence of self. For the first time, and by its own initiative, the infant attempts to control relationships with its environment and emerges from this attempt with independence and as a social being. Experience of success or failure begins with reflex responses and their conversion to reactive responses. Perceptions by the senses evoke more and more complex motor reactions. These require in turn a higher degree of organization of reflexes by the inhibition of some perceptions over others. The blueprint for much of this early selection is established by the genetic coding affecting all development, by the constitutional endowments, and by the life experiences. However, the results of this emerging selection are a distinctive combination for each individual and the beginnings of an independent existence in relation to self rather than others. This early relatedness makes the self forever the most significant object of life. The strength of this relatedness becomes part of the strength for life. It permits meaningful interactions with environment and their repetition. It makes possible learning from experiences. Above all, it introduces the infant to relationships with others through the existence of itself.

The nature of the early interactions of the infant with the caring parent does much to influence the role of inhibition within future development. There may be excessive reinforcement or failure to encourage selection by inhibition. There may be variability of interaction, so that no selection may emerge as a distinctive pattern. Appropriate reinforcement does much to encourage and facilitate this essential process and makes consistency in early infant-parent relationship one of the most important attributes. It is easy to see how these same conditions have broad application to the care of the retarded. Part of the disturbance of many of the retarded is vested in some of their own failures within this critical stage of development. Their selection by inhibition is poor. They preserve these earlier forms of reactions. They tend to regress to some of these patterns of response when under stress. Their concepts of themselves are poor and often inadequately defined. Persons concerned with helping and caring for the retarded must compensate for this developmental inadequacy by an understanding attitude and consistency of approach. It is never too late to introduce these essential ingredients to the nurturing care of our immature and dependent.

Severe disturbances of this inhibitory phase of sensory-motor organization are accompanied by varying degrees of retardation and inhibited behavior and communication. The genetically and constitutionally deviant show a generalized state of inhibition that permeates all of their functions. Others show their potential by isolated functions but never achieve that potential. Yet others are victimized by an ever-present inhibitory state that turns possible success into failure, interrupts learning, and frustrates teaching. Impulse becomes related to an inadequate self. Relationship with others is inhibited so that there is an appearance of withdrawal and emptiness. Behavioral responses are meager. Communication is limited by the poor development of expressive language and speech. Those subjected to circumstances that reinforce the inhibitory phase in spite of genetic and constitutional adequacy may demonstrate their disturbance not through retardation but by way of the inadequacy of self.

THE PERIOD OF SENSORY-MOTOR ORGANIZATION: THE EXCITATORY PHASE

The growing interaction between the developing self and the complexities of an expanding environment exposes the infant to an ever-increasing number and variety of stimuli. There must be a general quickening of ability to respond in order to meet this new demand. Need introduces the excitatory phase of sensory-motor organization. For only with new capacities is the infant able to cope with the rapidly changing circumstances of its existence. The inhibitory process fulfills the necessary role of bringing some order to impulse and reflex response, as well as beginning the internal organization of the infant. However, it reduces environmental input and interferes with a much needed acceleration of reactions to both internal and external events. A new order of things is required. The infant begins to be stimulated by its perceptions in a compensatory manner. A new sensitivity emerges, with attention given to every environmental cue. The established priority of reflexive responses gives way to reactive ones. Gratification begins to shift to new combinations. The hunger, crying, sucking reflex needs may be satisfied by feeding. But the infant's reactive needs now include touching, holding, rocking, cooing, smiling as the accompaniments for a satisfactory feeding. The integration of all these cues is dependent on a higher order of organization. It is dependent also on a more rapid form. The excitatory phase serves these purposes well.

There are many special characteristics to this phase. The infant responds to everything and everyone. Discrimination is almost lacking. Each sound, touch, and movement evokes a response. Anyone can feed it as long as he satisfies the hunger. Anyone can change the diaper as long as the discomfort is relieved. Reflexes run into each other. They become joined and sometimes interfere with each other. Feeding the very young infant will stimulate a gastrocolic reflex that causes a bowel evacuation. The evacuation may interrupt the continuity of feeding. This period takes on kaleidoscopic proportions. Everything changes, runs together, and then separates. It has the appearance of excesses. The infant not only eats but may eat beyond its capacity and regurgitate what it has eaten. Sometimes one response substitutes for another spontaneously and inappropriately. The hungry infant finds its thumb and sucks it. This act does not satisfy the hunger, but the sucking simulates feeding related to satisfying hunger and the infant is satisfied momentarily.

All of these sequences take place very rapidly. They appear and disappear. Some remain because they meet the genetic, constitutional, and reflex needs of the infant. Others remain because they meet the combined needs of infant and parent. The reinforcement by the parent helps overcome the lack of infant discrimination. It helps separate infant reactions by preventing them from interfering with each other. Parental limits minimize excesses and curb inappropriate substitutions. Parental determinations help confine the rate of change to reasonable proportions.

The recruitment of excitation marks another active expression by the infant toward self-determination. But the horizons of this determination extend now to all objects and experiences within the scope of the infant's perception. Whereas the reflex phase of sensory-motor organization is impulse-related and the inhibitory phase is self-related, the excitatory phase is object-related. It uses all that has taken place before while incorporating as many objective experiences as rapidly as possible to help define further the infant to itself and provide new resources for coping with relationships. It makes stimulation an essential ingredient of development. Without it, the infant becomes slowed by inhibition and disorganized by impulse. It makes the infant-parent relationship a most significant one. Without it, stimulation is lacking, discriminatory ability poor, reactive responses excessive or inappropriate, and the rate of developmental progression altered. This early combination of inhibition and excitation may account for one of the universal rhythms of life while making hyperkinesis (overactive and poorly organized behavior) a common infantile and childhood experience. A prolonged hyperkinetic state may have serious developmental repercussions. It may persist to the point of endowing its special features upon the character of the individual, or to the point of disturbance when it becomes identified as a hyperkinetic behavior disorder. It may disrupt development by such poorly ordered functions that a generalized state of retardation comes into being. The genetically and constitutionally deviant are more likely to fall prey to this type of early-determined disturbance, as well as other types.

The nature of these disturbances of the excitatory phase of sensory-motor organization places stress on the quality of nurturing and begins to quantify it. How much and how little nurturing becomes important. Whether it is offered in a sustained and consistent form takes on new meaning. Decisions of what should be responded to and reinforced achieve a new significance in creating a meaningful harmony between inhibition and excitation. The nature of the infant's object-relatedness begins to be molded by the determinations of infant-parent interaction.

All of these general truths of early infant care are reflected and become magnified by the needs of the retarded. Many of them have extensive problems with their object-relatedness as a result of their defects or developmental disharmony. Their care and programs require emphasis on helping them by stimulation to achieve better object-relatedness through improved discrimination, more appropriate responses, and the harmony of time and place within life.

THE PERIOD OF INDIVIDUATION

The early sensory-motor organization provides the infant with the objective dimensions of life. By its own growing sense of self and independence, the infant brings into being that of others. But the infant must learn to discriminate between itself and others if it is to survive as a distinct entity. This developmental need leads the infant to its period of individuation, forever establishing relationships with others as an essential part of life. The period of individuation is marked by the importance of human relatedness.

All that has taken place within maturation is recruited for this developmental task. The recognition of change, the ability to select, the dominance of inhibition over excitation, the control of impulse, the awareness of self, the object-relatedness —all begin to provide the infant with the ability to discriminate between the familiar and the unfamiliar. All permit the infant to experience the known with increasing certainty and assurance. All endow the infant with a growing strength for action and existence. No longer is it a question of *to be or not to be*. It is a matter of *I am*. And if I am, who are you? What is your relationship to me? Will you respond to my needs? Can I depend upon you? Do you exist with any constancy? Will you change? Can you cease to exist? If you cease to exist, do I?

The early patterns of infant behavior reflect many of these questions. There is an abrupt transition of behavior by attachment to the familiar. The infant seeks to reproduce known experiences. It responds to a smile by smiling. It smiles and searches for a responding smile. It cries to be fed or held and becomes frustrated and tense when it is not. It begins to demand human relationship. And suddenly it begins to demand familiar relationships. It will not smile for everyone. It will not be soothed by everyone. It begins to demand the particular —the known. This discrimination becomes a reflection of the emerging sense of self. It becomes the index of individuation. The infant cries when left alone. It becomes aware of presence or absence of people more than things. Now the infant demands relationship by making its own presence known.

This process of individuation places an increasing responsibility on the caring parent. Demand must be responded to or be ignored. Response cements the parent-child relationship and intensifies all of the preceding interactions. Lack of response leaves the developing infant to its own disharmony, and it can rely only on its poorly evolved controls and balances. The inappropriate dominance of early forms of reactions limits the infant in its relationship to others and interferes with all subsequent communication. In such instances, retardation appears as a result of the breakdown of the ability to perceive and express. When human relatedness fails to develop properly, the subtle equilibrium of development can be preserved only by going back to some of the earliest modes of functioning.

Nearly all retarded individuals, as well as many of the disturbed, show some alteration of their capacity for human-relatedness. They tend to be more self-centered. They seek relationships, but mostly for their own needs. They sometimes appear to have a better ability to relate to things than people. They frequently use things as an instrument for seeking relationship to people (the use of transitional objects). An object is used to negotiate relationship. They bring their teacher an apple in place of good performance. Their preoccupation with themselves extends to their physical dimensions. They seek bodily contact in order to be felt more than to feel. They more easily become preoccupied with their own bodily sensations than with interactive experiences. Their thinking reflects this same tendency, so that their fantasies interrupt their attempts to deal with realities. These patterns exist to varying degrees in all of us. They are well established in the retarded, who have not themselves resolved the problems of their individuation because of early handicaps. They must be helped by attitudes based on understanding the developmental needs of this period of individuation, and with relationships determined by this under-

standing. The rewards of these efforts will come from their developmental progression more than from the immediate interactions.

THE PERIOD OF SEPARATION

Individuation can be achieved only through the process of separation. It is never the parent who first requires independence of the infant. It is always the infant, through its developmental needs, who makes the initial demand. *Accept me as I am and not as you would like me to be* evolves into *Accept me as I function, not as you would like me to function.* Then, *Accept me as a dependent relationship.* And finally, *Accept me independent of this dependency.* The individuation process is so geared to the infant-parent relationship that its very existence creates a greater state of dependency. Not only is the presence of each other demanded, but the absence of one from another becomes unthinkable. To the infant, separation from the parent represents a loss of part of itself by way of loss of the familiar and expected. It represents an acceptance of new experiences before the old have been consolidated. It represents change within relationships when the old have not yet fallen into place. To the parent, separation from the infant represents a possible loss of identity as parent. Anxiety is born out of this potential, joining the period of separation to affect just as the period of individuation and sensory-motor organization are linked to relatedness and impulse control respectively.

This separation anxiety, born out of the potential loss of self, extends to all meaningful experiences. It introduces emotional content to events. The degree of its presence or absence alters the perception of experiences. It begins to motivate the relatedness of the infant to objects and people. It gives special meaning to familiar relationships and makes familiar relationships something special. It becomes the forerunner of other kinds of emotions. It supplies affect to the self and permits feeling to be attached to all objective experiences. It brings into being such complex emotions as love, through attachment to relationships; anger, through frustration with relationships; hate, from the destruction of relationships; and fear for the integrity of relationships of others with self.

All of us have our own anxiety of separation. The retarded have more. Their defects assault their integrity and prevent them from achieving the security of developmental completeness. Their inadequacies help them to hate themselves because of their fragmented and incomplete existence. Their disturbed functions anger them because of their inappropriate responses. Their dependency on others gives them their inheritance of unfulfilled love through their inability to give as much as they need to receive.

It is the developmental period of separation that defines the emotional attitudes required by the retarded. They need our love and affection not because of what they are but because this is their need within relationships. They need relief from their anger and frustration by what we do and not by what we expect them to do. They need our acceptance and inclusion within family and community to counteract their hatred of themselves. They need our admiration of their limited achievements to give them a sense of their own integrity.

THE PERIOD OF ADAPTATION

The final period of infantile development is heralded by the success of individuation and separation. The integrity of the infant is tested repeatedly by an ever-changing environment made more complex by the infant's own progression. Its perceptions and responses become more profoundly individualized. Its relationships become more distinctly a matter of special preference. Its reactions and behavior become colored by emotions. Its interactions demand expression through communication. No longer can the demands of self be only in terms of "I" or "me." Conscious thought as well as emotion contributes to the selection of experiences, since so many are possible. Attention must be paid to the best combination of relationships making behavior selective and expressive.

This capacity for thinking represents the most significant infantile adaptation to life. It helps the infant to conceptualize itself as a functioning unit. It permits the growth and change of concepts relative to developmental experiences. It encourages the infant to rely upon its own resources for interactions. Subsequently it opens the way to the more economical systems of learning by imitation and by being taught rather than the trial-and-error process of experience alone. The organization of thoughts reflects the developmental progression. The earliest thinking is completely self-centered and functional. I am hungry. I am uncomfortable. I want. The first appearance of expressive behavior is in relation to these basic functional needs. The first words of the infant are symbols of this early expressive behavior and the relationships that fulfill the needs. Mama. Dada. Milk. Eat. All are among the first spoken symbols learned to express the complex relationships of self to significant environment. These first thoughts are highly concrete and reflect the organization of functions and the dimensions of experiences. This concreteness of thinking dominates the early stages of development. The actual perception and response becomes the only reality. There are few or no abstractions possible. It's a "Me Jane, you Tarzan" existence.

This pattern of thought organization remains dominant through much of the life of the retarded. Its persistence handicaps them in the movement toward abstract thinking. Most of our intelligence tests are so weighted by their own progression in the direction of abstractions that they tend to generate by their design what comes to be recognized as retardation of thought. Many individuals who have low scores on intelligence tests appear to have better resources for daily living than their scores (IQ) would indicate. This discrepancy may be the product of the abstractions contained in our attempts to measure intelligence. In a similar manner, the more numerous abstractions of an industrial society with its complex interrelations of production, distribution, and consumption serve to make concrete thinking a defect. More of us can master the thoughts involved with tilling the soil than tinkering with the machinery that tills the soil. And so progress generates retardation by the very nature of thought organization. Unless we are willing to respond to this contradiction by incorporating within our progress the acceptance of an increasing number of such individuals, as well as the means for their productive existence, we will find the retarded to be a greater and greater burden. We cannot much longer tolerate the pollution of progress that creates "misfits" and discards them into human junk piles by classifying them as mentally retarded.

An awareness of the concrete nature of the thought of the retarded opens the door for improved communication with them. Simple, carefully delineated instructions are better understood and capable of being followed. Teaching and learning become more successful. A task broken down into component parts can be completed with greater ease. A clear presentation of the realities of an experience evokes better comprehension because nothing is left to the imagination. The poor boundaries of imagination do the retarded a disservice. The combination of concrete thinking with imagination tend to make fantasy a reality for them, so that suggestive rather than specific instructions lead to confusion and inappropriate responses. Imitative behavior is a strong component of early learning. However, the imitation of the retarded is concrete, so that they do as we do rather than what we say we are doing. A good example of this type of behavior can be seen in their imitation of dress and customs. They make an absurdity of some of these by seemingly carrying things to an extreme, when all that is taking place is a concrete representation of what is seen and heard. The retarded need routine and the familiar. Both are well defined and concrete.

This period of adaptation during the stage of infancy serves to bring into focus all of the resources needed for independent survival. It cements the contract for living with the acquired resources of genetic and constitutional origin and with the developing self. It consolidates the developmental patterns of infancy, permitting their utilization for more sophisticated forms of perception, movement, feeling, and thought. Any preserved immaturity results in some kind of retardation, depending upon which functions are altered and how behavior and communication is affected.

Perceptual systems are related to the objects of self and environment. The growing infant must perceive itself first in order to become related to its environment. It does this in a concrete manner, resulting in the formation of a body image. This perception incorporates all that has gone before, as well as the current physical dimensions of mass, size, shape, parts, and other anatomical characteristics. Developmental experiences are reflected in the emergence of this body image, which is complete or incomplete and adequate or inadequate, depending on what has taken place. The sequence reflects the nature and nurturing of both fetal and infant stages of life. Thus the very young child conceptualizes itself as a solid mass, differentiating into a globular mass, into a head and body mass, into a head and body mass with extremities, openings, internal contents, and more and more parts. This sequence is well established and important to the concept of the emerging self. Defects, deviations, and arrests of this sequence occur commonly among the retarded and impair their image of themselves to a significant degree. The ability to handle this body-image formation appropriate to developmental needs becomes another important infantile adaptation. Failure to acquire a well-defined perception of self impairs the ability to perceive the surrounding environment. The dwarf grows in a world of giants. The weak grow in a world of the strong. Many of our retarded are both dwarfed and weakened by their early retardation. This is manifest both within the dimensions of their body-image formation and their self-concepts. Approaches to them must take this into consideration.

The retarded must be helped to know the dimensions of their own body at each stage of life. As infants, they must be encouraged into a physical self-awareness by being held, touched, fondled, rocked, and encouraged to movement. Their defects tend to make them passive, undemanding, or unpleasantly demanding. There is a greater tendency for avoidance of contact under such circumstances and they are robbed of what is needed. As young children, the retarded must be encouraged by planned and appropriate motor activity because movement serves to integrate their sense of parts to the whole and provides a more complete awareness of self. Their awkwardness and failures discourage such efforts from themselves and others, and they are again deprived of these growth-stimulating experiences.

As older children and adolescents, the retarded tend to be segregated and isolated by their clumsiness and poor performance. They are more often left to their own determination, which is colored by their failures. Again inertia and limitation of movement result and inhibit many of the natural activities serving as nurturing stimulants. As adults, the retarded are excluded from most physical activities by their ineptness, so that they often have to regress to earlier forms of rhythmical motor activity for their gratification of the universal need for movement. Many of our institutions and practices for the care of the retarded are by their nature, and sometimes by their design, limiting of physical activity, and therefore regressive.

It has long been known that movement creates perception by introducing change. Our retarded should be recognized as victims of the lack of movement—not only physical but all kinds: developmental, environmental, emotional, social, and intellectual. Their perceptual abilities waste away with this lack of movement. They must be approached with an awareness of this problem so that efforts can be directed at expanding rather than constricting their exposure to new perceptual experiences of all kinds. All such exposure serves to stimulate a greater awareness of self and, by the accompanying growth, an increased capacity for new perceptual experiences. This sequence is the essence of learning. The interruption of this sequence is retardation. Its disruption is learning disability. All programs for the retarded must somehow respond to their chronic need for perceptual stimulation and movement at every stage of life. The limiting of such stimulation and movement can only serve to inhibit developmental progression or even introduce regression.

The emergence of a self within the concrete dimensions of a body image and functioning sensory motor apparatus not only facilitates an awareness of the object realities of self and environment but also permits the attachment of feelings to them. It is no longer *to be or not to be*, or *I am*. It is *If I am, who am I? Am I good, bad, or indifferent? If I am what I am, what's it to you?* Acceptance, rejection, approval, disapproval, and all the other subtleties of relationships are introduced, making feelings another important adaptation to life. For without the ability to experience such feelings, there is no resolution possible to the developmental question of *If I am, who am I?* The awareness of feelings serves to reinforce and quantify the infant's existence. It doesn't really matter what the feelings are so long as they exist. For it is their existence that reinforces the infant's existence. This reinforcement by way of feelings cements together self, perception, and movement so that they are forever joined together within each of us and relate us to our environment in a meaningful way.

The absence of this cement preserves an "if" quality within subsequent development. It breeds an unrelatedness. Existence and identity are preserved but not well integrated with events or interaction. Experiences may or may not have meaning. Learning may or may not take place. A subtle form of retardation may result within this developmental disturbance, manifested by the seeming loss of learned skills, the failure of memory, and the inability to apply known experiences to new situations. These functional disturbances of the ability to learn may be seen in the genetically and constitutionally damaged as a result of their deficits. The same kind of overall disturbance without the accompanying defects and general retardation can be seen in others who have been reared in an emotionally sterile climate. Very young children reared in institutional settings have suffered from this kind of handicap. Some of them are retarded as a result of the absence of emotional stimulation. Retarded individuals remain developmentally vulnerable to their emotional climate for a much longer period of their life. Practices and programs for the retarded must recognize this special vulnerability if they are to prevent the loss of learned skills and preserve memory and ability to adapt to new situations.

These adaptations of infantile life—the capacity for thinking, the conceptualization of self, and the ability to feel—are the result of a complex set of developmental events. An understanding of some of the circumstances affecting their outcome provides many of the fundamental principles that need to be recruited for the care of the retarded of all ages within their family or community.

Stages of Infantile Development

Stage	Relation
I. **Period of Sensory-motor Organization**	
(a) Reflex Phase	Impulse-related
(b) Inhibitory Phase	Self-related
(c) Excitatory Phase	Object-related
II. **Period of Individuation**	Human-related
III. **Period of Separation**	Affect-related
IV. **Period of Adaptation**	Environmental-related

CHAPTER VI

Later Stages of Human Development

The perceiving, moving, feeling, thinking infant blossoms quickly into a growing child. Each infant develops its own special combination of the acquired ingredients that provide it with a distinct identity. Within a matter of weeks after birth the rapidly growing infant emerges as a recognizable infant child who can be distinguished from all others. The parts are similar, but the combinations of parts and uses are different. These differences become the special features of expressive behavior that permit us to know ourselves and be recognized by others. All smiles are smiles. But one child's smile is different from another's. All walking is made up of similar movements. But most children can be identified by the way they walk. The same applies to feelings and thoughts. Thus behavior emerges as the expression of perception, movement, feeling, and thought.

All behavior is developmentally determined so that it is sequential and identifiable with the stages of life. The early reflex movements become the exploratory movements of the infant, become the purposeful movements of the young child, become the play movements of the older child, become the expressive movements of the adolescent, become the work movements of the adult. Stages of life are established arbitrarily by the process of selection and grouping of behavioral characteristics, and by the dominance of some features over others. The developmental stages of life after birth have been generally accepted to be infancy, early childhood, late childhood, puberty, adolescence, maturity, and senescence. Each of these stages has behavior and communication that distinguish it from the others.

The earliest phases of infancy have been described already in terms of their essence—the appearance of relatedness. This relatedness is present to a greater or lesser degree in all subsequent stages of life. It becomes part of the developmental endowment just as genetic characteristics provide a hereditary endowment and constitutional characteristics provide a prenatal endowment to life. These endowments establish some of the characteristics from which the patterns of behavior and communication come, while yet others come from the different stages of life. The recognition of retardation becomes dependent on an awareness of what type of behavior and communication is expected, and when.

INFANCY

The physical behavior of the infant progresses rapidly within this stage from random to purposeful movements. The appearance of mass body movements permits the infant, by eight weeks of age, to balance its head when held in the upright position or to lift its head and chest when lying on its stomach.

The hand grasps objects and can be brought to the mouth. There is response to sound with turning of the head. There is recognition of the parent and feeding by bodily activity. There is a growing awareness of the familiar. Communication is through crying and generalized body movements.

By twelve to sixteen weeks of age, behavior becomes responsive and expressive of need. Eating, and everything associated with it, becomes obvious and easily recognized. Hunger is visible through behavior. The satisfaction of hunger evokes clear responses. There are more and more efforts at total body movement marked initially by the success of turning over from stomach to back and then the reverse. The infant can now be propped and is able to maintain itself in the upright position by a new equilibrium between the flexor and extensor muscles of the back and neck. Objects can be searched out, reached for, and grasped. Smiles evoke smiles. There is the beginning of experimentation with sounds, many of which are imitative in nature. There is the first appearance of concern or anxiety with separation and early signs of clinging. Recognition extends to distant objects as well as those close at hand, but responses give priority to the experiences closest to the physical self.

This first phase of infancy is characterized by the appearance of purposeful and imitative behavior related to self; the beginning of balance between flexor and extensor muscles, permitting intentional movements, and the assumption of the upright position; the emergence of far receptors so that taste, touch, and smell are joined by sound and sight as important; and the introduction of emotional content by anxiety of separation from the familiar.

These developmental changes, with their behavioral accompaniments, pave the way for the appearance of new sequences. By six months the infant is able to pull itself up, sit, support itself when held in a standing position, and bounce up and down. There is experimentation and interaction with things and people. A toy or rattle is held and played with. Things are searched for and found. Their presence or absence makes a difference. The infant now cries when left. There is response to the behavior of others. The infant can be frightened, soothed, or frustrated. There are more experimentations with sounds, but now with the more obvious intent to communicate. This next phase of infancy is characterized by the preference for the upright position, the beginning of the dominance of sight over all other receptors, and a growing dependency on the familiar.

Now everything becomes dominated by movement and the emerging balance between the flexor and extensor muscles making this movement possible. By nine months the infant is able to pick up things between thumb and finger, as well as to grasp and let go of objects. Sitting for long periods of time without support is possible, as is the task of pulling to the standing position without help. Toys are played with and can be purposefully manuevered. Many imitative movements are possible. Whereas at an earlier phase this imitative ability appeared to be limited to the head parts through the infant's responding to and copying facial expressions, now the infant is able to imitate arm movements, such as splashing in the tub, waving "bye-bye," and playing "pat-a-cake." The earlier rostral dominance begins to give way to the new ability of a more balanced rostral-caudal utilization of all parts of the body. Creeping and crawling appear and introduce the body mobility, which alters dramatically and forever the infant's existence.

This ability for movement endows the infant suddenly with new environments and infinite possibilities for change by its own action. The responsibility is awesome and the infant reacts accordingly. Clinging, dependent behavior emerges, accompanied by shyness with strangers and crying when left. This mobility is recruited alternately for exploration and attachment. Suddenly there is negativism toward new experiences. There is a search for sameness because of the comfort of the familiar. The infant begins to imitate sounds and sometimes uses one- and two-syllable words. There is recognition of name and approval and disapproval.

By the end of the first year the upright position and mobility become an established way of life. The infant stands alone and may begin to take a few steps with help. There is free movement by creeping and crawling. There is a priority of response to sounds and sights. All parental activity becomes a stimulus. There is an attraction to the rhythmical sounds of music. The television image becomes a magnet, as does a mirror, attracting the infant to their every movement. Toys take on new dimensions of space. They need to be moved and examined, and their different possibilities explored. Inside and outside are added as one of the possible dimensions. Objects are put into and taken out of containers. The spoon is held, brought to the mouth, and its contents licked and swallowed. Drinking from a cup appears. The rhythms of life as shown by eating, elimination, waking, and sleeping become regulated into well-defined and stabilized patterns. Attention-getting behavior is present in increasing amounts, and this kind of activity gives way to the more efficient forms of verbal communication, with speech beginning to emerge more rapidly as the preferred mode of expression. Instruction becomes possible not only by conduct and imitation of conduct but also by command. "No" and "yes" take on significance extending beyond approval and disapproval. They also become part of the emerging child's own equipment for selection. This middle phase of infancy is characterized by the preference for the upright, for the new equilibrium between flexor and extensor muscles, for mobility, for sound and sight, for space, for active communication, and for conflict with dependency.

The second year of life becomes a period devoted to the

consolidation of all of the gains of infancy and the preparation for the demands and responsibility of childhood. By eighteen months the infant is walking and beginning to run awkwardly, with a wide-based gait. Space assumes the new dimensions of up and down, sideways, backwards, and around, as well as horizontal, vertical, and in and out. The infant-child begins to walk up and down stairs, sits by backing or sidling into a chair, pushes and pulls moveable objects, and builds with blocks. Order, purpose, repetition, and sequence begin to dominate much of behavior. The infant-child lends itself to cooperating with dressing and undressing, feeding, and toilet training. Routines of all kinds become important. Many of the activities must be repetitive, and this repetitiveness becomes part of the infant-child's behavior.

The growing awareness of self and environment intensifies both the dependency and independency, and all behavior reflects this. There are the attachments to parents, to stuffed animals, to dolls, or objects of their own choice. The inanimate can be made animate by some of the needs and attachments. Picture books with familiar objects become something special. Imitation becomes stronger. The infant-child begins to mimic everyone. There is an awareness of other children, but play is limited to the solitary level or participating in things initiated by an acceptable adult. Some possessiveness emerges. Verbal instructions are understood. Language through speech becomes better established, more used, and more meaningful. Vocabulary mushrooms from a few single words reflecting familiar objects or activities to many words and simple groupings. Words are used as expressions of needs and the pronouns "me" or "mine" may appear. There is jargon in the form of imitated and repeated sounds, and considerable repetition of sounds and words sometimes resembles stuttering. This phase of infancy is characterized by organization, order, and routine. It brings into being a child capable of moving toward independence, with feelings for others as well as itself, and distinctive behavior and thought.

Retardation during infancy becomes identified by the alterations of the basic characteristics of this stage of life. Progress is slowed. Purposeful behavior related to the infant's existence and survival does not emerge early or clearly. The cry is weak. Sucking is poor. The need for feeding (hunger) is badly defined. Basic patterns of organ-systems functioning are variable and unpredictable. The transition to a flexor-extensor equilibrium takes place slowly and irregularly. This alters the rate of progress of all motor activity involved with sitting, standing, crawling, and walking. The dominance of near receptors (taste, touch, and smell) persists longer than it should, so that the recruitment of the far receptors (hearing and sight) takes place slowly, changing the response patterns of the infant. It is less attentive to external stimulation for longer periods of its early development. Bodily sensations remain more important than interactive experiences. The ability to differentiate is impaired, and the awareness of self and the familiar appears much more slowly, so that the emotional content of the anxiety of separation is meager. Spatial organization lags. The horizontal takes precedence over the vertical, and the entire progression to the upright position of standing and walking is slowed by this and also by any imbalance between the flexor and extensor muscles. The other dimensions of spatial perception are altered equally, so that the spontaneous, exploratory behavior of the infant is inhibited, limiting the awareness of its surroundings. Also the emerging order, purpose, and sequence of development appear slowed and, with them, the recruitment of behavior for fulfillment of needs and expression. Thus communication, in all forms—expressive behavior, symbol formation, language, and speech—is nearly always impaired. Dependency, once established, is sustained and without conflict. Independent behavior is slow to appear. Separation anxiety may become intensified, so that clinging and inability to accept the unfamiliar become part of the expressive behavior of the retarded infant. Order and routine are sacrificed to satisfy dependency needs.

Efforts in behalf of the retarded infant must reflect its needs more than its desires or those of its parents. Progress cannot be accelerated except by fulfilling the developmental tasks of the moment. Careful attention must be given to identifying and correcting, where possible, any underlying defect of heredity, constitutional makeup, or relatedness. The correction of the first two types of defects rests with efforts directed at earlier stages of life and carried over into infancy. The correction of defects of relatedness requires sensitivity to the delicate harmony of early infant-parent relationship. Alterations of this relationship may occur as a result of family chaos, physical and emotional illnesses, events leading to early prolonged separation, and variable infant-rearing practices. Special mention should be made of the impact of illness on the course of infancy. Postpartum depressions of the mother may alter the maternal-infant relationship to a degree that may affect the early relatedness of the infant. Similarly, protracted illnesses of the infant may alter the infant-maternal relationship in a like manner. Extra supportive efforts are needed under such circumstances if retardation of infant development is to be avoided.

Order and organization are essential to the rapid developmental progression within infancy. The retarded infant-child demonstrates a lack of order and problems of organization. For example, sucking involves pulling in the tongue, while licking involves its protrusion. Sucking is far more vital to eating and living than is licking. Yet some infants seem to prefer the licking of objects or become tongue-thrusters. This reflects a disturbance of both order and organization on a very primitive level. Some of the more seriously retarded demonstrate this early disruption of developmental progression throughout their lives by their tendency to protrude their tongues. Another example of this kind of disruption occurs within the acquisition of speech. Speech is a function of synchronized muscle movements and its appearance is related to general motor organization. Thus talking and walking, both of which are a reflection of motor organization, appear usually within the same developmental time interval—at about one year of age. Some retardations reflect a general lack of motor organization and both walking and talking are delayed. Other kinds of retardation reflect a disturbance of order alone and there is a marked discrepancy between the beginning of walking and talking. This kind of disruption of order may compound other developmental sequences dependent on the appearance of speech.

The result of this pyramiding is the subtle spread of disorder, very much like the waves caused by a pebble thrown into the stillness of a pond. Interventions directed at such disturbances of order must be timed appropriately to minimize their secondary effects. This concept of timing of interventions is an essential ingredient of successful programs for the retarded. Late remediations may be the equivalent of retrieving the pebble out of the pond but not altering the effects of the waves.

Yet other ingredients of programs for the retarded can be gleaned from the knowledge of the nature of retardation within infancy. Purposeful, sequential, and related instructions and tasks are essential. Ample opportunities for motoric behavior and expression through movement are needed. The inadequacies of the distant receptors of hearing and seeing must be respected and anticipated by the use of learning activities of doing. The apprenticeship model of teaching the retarded is far more effective than is the classroom. Yet so many of our programs for them remain anchored to classroom techniques of group instruction, demonstration, and abstract representations. Learning by imitation is an effective method for the retarded. But we still isolate them within specialized programs where they are more likely to imitate each other rather than the teaching models.

Many of the retarded have persisting evidence of their early-determined problems of spatial organization. They need clearly defined physical boundaries for living, learning, and working. Many programs tend to separate and compartmentalize these differing but not different aspects of life for the retarded. Moving them from one place to another inhibits their ability to recruit what they have learned in one place for use in the other. Their living must be combined with learning and working, just as their learning must be combined with living and working, just as their working must be combined with living and learning. Some of our best programs for the retarded take pride in the excellency of their school and work programs without ever giving thought to the separateness of each from the other, and both from the living experience.

EARLY CHILDHOOD

The progress of infancy equips young children for their independence. Their motor skills are well established after two years of age. The children walk and run well alone. They can go up and down stairs with ease. They turn the pages of books one at a time. Large beads can be strung easily. Scissors can be used in an awkward manner. Objects and toys are used appropriately. There is imitation of everyday household activities. They assist in dressing, rather than just cooperating. They prefer to feed themselves. Toilet needs are indicated and many children become trained between two and three years of age. Much of their behavior is now discriminating. There are preferred toys and activities. Parallel play appears. The two- to three-year-old child likes to play near other children but not with them. Family routines become acceptable. There is a seeking of approval and a reaction to disapproval. Emotional responses become varied, with signs of affection, pity, concern, guilt, happiness, and sadness. Speech ability develops rapidly. There is less jargon. Sentences are used. Curiosity becomes verbal with the introduction of "what." Their expanding imagination attracts them to listening to stories.

By three to four years of age, the manifest skills of the acquired behaviors and communication are very much evident. Now children are active, lively, and agile. They can skip, climb, ride a tricycle, throw a ball overhand. Balance is excellent. They can carry a glass of water safely. Play is more imaginative, constructive, and often cooperative. It is reality-oriented and involves role-playing. There is a good deal of drawing, some of which involves human figures. Details of parts of the body related to the whole begin to appear. Children have a rather complete concept of themselves now and begin to have the ability to conceptualize the inside of their body as well as the outside. The ability to trace lines reflects the appearance of fine motor control, in addition to their gross motor accomplishments. The average four-year-old can dress and undress with little assistance and can manage buttons, zippers, and sometimes shoelaces. Children's internal order is reflected by a growing interest in external order. They begin to brush their teeth, wash their face, put away toys, and care for their personal belongings. They not only feed themselves but can also participate in serving. They have distinct preferences for foods, clothing, and daily routines. They demand the right to participate in decisions concerning themselves. Toilet use is completely self-determined and only a few children continue to wet their beds after four years of age. Nap periods disappear and are replaced by periods of quiet activity. Sleep at night is usually uninterrupted. There may be occasional nightmares.

Cooperative play becomes well established and the company of other children is preferred to that of adults. Group activity is enjoyed and there may be a special friend. Social involvement becomes heavily invested in verbal communication. Active interchange of thoughts and ideas permeates their expressive behavior. Children brag, boast, and exaggerate. They articulate events and happenings. They make up stories. There is experimentation with ideas. No longer do their thoughts and speech reflect the concrete nature of their day-to-day existence. They become more aggressive and test the boundaries of adult authority. There is a new kind of negativism, which coincides with the emergence of an independent self. "I" becomes one of the most important words of their expanding vocabulary. Lengthy conversations become a favored activity. Sentence structure is complete, though there may be misuse of words and grammatical errors. Now "what" is joined by "how" and "why." Their imagination works overtime. Tall tales join truth and make-believe. The ability to bring order extends to the repetition of numbers and counting from one to ten. Speech is now appropriate, with all vowels and consonants mastered. There may be occasional lapses into baby talk.

By five years of age, behavior is more purposeful. It is goal-oriented and well controlled. Physical activities are complicated and skillfully performed. Right- or left-handedness is clearly established. Competitiveness within play makes its appearance. Imagination begins to show order through involvement with dramatic play. Now roles are chosen and assigned. The relationship of things and people to each other are included, so that games have objectives, rules, beginnings, and ends. Symbol formation extends from the spoken word to picture drawing and writing. Interest develops in the letters of the alphabet and in written words. The meanings of things are sought. Singing, dancing, and acting become part of everyday pursuits. The responsibility for personal care of self is demanded within the context of the growing sense of independence. The boundaries of space and time expand to ventures into the neighborhood, visits to the homes of friends, and a growing interest in school.

Children of this age begin to develop an appreciation of relative values. There is an interest in larger and smaller, older and younger, stronger and weaker, shorter and taller. They become more aware of the differences between themselves and others. Being a girl or a boy is important to them. There is a growing awareness of sexual differences accompanied by an increasing consciousness of their own bodies and a desire for privacy. There is the beginning of a preoccupation with the significance of close relationships. Curiosity leads them to explore and test the differences between relationships. They become preoccupied with what goes on between mother and father. They insert themselves into family relationships by their imagination through dreams, stories, and behavior. They show an interest and awareness in the different roles of everyone around them. The children begin to have a sense of time, with an awareness of a past, present, and future. No longer is their life made up of what is. It now becomes involved with what may be.

All of this heightens the range of their emotional existence. All their different feelings and attitudes toward life can be seen in their behavior as they begin to show their adaptations (defenses) to these feelings. They begin to demonstrate an ability to tolerate and handle their own emotions. But this ability is poor and most young children remain emotionally volatile. They cry and laugh easily. They swing rapidly from one mood to another. All of the dimensions of feelings and thoughts are now present but poorly controlled. The children need to venture forth into the world and away from the family before they achieve a proper harmony of their inner self with the world around them. This developmental task is completed in the later stages of childhood.

Retardation during early childhood becomes identified by the alteration of many of these sequences and the failure of some of them to appear. It is not only that progress is slowed; it may begin to be different. The severe retardations associated with genetic and constitutional defects and disturbed relatedness show few of these developmental progressions. The retarded children's failure to develop a significant and meaningful self arrests and distorts the evolution of expressive behavior and communication. Severely damaged young children have their expressive behavior limited to their bodily needs and functions. They remain related primarily to themselves, so that their communication becomes locked to these needs and functions. Thought and language have no relationship to others and therefore speech as a representation of the common language among us fails to appear.

The less severe forms of retardation show all kinds of variations of developmental expectations during early childhood. These variations are more obvious in the physical behavior and social responses of children but are equally present within the emergence of their thoughts and feelings. The overall picture is usually one of immaturity. Skills are present but are not quite up to expectations. One of the most important indicators of retardation rests with the appearance of speech, since it is the end point of expressive behavior. Delay in the acquisition of speech should not, however, be viewed by itself as an index of retardation. Such delay must be accompanied by other identifiable disturbances before its full significance as an indicator of retardation is judged.

The subtleties of retardation within this stage of life exist within the nature and order of appearance of things. For example, motor skills may be altered by the persistence of earlier-determined patterns. Or there may be a lag in the appearance of lateral dominance (left- or right-handedness), so that the child continues to use both sides of the body, failing to develop the appropriate skills of one side over the other. The slowing of the formation of body image may lead the child away from the expected preoccupation with form, structure, and internal content, so that spatial boundaries develop more slowly and are altered. The persistence of concrete approaches to things may inhibit the use of imagination within evolving thought organization. Emotional responses may be similarly altered. Thus retardation of early childhood comes to be identified by maturational lags that may be general or specific.

Interventions must be geared to early identification of these maturational lags in order that their effects may be ameliorated where possible. They cause an attrition of behavioral skills much needed by the growing child to complete the developmental tasks of later stages of life. The strengthening and reinforcement of their own attempts at adaptation to their defects may help some. Others need to be aided by the exposure to experiences that promote achievement. Yet others need stimulation and encouragement in place of demand and criticism. The early recognition of defects alters the levels of expectation and permits more appropriate kinds of activities. Proper supervision of these activities may replace failure with success. Within the hierarchy of development, success breeds success just as failure breeds failure. Success breeds motivation and self-confidence. These are essential ingredients for progress among the retarded.

Another aspect of this early childhood development is the progress toward order and relationships. The retarded respond best to efforts that help them with the achievement of both. Their own disabilities leave them poorly equipped to bring order into their living experiences. They must be helped by exposing them to an organizing and ordered existence. Their immaturity sets them apart from the opportunities for many needed social experiences. They must be helped by planned and supervised group activities that maintain them within the mainstream of life. They must not be permitted to be shunted into isolation or to withdraw there. Their immaturity creates social difficulties within a comparable age group. However, their placement with younger children permits many similar levels of performance, so that a kind of social parity results. This kind of placement can provide some of the much needed social stimulation for early childhood.

Particular attention must be paid to their problems with relationships. Their maturational lags preserve many of the earlier characteristics of relatedness. This requires efforts by others to overcome their difficulties of interacting with things and people. A reaching-out approach is necessary. The retarded need more from us. It is difficult to spoil them by overprotection or too much love and devotion. It is easy to rob them of their birthright to life by demands for performance and conformity.

LATE CHILDHOOD

The achievements of early childhood provide a sense of independence that must be consummated by experiences both within and outside of the family. By six years of age there is almost complete physical independence. Children are well balanced and have good coordination. They run fast, climb well, ride a bicycle, and are capable of handling themselves without supervision. They search for and enjoy all kinds of physical activities. The interests of boys and girls become markedly different. The boys become involved with the more active pursuits of playing ball, tag, wrestling, and other movement games. The girls prefer doll play and less physically demanding activities. They both enjoy handicrafts, making things, and creative activities. They are completely self-sufficient within the home. They now seek out and find their own friends. They are more aggressive with their peers. Above all, they are now capable of living by rule and order. They are ready for the demands of organized social interaction of peer group and school during the remaining years of childhood.

They are ready for this new phase of living outside the family not only by physical endowment and social development but also by their emotional stability and thought organization. Their sense of self has reached the point of assertion. They accept separation from the protective warmth of the family. They can tolerate the substitution of others' authority. Their aggressiveness permits them to satisfy their own needs within new situations. The integrity of their emotional development allows them to adapt to a more impersonal climate and yet fulfill themselves by sublimating their intimate emotions within the more general circumstances of peer group and school. They form attachments to teachers as if they were substitute parents. They seek satisfaction from peer associations in a manner that reflects their needs. One friend is their confidant. Another is their outlet for aggression. Yet another may be their protector or protected. Their need for emotional gratification within this new world of relationships has many outlets and, typically, the children of early school age move in many directions in order to satisfy this need. It helps generate motivation for compliance to the social order of life outside the family and for learning within this new setting.

The thought organization of children undergoes a similar transition, seemingly preparing them for the more formal teaching-learning experience of school. The concreteness of early thought, which made learning by imitation so easy but limited in its scope to events of the moment, is replaced by the breadth of imagination and a new capacity for abstract thoughts. The process of creative thinking unfolds through a new ability to understand concepts and principles. Space and time can be conceptualized and no longer have to be experienced directly. The children now know "where." They know and can remember their home address while they are at home or in school. They can tell time. They know that there is a time for home and a time for school, and they are not made anxious by their separation from home. They are able to conceptualize the past, the present, and the future. The children now know "when." They can place events within the perspective of time. They are better able to accept rules because time poses limits to rules. They are better able to accept their own imagination because space and time pose limits to their imagination. And the teaching-learning process of the schoolroom requires the child both to feel at home and to bring his imagination there.

This ordering of space and time within the dimensions of thought is accompanied by many subtle changes of the resources and behavior of the children. They become available for formal teaching and its rules. They are able to sit quietly and follow instructions. They are able to incorporate the order of reading, writing, and arithmetic. They can apply the learned principles to other areas of knowledge. They develop hobbies and special interests. They collect things, applying the concepts of similarities and sequence. They participate in club activities. Their behavior begins to be influenced by each other and early groupings take place. They begin to seek each other out through similar interests. The interests of girls become grouped and separated from those of boys, as does their social living with each other. They are made anxious by each other's presence. Some of this same behavior takes place within the family as well. The girls move into the orbit of the mother as the boys move toward strong identification with the father. Part of the harmony of existence of this stage of life comes from this separation into male-female identifications. This process helps further the concepts of self and prepares the children for the social order vested in the differences between the sexes.

The children's preoccupation with themselves reflects much of this same process. They fluctuate from one extreme to another. They go through periods of active involvement and then withdrawal. They seek relationships and then discard them. They become lost in both the realities and imaginations of their lives. They daydream about the present and the future and seem to want to get away from their past. They are made uncomfortable by immature behavior, so that they tend to separate themselves from younger children as well as the immaturity of the retarded. This stage of late childhood witnesses the active segregation of retarded children by other children, more as a result of the discomfort of the children with themselves than of discomfort with the retarded.

All of these developmental changes need a long time interval for their fulfillment, so that the rate of change within the children slows down. Development, which has been characterized by its rapid progress, now seems to crawl, and its potential for causing change appears latent. But this is only appearance, since maturation proceeds through quantifying rather than qualifying behavior and communication. Different forms of physical, social, emotional, and intellectual growth appear, forever distinguishing each of us from the other while preparing the child for the responsibilities of his or her maturity.

Most retardation stands exposed during this later stage of childhood. Whereas the severe forms of retardation associated with genetic and constitutional defect and disturbances of relatedness are identified by early childhood, the less severe forms are lost or hidden within the family. They remain undetected because immaturity and dependency are expected behavior from children within the family and few of us have the ability or desire to distinguish our young as more immature or more dependent than others. There is also a greater tolerance built into the structure of the family for the milder degrees of retarded function and behavior. The familiarity within family life minimizes the impact of retardation on communication, and expressive behavior compensates for any defects within the language and speech of the young child.

The rapid transitions of social existence and thought organization during late childhood ring up the curtain on a drama of separation of the retarded from family and peers. Our industrial society has dictated that all children must move into its institution known as "school" during this stage of life, ready or not. Thus any prolonged state of dependency on family becomes a disturbance visible to all outside of the family and is labeled as such. At the same time, the developmental transition of identifying and grouping with peers serves to magnify the immaturity of the retarded. The subtle, and sometimes not so subtle, differences of physical and social behavior of the retarded sets them apart from their peers. This separateness is hastened by the selectivity of the grouping by peers and the institutional practices of our school system, which also operate by grouping.

An equally potent force contributing to the separation of the retarded is their qualitative difference of thought organization, which lends itself poorly to the new learning-teaching procedures. The concreteness of thought of the retarded, with its reliance on the here and now and on imitation, does not operate well for group instruction, comprehension of abstract ideas, association of facts, and the many other variables of sophisticated learning and teaching. The net result is further separation from both group and system. Nor can the retarded return easily to the safety of their family, which has also undergone many changes. They stand isolated and alone, singly or in small groups, vulnerable and exposed as much by what takes place around as within them.

Intervention should not be geared as intensely to the

identification of the retarded, although much of the efforts of our special services within our school system continue to be devoted to this. The retarded stand out by their very nature. They need more of our efforts to minimize their isolation and segregation by peers and systems. They need teaching systems that respond to their learning requirements. They need a greater reliance on individual instruction. They need the opportunity to learn by doing rather than saying. They need help with their attempts to remain in the mainstream of life, so that more of them can become socially productive and self-sufficient.

PUBERTY

Nature demands the unfolding and exposure of its products while the rhythm of life within maturation pushes one or another aspect of development into ascendancy within the different stages. The physical aspect bursts forth in all its glory in puberty as the social, emotional, and mental processes continue to distinguish the varieties among us. The return to the dominance of the physical reintroduces some of the same equalities of the earliest stages of life. The changes of pubescence are the same for all, regardless of the variety. All children respond to the new hormonal balances and begin to show the physical changes of form that are universal experiences. Boys and girls develop their distinctive secondary sex characteristics, furnishing visible evidence of a maturity not necessarily equaled by their social, emotional, or mental development.

The rate of physical change within puberty is different for girls and boys and shows many chronological variations as well. Some enter puberty early and others late. Girls experience their pubescence earlier than most boys, so that the separateness of the sexes appears hastened by this difference. The earlier and more obvious physical changes occurring among some catapult them more quickly into new social and emotional circumstances. Their mental abilities are not as important to their developmental progression and give way to the other abilities. This changing relationship brings new and different priorities to behavior and communication. Grouping of pubescent children becomes determined more by physical and sexual characteristics. Girls stay with girls, as do boys with boys. They seek each other out and cling to each other. Their relationships with each other are determined by the visible similarities and new impulses associated with sexual development. The relationships with adults are determined in a like manner. Within the family, the girls rediscover their father and the boys their mother. Outside the family, the secret crush attaches the pubescent to teachers, movie stars, pop idols, and other heroes.

The common physical and sexual interests of puberty often serve, for a time, to minimize the distinctions of mental capacities. The physically well developed retarded girl or boy can sometimes achieve a high order within the transitional grouping of puberty. They may do so by way of their concrete representation of this moment in life and their ability to imitate what some believe to be the behavior of maturity. There may even be moments of short-lived glory. Pubescence is both a stimulator and equalizer of developmental progression. It achieves this, however, by reordering some of the priorities more than by altering the resources of the individual.

Approaches to the retarded should reflect this reordering of priorities. Too often our procedures with them remain locked in the same mold. We continue to try to teach them reading, writing, and arithmetic when they need exposure to learning through living and doing. We maintain them in groupings that keep their retardation visible rather than permitting them to merge with others by whatever resources they can recruit. We participate in limiting their opportunities for associations within family and community and rob them of their heroes. All programs for the retarded must contain the flexibility of offering new opportunities for living and learning if they are to avoid the destructive power of rigid, institutional practices.

ADOLESCENCE

The resources endowed to children by nature and nurturing must be integrated and refined for the responsibilities of maturity. This can be only through trial and tribulation, making adolescence a period of experimentation. This experimentation has the purpose of rediscovering the potential and resources of the self while finding the benefits of the surrounding world. It doesn't always work out appropriate to desire, but this developmental task of adolescence remains no matter what the outcome. Function, behavior, and communication are combined and recombined in many different ways, making the adolescent unpredictable. There may be a quality of infantilism one moment, childishness the next, then pubescent explosiveness, followed by adolescent maturity. There are periods of pure impulsive actions, and others of intense relatedness, or of unrelatedness. Sometimes adolescents appear inhibited and withdrawn. At other moments agitated excitement dominates their behavior. They can be completely self-centered while concerned with the problems of the world. Emotions run high and deep but change so fast that they may barely touch the surface of events. Thoughts encompass the universe by their achievement of the full range of imagination and capacity for abstract thinking. All the dimensions of life become exposed to adolescents through their own developmental progress, and they test them, as well as their own mettle. They do this in a repetitious manner, seemingly not learning from experience while attaining new heights of knowledge. Their experimentations are physical, social, emotional, and intellectual. Their sexual explorations with each other help refine their identity to themselves while preparing them for the adult roles of marriage partners and parents. Their strong involvement with social groupings and causes serves again to refine their identities to themselves while preparing them to accept the rules and order of the society in which they must live. Their emotionality exposes them to all the nuances of feelings, bringing them to a better awareness of their own needs and those of others. Their intellectual explorations help them toward a selection of a model of work designed to sustain them through later years.

The successes and failures of the experimentations and selections of adolescence are the important determinants of the forthcoming maturity. Regretfully, the retarded come to adolescence handicapped by their own developmental incompletion, leading to failures with many of their experimentations and an inability to make appropriate selections. More often than not, these circumstances make adolescence a shambles for the retarded unless they are guided properly. They bring poor impulse control to an impulsive period of life; their own variations of relatedness to periods of variable relatedness; their built-in inhibitions to periodic inhibition; their poor controls to moments of agitated excitement; their emotional immaturity to poorly defined emotions; and their concrete thinking to the symbolic, ritualistic behavior reflecting the abstract quality of adolescent thought. They imitate out of need but are unable to select appropriate to need and become vulnerable to the consequence of their selections. Also, they are judged by these consequences rather than by their retardation. Thus it is the retarded member of the joy-riding gang of adolescent boys who gets caught for "stealing" the car. Or it is more likely that the retarded girl "gets caught" for experimenting with the natural impulses of this period of life.

This merger of the qualities of retardation with those of adolescence helps define yet another important aspect of interventions in behalf of the retarded. Their need for sympathetic and well-defined guidance is essential to their integration with society. Our present concepts of guidance have been focused more and more on vocational efforts alone. But the retarded need guidance in all areas—physical, social, and emotional, as well as vocational. They need help with their selectivity, values, and attitudes through a much longer period of their life. The family had always provided this to its young and dependent members. If we develop community programs to support or substitute for the family, these ingredients must be incorporated within such programs. There is no way to circumvent this protracted need for guidance by the retarded. Moreover, it suggests that the apprenticeship system of teaching and learning may have to be preserved to a greater degree than it has, if we are to make room for the retarded within family and community.

MATURITY

The achievements of development are marked by maturity. However, the infinite variations of developmental events make maturity a highly individual state within each of us. Categorization of maturity is difficult. It has special characteristics, specific interests and skills, different forms of behavior and communication, personalized needs, and many other distinctive qualities that distinguish each of us from the others. Individualization and specialization are the result. These are combined with all the consummated patterns of maturation, providing an adaptability that offers the potential for harmony between self and environment. Frustrations can be tolerated. Relatedness can be preserved. Emotions can be modified. Environment can be organized and controlled. Reality and fantasy are perceived separately and rarely confused. Thinking is recruited for living and working. The degree of the achieved harmony provides an index of maturity.

Retardation of any kind limits the possibilities for this harmony. Adaptability is modified or impaired. Immaturity hampers individualization. Generalization dominates the movement toward specialization. The severely handicapped never come to any maturity. Their needs must be met by others. Their lives must be ordered for them. Their environment has to be modified to provide some opportunity for a tenuously balanced existence. The changing nature of contemporary family life no longer offers the resources for care of the severely retarded, so that residential institutions provided by others within the community become the principal means for their care. Fortunately this group is the smallest among the retarded, representing about 10 percent of the total. The ability to meet their needs is usually an accurate index of an overall ability to meet the needs of the much larger group of moderately to mildly retarded.

The less severely retarded do achieve some level of maturity. They take much longer getting there. Their course is erratic and unpredictable. Most important, their maturity is uneven. They may come to an adequate degree of physical and social maturity while remaining emotionally and intellectually immature. Any combination is possible. It is this variability that confuses the efforts to identify and classify retardation. It causes the retarded to be segregated into different programs and places. It fragments services into separate efforts directed now at physical needs, now emotional, now social, and now intellectual. It encourages the movement of the retarded from one program to another, so that they become lost within the movement. It per-

mits their exclusion by changing their identity from one form of retardation to another. Sometimes this variability of retardation may become a significant asset within adult life. A well-endowed physical self with a poorly endowed intellectual self and emotional immaturity can be a winning combination in certain circumstances of adult living. However, these circumstances are dependent on factors extraneous to the individual. But adult existence does provide an infinite variety of conditions offering many opportunities to those who are identified as retarded. We must not permit such identification to rob the retarded of their right to search for their niche in life. By our efforts, we must help sustain them to achieve the levels of their potential that represent their maturity.

SENESCENCE

The cycle of life is completed by senescence. It brings equality to those who survive to this stage of existence. All have the same problems and needs. No longer are abilities or achievements as significant. Well-being, the simple comforts of life, and acceptance are the important determinants.

Few of the severely retarded reach senescence because of their greater vulnerability to all the stresses of life. The majority of the less retarded come to their aging, as most of us do, with the successes and failures of life hidden beneath the reality of need for care and acceptance. The simple truth of the retarded is their need for this care and acceptance for a longer period of their lives.

CHAPTER VII

Disturbances of Human Development

Retardation has been identified as the result of arrests or disturbances of developmental progression. The impact of these arrests or disturbances may be general or specific, depending on their occurrence in time (when) and place (where) within the sequence of the progression. The earlier disturbances cause the more generalized and usually more profound forms of retardation. The later disturbances cause the more localized and usually more limited forms of retardation. In attempts to identify and classify the reasons for retardation and its nature, causes and effects must not be confused with each other. Such confusion has occurred in the past and continues to represent a problem to our approach to retardation. Major efforts are being made throughout the world to deal with this problem, which has preoccupied all who are devoted to the care of the retarded. Recently much of this effort has taken the form of professional meetings geared to making recommendations for the forthcoming ninth revision of the *International Classification of Diseases* in 1975.

Anticipating this revision, the American Association on Mental Deficiency released its current *Manual on Terminology and Classification in Mental Retardation, 1973 Revision.* This esteemed organization, which is approaching its centennial year, published its first manual on classification in 1921 and has issued several revisions during the intervening years. Its present definition of mental retardation reflects many of the changing attitudes toward disturbances of human development that have become associated with the concepts of retardation. It makes no reference to etiology and places the upper age limit of the developmental period at eighteen years. Adaptive behavior is defined "as the effectiveness or degree with which the individual meets the standards of personal independence and social responsibility expected of his age and cultural group." Deficits in adaptive behavior are linked to major stages of development, including sensory-motor, communication, and self-help skills and socialization (ability to interact with others) during infancy and early childhood; application of basic academic skills in daily-life activities and of appropriate reasoning and judgment in mastery of the environment and social skills (participation in group activities and interpersonal relationships) during childhood and early adolescence; and vocational and social responsibilities and performances during late adolescence and adult life. Their behavioral classification is divided into measured intelligence and adaptive behavior and their medical classification follows the *International Classification of Diseases, Eight Revision,* of the World Health Organization, 1968, and the *Diagnostic and Statistical Manual of Mental Disorders, Second Edition,* of the American Psychiatric Association, 1968. This classification includes the major categories of infections and intoxications, trauma or physical agents, metabolism or nutrition, gross brain disease (postnatal), unknown prenatal influences, chromosomal abnormalities, gestational disorders, psychiatric disorders, environmental influences, and other conditions.

There is a growing agreement that the current classification of mental retardation is inadequate. A principal suggestion for change is the adoption of a multiaxial scheme. This scheme would consist of three axes: (1) the intellectual level; (2) the associated or etiological factors; (3) a clinical psychiatric system. This multiaxial scheme requires the classification of retardation to include degree, organic aspects, psychiatric and behavioral aspects, and psychosocial aspects. Within these considerations, there is an increasing dissatisfaction with measures of intelligence. It has been recognized that intelligence is not a fixed and immutable quality; that prognostications about future intellectual development are uncertain; that assessments of intelligence be related to current level of functioning without regard to the nature or causation of retardation; that intelligence scores should not be used in isolation but with the clinical judgments of the social and adaptive behavior of development; and that intelligence tests might even be inappropriate for populations in which social and cultural factors were quite different from those found in the populations on which the tests were standardized.

There appears to be general agreement that the degree of retardation is identified best by the categories of "mild," "moderate," "severe," and "profound." Another consideration includes the recognition of mental retardation as a symptom and not a disease. However, the concept of mental retardation as a specific entity has become so fixed within systems of classification, the history and schema of scientific knowledge, the organization of services, and the social and political structure of the countries of the world, that classifications must continue.

Attempts to separate different forms of retardation date back to the last century. Various criteria were proposed for etiology (cause), such as congenital or acquired, and for degree (effect), such as idiocy, imbecility, or feeblemindedness. At that time the selection of criteria depended largely on the purpose the classification was to serve. Now the selection depends largely on what can be negotiated among the many different professional disciplines devoted to the care of the retarded. Classification has always been a cardinal problem of specialization. There is general agreement for the grouping of principal factors causing developmental defect. These are as follows:

1. Hereditary or familial traits resulting in general metabolic disturbances, or those affecting the central nervous system in a special way (genetic).
2. Embryonic or fetal disturbances reflecting the harmful influences acting upon the parents, especially the mother (constitutional).
3. Infectious, toxic, traumatic, and nutritional difficulties during the birth period (environmental).
4. Infectious, toxic, traumatic, and nutritional difficulties during the life after birth (environmental).

The existing classifications of retardation are based on these factors, and it is proposed to offer here a dictionary of the associated conditions and terminology rather than providing another variation on this theme. More formal classifications are readily available in the aforementioned manuals and the numerous reference books on the subject and within the *International Classification of Diseases.* No attempt will be made here for this listing to be all-inclusive, since any disturbance within the range of human experience is capable of affecting developmental progression, causing retardation. Also, different styles of nomenclature at various periods of the history of this subject have resulted in different names being attached to the same entities. This dictionary is made up of a listing of conditions as they have appeared in some of the contemporary literature on the subject. The list is coded for the nature of causation and severity of the retardation. The code symbols coincide with developmental time and space sequences that may involve more than one interval.

G	Genetic
C	Constitutional
E	Environmental

The code symbols for severity have been selected to coincide with the accepted categories.

mi	mild
mo	moderate
se	severe
pr	profound

The most common conditions associated with retardation will be described briefly. The less common will have notations for purposes of identification. The list is weighted with the less common conditions because of their concrete nature and the frequency of their mention within the subject of retardation.

DICTIONARY OF RETARDATION

Acrocephalosyndactyly. G & C. mi–pr. SEE Apert's Disease.
Acrocephaly. A malformation of the skull with the head pointing toward the front.

Acute Infantile Diffuse Sclerosis. G. se–pr. SEE Diffuse Cerebral Sclerosis.

Adenoma Sebaceum. Small shiny, waxy, or reddish elevation of the skin, usually distributed over the face and seen in tuberous sclerosis.

Alpers's Disease. G. se–pr. A progressive neurologic disorder of infancy beginning with convulsions, then showing arrested development, blindness, generalized rigidity, and with a fatal outcome.

Amaurotic Idiocy. G. se–pr. Characterized by a disturbance of lipoid metabolism resulting in intracellular deposits of abnormal substances, mainly in the brain and retina. Accompanied by retardation and visual defects. There is an infantile type (Tay-Sachs disease) in which the neurological and ophthamological abnormalities develop within several months of birth. There is a juvenile type (Spielmeyer-Vogt disease) in which the symptoms are similar but onset is delayed for several years and progresses more slowly.

Anaclitic Depression of Infancy. G & C & E. mi–pr. A developmental disturbance of infancy reflecting the inhibition of relatedness and functioning. Retardation may result from persisting depression.

Anencephaly. G & C. se–pr. Failure of the brain to develop. Usually fatal.

Anoxia. Lack of oxygen to the developing fetus. May cause damage to its central nervous system, resulting in retardation.

Apert's Disease. G & C. mi–pr. Craniofacial dystosis with syndactylia. There is a high, wide, and short cranium associated with malformation of the fingers and/or toes. Retardation is usually present.

Aphasia. C & E. mi–pr. A developmental disturbance of language and speech. May be motor or sensory in origin. A common finding among the severely and profoundly retarded.

Arachnodactylia. G & C. se–pr. SEE Marfan's Syndrome.

Arginosuccinicaciduria. G. se–pr. Disturbance of protein metabolism involving arginine. Accompanied by retardation, convulsions, friable hair, ataxia, and argininosuccinic acid in the urine. Defects in myelination of nerves occur.

Aspartylglucosaminuria (AGU). G. mi–pr. A disturbance of glycoprotein metabolism accompanied by retardation and coarse face, short stature, and skeletal and skin abnormalities.

Ataxia-telangiectasia. G & C. mi–pr. A disturbance characterized by the appearance of clustered blood vessels within the nervous system, eyes, and skin, as well as progressive cerebellar signs and retardation.

Autism. SEE Infantile Autism.

Autosomal Dominant. An inheritance pattern in which one gene from either parent determines the characteristics associated with that gene.

Autosomal Recessive. An inheritance pattern in which similar genes from both parents determine the characteristics associated with that gene.

Battered Child Syndrome. E. mi–pr. Brain damage resulting from physical beatings about the head of infants and young children. A growing awareness of the existence of this completely preventable disturbance has resulted in statutes requiring medical reporting of physical abuse to children. This kind of abuse or neglect has been found, since reporting has been instituted, to be more common than had been thought. Retardation is associated with the more severe forms.

Brain Damage. G & C & E. mi–pr. Injury to the brain may occur at birth or during infancy, resulting in retardation. Head trauma is common during these periods of life. The traumas may cause extensive damage because of the vulnerability of the developing brain and the incomplete protection offered by the softness of the bones of the skull. The brain of the fetus and infant is vulnerable to infection and to toxins, with resulting damage accompanied by varying degrees of retardation.

Cerebral Gigantism. G & C. mi–mo. A developmental syndrome associated with mild retardation, excessive height, and mild damage to the central nervous system.

Cerebral Lipidoses. G. mi–pr. Disorders of the metabolism of sphingolipids (fat metabolism of the brain) with accumulation of one or more of these compounds within the brain tissue. Accompanied by retardation.

Cerebral Palsy. G & C & E. mi–pr. Disorder of the nervous system characterized by disturbances of motor function. May be accompanied by sensory disturbances, seizures, mental retardation, learning difficulties, or behavioral disorders.

Childhood Schizophrenia. G & C & E. mi–se. A disturbance of childhood reflecting a general disorganization of developmental progression, so that unusual patterns of behavior and communication appear. Retardation may be one of the manifestations of this disturbance.

Chromosomal Aberrations. G & C. mi–pr. Varying forms of general retardation are associated with morphological abnormalities of chromosomes. A number of these are listed under identifying names, such as Down's syndrome.

Chromosomes. Small bodies consisting of chromatin found within the nucleus of the cell and serving as the carriers of the genes. Human chromosomes have been identified by shape and numbers (for example: trisomic–21), inheritance pattern (dominant or recessive), sex-linked (x and y), genetic content (segregating and polygenic traits), and some of their abnormalities. Their characteristics have also been associated with their forms of transmission (mosaic parents and translocation carriers).

Citrullinuria. G. se–pr. Disturbance of protein metabolism involving citrulline. Accompanied by impairment of the central nervous system, with convulsions and retardation.

Convulsive Seizure Disorders. G & C & E. mi–pr. Disorders of control of impulses of the central nervous system characterized by convulsive seizures, frequently with loss of consciousness, and disturbances of the sensory and motor systems. They are disorders accompanying brain damage and are identified by direct observation and the appearance of typical brain-wave patterns on the electroencephalogram. Treatable with anticonvulsant drugs.

Craniofacial Dysostosis. G & C. se–pr. Crouzon's disease. A malformation affecting head, face, and nervous system, with accompanying retardation.

Craniofacial Dysostosis with Syndactylia. G & C. se–pr. SEE Apert's Disease.

Craniostenosis. G & C. mi–pr. Abnormality of growth of the cranium accompanied by brain damage and retardation.

Cretinism. G & C & E. mi–pr. This is related to a glandular disturbance of the thyroid function during pregnancy and associated with a lack of iodine intake. Lethargy, irritability, anemia, constipation, and retardation of growth of the infant are among the earliest signs. A small percentage of cretins have nonendemic familial goiterous cretinism and genetically determined defects in thyroid synthesis.

"Cri du Chat" Syndrome. G & C. mi–pr. A chromosomal aberration connected with delection of the short arm of the fifth pair of chromosomes. It is accompanied by retardation.

Crigler-Najjar Syndrome. G. se–pr. A disturbance of pigment metabolism involving a deficiency of glucuronyl transferase and incapability of converting indirectly acting bilirubin into the directly acting form. It is accompanied by retardation.

Crouzon's Disease. G & C. se–pr. Craniofacial dystosis. Characterized by a cranial deformity associated with retardation. Physical abnormalities include a thin, acrocephalic skull, prognathism, exophthalmos, and optic atrophy.

Cystathionuria. G. se–pr. Disturbance of protein metabolism. Accompanied by retardation, congenital anomalies, pituitary disturbances, and cystathionine in the urine.

Cystinosis. G. se–pr. Also known as Lignac's syndrome. It is a metabolic disturbance accompanied by excessive storage of cystine crystals in the body. It is autosomal recessive. Symptoms appear after six months of life with growth failure, weakness, and generalized debilitation. Few of the afflicted survive past childhood.

Cytomegalic Inclusion Disease. E. mi–se. A congenitally acquired infection resulting in a general, systemic disease characterized by the presence of intracellular inclusion bodies involving any organ system. Permanent cerebral damage is often present in infants who survive.

De Grouchy's Syndrome. G & C. mi–pr. A chromosomal aberration involving the deletion of the short arm of the eighteenth pair of chromosomes. It is accompanied by retardation.

De Lange's Syndrome. G. se–pr. Small-statured individuals with bushy eyebrows, upturned nose, wide upper lip, hypertrichosis, and skeletal abnormalities.

Diffuse Cerebral Sclerosis. C & E. mi–pr. Also known as Schilder's diffuse sclerosis, encephalitis periaxialis diffusa, and global demyelinization. It is a demyelinization disease of the central nervous system occurring with greatest frequency between ages five and ten years. It is accompanied by convulsions, disorders of gait, progressive impairment of intelligence, and memory defects.

Down's Syndrome (Mongolism). G & C. mi–pr. A chromosomal aberration involving a trisomy of the twenty-first pair of chromosomes. It is the most common disease entity of retardation, with a rate of occurrence of about one in six hundred live births. Diagnosis is usually made in the first year of life. Stature is reduced. Limbs are hypotonic. The head tends to be small. There is a characteristic facies including slanting eyes, epicanthic folds, squint, Brushfield's spots (white specks) in the iris, and small nose and ears. The little finger of the hand tends to curve inward and there is a wide gap between the first and second toe. A single transverse palmar crease is present, often accompanied by characteristic dermatoglyphic patterns of the palms and soles. There is a high incidence of congenital abnormalities of organ structure. Mortality rate is high, with expectation of life at birth being about twenty years. The degree of retardation is variable but always present.

Dwarfism. G & C & E. mi–pr. Generalized growth failure due to different causes. Hormonal and nutritional failures are among the significant causes. Retardation is associated with the general growth failure.

Dyscrania. G & C. mi–pr. Abnormalities of growth and development of the head and brain, accompanied by brain damage and retardation.

Dysmaturity. C & E. mi–pr. Resulting from intrauterine growth retardation. Birth weights of less than 2,000 gms. (4 lb., 7 oz.) and a gestation of 36 weeks or more. Ranges from microcephaly with dwarfism to mild growth deficiencies. Other anatomical defects are frequent, with retardation.

Edward's Syndrome. G & C. se–pr. A chromosomal aberration connected with a trisomy in Group E of the eighteenth pair of chromosomes. Accompanied by retardation.

Embryopathia Rubella. C & E. mi–pr. Rubella during the first trimester of pregnancy may cause varying degrees of retardation and developmental abnormalities in the embryo and fetus. SEE German Measles.

Encephalitis. E. mi–pr. An infection of the substance of the brain due to many different viral, bacterial, and toxic agents. Any resulting brain damage may be accompanied by retardation.

Epilepsy. G & C & E. mi–pr. A disorder of the control of impulses of the central nervous system characterized by convulsive seizures, loss of consciousness and disturbances of the sensory and motor systems. They are disorders accompanying brain damage and sometimes complicated by retardation. Treatable with anticonvulsant drugs.

Erythroblastosis. G & C. mi–pr. A breakdown of the red blood cells of the newborn infant (kernicterus) with Rh or ABO incompatibility with the mother. Exchange transfusion at birth can be life-saving and prevent damage to the infant's central nervous system.

Friedreich's Ataxia. G. mi–se. Also known as hereditary spinocerebellar ataxia. It is a hereditary disorder transmitted as an autosomal recessive gene. It usually starts between seven and ten years with stumbling, disturbances of gait, loss of position sense, curvatures of the spine, and other neuromuscular disturbances. The disorder is progressive and accompanied by gradual deterioration and retardation.

Fructosuria. G. mi–pr. A carbohydrate metabolic disturbance with hyperaminoaciduria. Accompanied by retardation.

Fucosidosis. G. se–pr. A disorder of carbohydrate metabolism accompanied by marked retardation.

Galactosemia. G. mi–pr. A carbohydrate metabolic disturbance in the action of the enzyme galactose-L-phosphate-uridyl-transferase. Accompanied by retardation and a failure to thrive. Cataracts, hepatomegaly, and jaundice may be present, as well as retardation. Early treatment with a galactose-free diet has been successful in preventing much of the damage of this metabolic disturbance.

Gangliosidosis. G. se–pr. A disorder of lipid metabolism usually accompanied by severe retardation.

Gargoylism. G. se–pr. A genetically produced aberration of growth and development accompanied by retardation. There is a disturbance of both lipoid and carbohydrate metabolism, with the accumulation of abnormal substances within the cells of the body. There is a grotesque facies and deformed appearance. Other terms sometimes used include lipochondrodystrophy, dystostosis multiplex, and Hunter's or Hurler's diseases.

Gaucher's Disease. G. se–pr. A metabolic disturbance of cerebroside lipidosis. It is a progressive illness characterized by visceromegaly, head retraction, hypertonia, and failure of motor and intellectual development.

German Measles. C & E. mi–pr. Rubella during the first trimester of pregnancy may cause varying degrees of retardation in the offspring. Risk approaches 50 to 60 percent of major congenital malformation in the first four weeks and declines to 4 or 5 percent by the fourth month. Afflicted children tend to show hearing defects and retardation in physical, mental, and motor development with disorders of communication. Another term used is Embryopathia rubella.

Globoid Cell Leucodystrophy (Krabbe's Disease). G. se–pr. Disturbances of lipoid metabolism with severe retardation.

Grand Mal Seizures. G & C & E. mi–pr. A convulsive seizure pattern in which there is loss of consciousness and sensory-motor disturbances. It accompanies brain damage and is of frequent occurrence among the brain-damaged. It is identified by direct observation and typical brain-wave patterns on the electroencephalogram. Treatable with anticonvulsant drugs. SEE Epilepsy.

Growth Failure. G & C & E. mi–pr. The failure to grow has been recognized as having an important correlation to retardation. It is a multidetermined state.

Hartnup Disease. G. se–pr. Disturbance of protein metabolism with "neutral" amino acids present in the urine. Accompanied by retardation, ataxia, and pellagra-like rash.

Hemolytic Disease of the Newborn. G & C. mi-pr. SEE Erythroblastosis. Caused by passive transplacental transfer of a maternal antibody active against the red blood cells of the fetus and causing their breakdown, with possible damage to the central nervous system.

Hepatolenticular Degeneration. G. mi–pr. Also known as Wilson's disease. It is a progressive hereditary disturbance accompanied by damage to the liver and brain resulting in gradual deterioration and retardation.

Histidinemia. G. se–pr. Disturbance of protein metabolism of histidine. Accompanied by retardation.

Homocystinuria. G. mi-pr. Disturbance of protein metabolism of methionine. Accompanied by seizures, dislocated lens, thromboembolic phenomena, and retardation. Defects in myelination occur.

Hormonal Disturbances. C & E. mi-pr. A variety of hormonal disturbances of the mother may cause retardation of the developing fetus. Similarly, such disturbances within the fetal and infant periods may cause retardation.

Hurler's Syndrome. G. mi–pr. A metabolic disturbance of mucopolysaccharidoses with retardation. Prominent forehead, protruding tongue. Evidence of extensive neurological damage. Gargoylism.

Hydrocephaly. C & E. mi–pr. A multidetermined anatomical disturbance involving the growth of the brain. The disturbance causes the brain to enlarge, with the possible destruction of brain cells. Correction is possible in some instances by early surgical intervention.

Hydroxyprolinemia. G. se–pr. Disturbance of the protein metabolism of hydroxyproline. Accompanied by microscopic hematuria and retardation.

Hyperbilirubinemia. C & E. mi–pr. An excess of bilirubin in the blood of the newborn due to a variety of reasons. This excess may cause damage to the central nervous system, with retardation. Exchange transfusions can minimize and prevent the damage.

Hyperlysinemia. G. mi–pr. Disturbance of protein metabolism of lysine. Accompanied by retardation.

Hyperprolinemia. G. mi–pr. Disturbance of the protein metabolism of proline. Accompanied by anomalies of the genitourinary tract, renal disease, and retardation.

Hyperuricemia. G. mi–pr. Associated with the Lesch-Nyham syndrome. A rare sex-linked disorder of children. Often with retardation, involuntary movements, and self-mutilation. Characterized by excess formation of uric acid and absence of the needed enzyme, as in gout.

Hypervalinemia. G. mi–pr. Disturbance of protein metabolism of valine. Accompanied by retardation.

Imbecillitas Phenylpyruvica. G. mi–pr. SEE Phenylketonuria (PKU).

Immunopathological Disturbances. G & C. mi–pr. Incompatibility of the antigenic properties of the maternal and fetal blood with regard to blood types and rhesus factors, as well as hemolytic diseases of the newborn. Accompanied by damage to the central nervous system and retardation.

Infantile Autism. G & C & E. mi–pr. A developmental disturbance reflecting the inability of the infant to relate appropriately to self, objects and people. There is a functional retardation with many accompanying disturbances of behavior and communication.

Infantile Neuroaxonal Dystrophy. G & C. mi–pr. A disturbance of the development of the nervous system in which an abnormality of the conducting portion of the nerve cell (axon) occurs, with impairment of the function of the nervous system and retardation.

Infections. Severe infections may disturb the maternal-fetal balance during pregnancy with many disastrous effects on development. Severe infections during the first three to four years of life may cause damage to the central nervous system and retardation. These include viral and bacterial infections, such as influenza, measles, mumps, pneumonia, dysentery, encephalitis, meningoencephalitis, meningitis.

Joseph's Syndrome. G. se–pr. Disturbance of protein metabolism involving proline, hydroxyproline, and glycine. Accompanied by retardation, infantile convulsions, and increased proteins in the cerebrospinal fluid and urine.

Kernicterus. C & E. mi–pr. Jaundice of the newborn causing damage to the nervous system with athetosis, deafness, and retardation present in the more severe forms. Can be treated by exchange transfusions when detected early.

Klinefelter's Syndrome. G & C. mi–se. A chromosomal aberration involving the system of sex chromosomes (XXY). The abnormalities associated with this become apparent at puberty of males and include gynaecomastia, small testes, poor hair growth, and increased secretion of follicle-stimulating hormone, altering the masculinity. It is usually accompanied by a mild retardation and unstable personality.

Late Infantile Amaurotic Idiocy. G. se–pr. A disturbance of cerebroside lipidosis. Progressive. Similar to Tay-Sachs disease. Also known as juvenile-type or Spielmeyer-Vogt disease.

Laurence-Moon-Biedl-Bardet Syndrome. G. mi–se. Autosomal recessive transmission of a syndrome characterized by obesity, hypogenitalism, polydactyly, retinitis pigmentosa, and retardation.

Lead Poisoning. E. mi–pr. This toxic condition, plumbism, resulting from the ingestion of lead by the infant and young child (pica) is becoming more common with the extensive use of lead paints in households. The tendency of young children to mouth things results in the ingestion of the lead and its selective accumulation within bone and brain tissue. Its presence in excess may cause brain damage and retardation. It is completely preventable and can be treated by the use of chelating agents—penicillamine by mouth and EDTA by intramuscular or intravenous routes. SEE Plumbism.

Lejeune's Syndrome. G. mi–pr. A chromosomal aberration involving the deletion of the long arm of the eighteenth pair of chromosomes. Accompanied by retardation.

Lesch-Nyham Syndrome. G. mi–pr. Associated with hyperuricemia, excess formation of uric acid and the absence of the needed enzyme. It is a sex-linked disorder of children, often with retardation and self-mutilation.

Lignac's Syndrome. G. mi–pr. SEE Cystinosis.

Mannosidosis. G. se–pr. A disorder of carbohydrate metabolism with retardation.

Maple Syrup Urine Disease. G. se–pr. Disorders of protein metabolism of valine, isoleucine, and leucine. Accompanied by spasticity, myoclonic seizures, and retardation. Defect in myelination occurs.

Marfan's Syndrome. G. mi–pr. Arachnodactylia. A progressive spastic paraplegia occurring in children, the subjects of hereditary syphilis; the lesion is a myelitis involving the pyramidal tracts. Accompanied frequently by retardation.

Meningitis. E. mi–pr. An infection of the covering of the brain due to many different viral, bacterial, and toxic agents. Any resulting brain damage may be accompanied by retardation.

Meningocele. G & C. mi–pr. Anatomical abnormalities of the developing central nervous system accompanied by brain damage and retardation.

Metachromatic Leucodystrophy. G. se–pr. A disturbance of lipoid metabolism. A progressive disease usually starting in late infancy, with diffuse damage of the nervous system. Also known as sulfatide lipidosis.

Methemoglobinemia. G. mi–pr. A disturbance of pigment metabolism involving the blockage of the enzyme needed to convert methemoglobin into hemoglobin. May result in brain damage with retardation.

Microcephalus. G. pr. A growth failure of the brain with profound retardation.

Minimal Brain Dysfunction (MBD). G & C & E. mi. A disturbance of functioning with no specific evidence of brain damage. Usually accompanied by behavioral and communication problems resulting in occasional retardation.

Mongolism. G & C. mi–pr. A chromosomal aberration involving a trisomy of the twenty-first pair of chromosomes. SEE Down's Syndrome for details.

Mucopolysaccharidosis. G. mi–pr. A disturbance of carbohydrate metabolism accompanied by retardation.

Muscular Dystrophy. G. mi–pr. A muscle disease sometimes accompanied by some degree of retardation.

Neurofibromatosis (von Recklinghausen's disease). G & C. mi–pr. Characterized by nerve tumor formation that may involve many parts of the body. When the central nervous system is involved, retardation occurs. Sometimes accompanied by epilepsy.

Niemann-Pick Disease. G. mi–pr. One of the disturbances of lipoid metabolism and known as sphingomyelin lipidosis. Four types are now distinguished on the basis of appearance of symptomatology. Symptoms include hepatosplenomegaly, progressive neurological deterioration, cherry-red spots in the maculae, and retarded development. Neurological symptoms start in early childhood.

Nutritional Deficiency. E. mi–pr. Nutritional deficiencies of all kinds have been identified with arrests and disturbances of development, as well as damage to the nervous system. The nature of the disturbance will depend on the nature of the deficiency and the time of its occurrence within the life span. Those occurring early in life may result in extensive damage, with severe retardation.

Oasthouse Urine Disease. G. mi–pr. Disturbance of protein metabolism of valine, leucine, isoleucine, methionine, phenylalanine, tyrosine. Accompanied by white hair, edema, unpleasant odor of urine, and retardation. Defects of myelination occur.

Parasitic Infections. G & E. mi–pr. All kinds of parasitic infections starting with conception and extending through early life may cause retardation. The more diffuse and profound effects occur at the beginning of the spectrum of life. Infections include syphilis, listeriosis, and others.

Patau's Syndrome. G & C. se–pr. A chromosomal aberration connected with a trisomy in Group D, thirteenth to fifteenth pairs of chromosomes. Accompanied by general retardation.

Pelizaeus-Merzbacher Disease. G & C. mi–pr. A disturbance of the development of the nervous system in which there is failure of proper myelination with impairment of the function of the nervous system and retardation.

Petit Mal Seizures. G & C & E. mi–pr. A convulsive seizure pattern in which there are momentary lapses of conscious awareness or behavioral responses. It accompanies brain damage. It may occur among the retarded with brain damage. It can be identified by direct observation and typical brain-wave patterns on the electroencephalogram. Treatable with anticonvulsant drugs. SEE Epilepsy.

Pharmacological Disturbances. E. mi–pr. Excessive use of drugs during pregnancy and throughout life has increased dramatically, and with it the potential for damage during fetal life and infancy. Metabolic, hematological, hormonal, or neurological disturbances are common. Overdosage or excessive use are the most frequent causes of toxicity.

Phenylketonuria (PKU). G. mi–pr. Disturbance of protein metabolism associated with blockage of phenylalaninehydroxylase. Suspicion of its existence is raised with the presence of an affected sibling. Serum phenylalanine determination should be obtained after the sixth day of life. Phenylalanine metabolites may not be detected in the urine until the sixth week of life. Diaper testing using ferric chloride is widely used but should not be performed until the second month of life where suspicion exists of this condition. Most individuals with PKU are severely to profoundly retarded. Behavioral disturbances are common, with autistic, withdrawn features and impulse disorders. They demonstrate abnormalities of their electrocephalograms and one-fourth have seizures. Abnormalities of myelination have been reported. Treated with low phenylalanine diets. Special diet may be discontinued after three years of age with little evidence of deterioration of mental development.

Plumbism. E. mi–pr. Lead poisoning affecting the nervous system, with brain damage and retardation as a result of the ingestion of lead (pica). Treated by penicillamine by mouth for the less severe cases and EDTA by the intramuscular or intravenous route for the graver cases. SEE Lead Poisoning.

Postmaturity. C & E. mi–pr. A form of dysmaturity. The period of pregnancy is prolonged excessively.

Prematurity. G & C & E. mi–pr. Termination of pregnancy prior to full term. Seventy percent of premature infants weighing less than 1,500 gm. (3 lb., 5 oz.) at birth have various physical, neurological, and mental disorders, with retardation, speech, and learning difficulties and behavioral problems.

Radiation Disturbances. G & C & E. mi–pr. Radiation may cause damage to the reproductive cells of the parents as well as direct damage to the embryo, fetus, and infant.

Retinitis Pigmentosa. G & C. mi–pr. A genetically produced aberration of development accompanied by deposits of a pigment in the retina of the eye, as well as different parts of the brain. Accompanied by retardation.

Retrolental Fibroplasia. C & E. mi-pr. Damage to parts of the central nervous system resulting from an alteration of the amount of available oxygen to the brain immediately after birth. Damage occurs to the retina, so that there may be some loss of vision or blindness. Retardation may accompany any brain damage.

Rh Incompatibility. G & C & E. mi–pr. SEE Erythroblastosis and Hemolytic Disease of the Newborn. It is a condition in which the mother has Rh-negative type of blood and the fetus has Rh-positive type of blood, causing antibody formation in the mother. This may result in destruction of the Rh-positive red blood cells, causing excessive amounts of blood pigment to accumulate in various organs of the fetus, with brain damage and retardation.

Rud's Syndrome. G & C. se–pr. Metal retardation with ichthyosis.

Septicemia. E. mi–pr. An infection of the bloodstream that may spread itself to any part of the body. Spread of such infection to the brain may cause damage to it and retardation.

Sjogren-Larsson Syndrome. G. mi–pr. Characterized by ichthyosis, spastic paralysis, and retardation. Due to an autosomal recessive gene.

Smith-Lemle-Opitz Syndrome. G. se–pr. A form of microcephaly.

Sphingomyelin Lipidosis. G. mi–pr. SEE Niemann-Pick disease.

Spina Bifida Cystica. G & C. mi–pr. A malformation of the nervous system accompanied by functional disturbances and retardation. There are skeletal malformations associated with those of the nervous system.

Spongy Degeneration (Canavan's Disease, von Bogaert-Bertrand Disease). G. se–pr. Characterized by onset in early infancy, progressive neurological signs, and megalocephaly with retardation.

Sturge-Weber Syndrome. G & C. mi–pr. Abnormal angioma-like growths affecting the central nervous system, with accompanying retardation.

Sucrosuria. G. mi–pr. Metabolic disturbance of carbohydrates involving an intolerance of saccharose.

Symbiotic Disturbances. G & C & E. mi–se. A developmental disturbance of infancy and early childhood reflecting an unusual attachment to objects and people, so that expected developmental progression is impaired. Retardation may be present, accompanied by disorganized behavior.

Tay-Sachs Disease. G. se–pr. A disorder of lipoid metabolism affecting the development of the nervous system and accompanied by retardation. The metabolic disturbance is known as gangliosidosis.

Toxic Disturbances. C & E. mi-pr. A variety of toxic factors, both exotoxins and endotoxins, in the mother may cause retardation of the developing fetus. Many of these same toxic substances may produce similar effects directly on the young infant.

Toxoplasmosis. E. mi–pr. A viral infection also known as cytomegalic inclusion disease. Its occurrence during pregnancy may cause retardation of the infant, with cerebral calcification, hydrocephalus, and eye involvements.

Tuberous Sclerosis. G & C. mi–pr. Abnormal growth affecting the central nervous system, with accompanying retardation. There is a typical rash of adenoma sebaceum, which appears somewhere about the third or fourth year of life. Epilepsy occurs frequently. Probable inheritance pattern is involved.

Turner's Syndrome. G & C. mi. A chromosomal aberration involving the system of sex chromosomes (XO). Characterized by shortness of stature, webbing of the neck, circulatory weakness, diminution of development of secondary sexual characteristics, amenorrhea, and infertility. Retardation is mild or not at all.

Tyrosinosis. G. se–pr. An inherited disorder in an autosomal recessive manner associated with a defect or lack of parahydroxyphenylpyruvic acid oxidase. Symptoms appear in infancy, with the main clinical features being cirrhosis of the liver and multiple renal tubular defects. There is failure to thrive, irritability, fever, and hepatomegaly. Liver failure is a common cause of early death.

Viral Infections. C & E. mi–pr. All kinds of viral infections starting with conception and extending through all of life may cause retardation. The more diffuse and more profound effects occur at the beginning of the spectrum of life. These viral infections include influenza, mumps, infectious hepatitis, cytomegalic inclusion disease, and others.

Wilson's Disease. G. mi–pr. SEE Hepatolenticular Degeneration.

Wolf's Syndrome. G & C. mi–pr. A chromosomal aberration in Group B that is connected with the deletion of the short arm of the fourth pair of chromosomes. May be accompanied by retardation.

CHAPTER VIII

Early Interventions

The prevention of retardation is the cornerstone of all intervention. The timing of these interventions has to be synchronized with developmental progression by the anticipation of the needs of each stage and period of life. Such anticipation may eliminate predetermined defect, encourage recognition of potential, permit alternatives, and recruit the full range of human experience and imagination for the requirements of development. Thus approaches to intervention must start with conception and progress with the sequence of life.

GENETIC COUNSELING

Genetic counseling is the process of identifying the possible impact of inherited and genetically transmitted conditions. It involves the exchange of information concerning genetic prognosis and associated problems. Genetic prognosis is centered around those disorders of birth with high-recurrence risks. It is designed to provide sufficient information to potential parents so that they can arrive at a rational, personal decision with respect to family planning. Individuals with known genetic disorders or parents who have been identified as harboring a genetic abnormality have the major responsibility for the prevention of genetically determined disturbances leading to retardation. The recent changes in social attitudes toward therapeutic abortions have increased the possibilities of preventing the birth of infants with serious genetic abnormalities. This has broadened the scope and importance of this kind of counseling.

Several approaches may be used to evaluate the role of genetic factors. One is the direct assessment of a known case through whom the abnormality is first recognized, followed by an extensive family investigation. This permits the construction of a pedigree. By comparing this pedigree with others representing similar clinical disorders, the mode of inheritance and the risk of the disease among relatives can be estimated. Another approach to measuring the impact of inherited factors rests with the complete assessment of all similar cases in a specified population group. This provides information on how the genes involved are maintained in the population. The application of this knowledge to a given condition indicates the parameters of risk, which can then be used for making judgments and counseling.

These methods have identified a number of genetic traits or characteristics for which there is an increased risk among relatives, compared with the general population. There is a greater concordance of traits in identical than in fraternal twins. The existence of a recessive trait is more likely with an excessively consanguineous parentage. The trait does not spread to nonrelated individuals. Many genetic traits have their onset at a characteristic age without a known precipitating event. Different populations show considerable variations of incidence of any trait. These characteristics can be utilized for estimating the possibilities and need for preventive intervention.

A number of distinct genetic mechanisms have been described that determine diseases, malfunctions, and variations associated with retardation. These include single genes that may be autosomal dominant, autosomal recessive, or X-linked recessive; chromosomal abnormalities; complex malformations; incompatibilities; segregating traits; and polygenic traits. It should be stressed that individual conditions are rare, with frequencies from one per ten thousand to one per one hundred thousand for single-gene traits and variably higher for the others. It has been estimated that approximately 5 percent of all live-borns have or will develop during life some disease or malformation with a recognizable genetic component. Only a portion of this percentage will have retardation associated with the genetically determined disability. It is no longer certain, however, that the retardation is the direct result of the genetic disability except in a relatively small percentage of the total. There is a growing body of evidence to suggest that the genetic disability contributes to a general vulnerability, and that the circumstances of life add the retardation.

The observable characteristics of any individual, relative to a particular trait (phenotype), is the sum of all the genes (genotype), the environment, and the interaction between the two. Phenylketonuria (PKU) represents a disorder in which the abnormal genotype is the principal cause of an abnormal phenotype. At the other end of a spectrum of cause and effect is a condition such as hydrocephaly. This condition does have a higher risk of recurrence among relatives but has a different kind of distribution, suggesting environmental causation with the presence of a susceptible genotype. Studies of retardation demonstrate the existence of this genetic spectrum of cause and effect. The severely and profoundly retarded are more likely to be affected for genetic or singularly organic reasons. The mildly to moderately retarded are more likely to be the product of multiple and interactive causative forces.

Each of the genetic mechanisms that has been listed has its distinctive characteristics that influence inheritance differently. Among the single-gene autosomal dominant, all affected offspring have an affected parent. Both sexes are involved equally. Mating with a nonaffected person has a reproductive frequency of the genetic trait of one half. Among the single-gene autosomal recessive, all relatives except siblings of affected individuals are usually normal. Both sexes are involved equally. Mating with a nonaffected person has a reproductive frequency of the genetic trait of one quarter. Consanguinity of parents of affected children is more common than in the general population. Among the single-gene X-linked recessive, except for male relatives in the female line, parents and other relatives are usually normal. All affected sons have carrier mothers. Affected males have normal sons, but their daughters are all carriers. Carrier females have normal and affected sons and carrier and normal daughters, with a reproductive frequency of one half for each.

The techniques for studying human chromosomes are a recent addition to the growing ability to identify factors associated with retardation. This study of human chromosomes has shed some light on the single most common specific diagnostic category of retardation—Down's syndrome, or mongolism. It has revealed the existence of a chromosomal aberration in all such afflicted individuals. Nearly all children with Down's syndrome are the offspring of normal parents and are born into families without previous known cases. This would suggest an autosomal dominant mutant with the mutation representing a single abnormal gene arising from a normal gene of either parent. The relatively high incidence of Down's syndrome suggests that genetic mutation cannot account for this syndrome in a satisfactory manner. However, the chromosomal evidence, when combined with the expected types and frequency of ova produced in a trisomic-21 female (having three number 21 chromosomes), provides a probable explanation of the occurrence of this condition. Other evidence for genetic factors can be found in twin studies. The concordance in identical twins is almost 100 percent. The concordance of Down's syndrome in fraternal twins is about zero percent. Family aggregation (the presence of multiple cases within a family in excess of random occurrence) of Down's syndrome does occur. About 1 percent of patients have a similarly affected sib. Evidence suggests that this family aggregation results from many causes, including translocation carrier and mosaic parents. The one factor most commonly associated with incidence of Down's syndrome is maternal age. There does seem to be a direct increase in frequency of the condition as a function of the mother's age. Paternal age shows no such association. All of this information provides a basis for family planning for the parents of children with Down's syndrome.

Incompatibilities are important genetic mechanisms that can result in retardation. The most common of these is Rh incompatibility. The union of an Rh-negative mother with an Rh-positive father results in all or a portion of the offspring being Rh-positive. There is an accompanying environmental component. The extent of antibody response stimulated in the Rh-negative mother by the presence of the Rh-positive fetus is related to exposure, so that the larger the number of incompatible pregnancies, the stronger is the antibody response. The maternal anti-Rh antibody produces fetal hemolysis (breakdown of the red blood cells) and erythroblastosis. This condition is treatable by exchange transfusion of the newborn, or even fetal transfusion. Without such interventions, the erythroblastostic infant develops kernicterus and brain damage, with retardation. Here is another important area of genetically determined damage that can be identified and prevented by appropriately timed interventions.

The application of genetic knowledge to the prevention of retardation can be directed at stopping a known harmful process, or at early case-finding and treatment where possible, so that the consequences of the harmful process are minimized or eliminated. Genetic counseling offers the opportunity to assess the risks of producing abnormal offspring and minimizes the potential for genetic defects. Skilled birth control information becomes an important part of the counseling service, since family planning is so often needed. The availability of competent laboratory facilities is also important in face of the increasing number of diagnostic procedures. There may be a need for additional medical interventions for implementation of recommendations arising from the genetic evaluation. In addition, the implication of damaged progeny represents a psychological assault on the self-image of adults, so that emotional support becomes another prerequisite of genetic counseling. All of these facets require a well-integrated use of professional services, which mandates genetic counseling to be part of the program of a medical center with a capacity to recruit each of the necessary services as needed.

Other preventative measures have become available in recent years. An increasing number of inborn metabolic errors have been identified. In some instances, appropriate treatments have been developed. Mass screening methods, as in PKU, have evolved. The purpose of such early identifications is to ensure effective intervention at a stage when retardation can be prevented. This emphasis on early diagnosis and treatment may lead to important new approaches. A parallel development has been the technique of registries and linkage procedures that facilitate the identification of high-risk infants very early in life, while providing a broad-based community organization devoted to identification, diagnostic counseling, and therapeutic services for individuals with genetic problems.

EARLY PREVENTION

The opportunities for prevention of retardation are many. Genetic counseling deals with conception from the viewpoint of genetic determination. Yet the progress in this field has served to reinforce our awareness of the far greater importance of environmental influences on the outcome of conception and subsequent life. There are many opportunities for prevention by physical means, and by relating such efforts to the different stages of life.

Proper nutrition ranks first among all the physical factors influencing gestation and postnatal existence. The physical well-being of the pregnant female is directly related to her nutritional state, as is the maturation and growth of her fetus. Malnutrition is one of the most common causes of infertility, miscarriage, and spontaneous abortion. It has been linked to all kinds of constitutional defects and growth failures. There is evidence correlating malnutrition during infancy to later retardation. Disturbances associated with chronic vitamin and mineral deficiencies have varying degrees of retardation associated with them. Many of these conditions are accompanied by irreversible damage to the central nervous system in early life. Nearly all of them are preventable by adequate nutrition, particularly during gestation and early infancy.

Bacterial, viral, and protozoan infections represent other major hazards for all stages of existence. Such infections of the mother during gestation, and of the infant, not only pose dangers to life but may have profound effects on its outcome because of the special vulnerability of the fetus and its immature nervous system to damage by infection. Developmental retardation is a common aftermath of such damage. Infections of an adult woman may cause sterility, infertility, spontaneous abortions, miscarriages, prematurity, and the full range of birth casualties. The products of such events have a very high incidence of damage, with secondary effects on their development leading to specific or generalized retardation. The known high incidence of fetal damage from rubella during the first trimester of a pregnancy has become an accepted medical reason for the interruption of the pregnancy. Syphilis during pregnancy has such proven damaging effects on the fetus that treatment of the newborn infant has become mandatory.

Nearly all of the developmental consequences of maternal, fetal, and infant infections are preventable by good prenatal and postnatal health care, as well as by early and determined treatment. We are blessed with an array of therapeutic agents that can master nearly every type of infection. Regretfully, too many of these go untreated, or are treated too late. The result of this "too little and too late" is the existence of many damaged infants who demonstrate some form of retardation later in life.

A number of treatable maternal metabolic and endocrinologic disorders may cause preventable defects with retardation among the offspring. These maternal disturbances include toxemias, diabetes, hypothyroidism, myasthenia gravis, and idiopathic thrombocytopenic purpura. Infants born to diabetic mothers have a higher neonatal morbidity and mortality, with increased congenital malformations and neurological sequelae. Good control of the maternal diabetes with anticipation of problems in the newborn results in a decreased risk of damage. The mother with hypothyroidism or goiter must be adequately treated during pregnancy if congenital malformations and retardation are to be avoided. Good maternal care during pregnancy is one of the cardinal principles of prevention of retardation.

In these days of worldwide concern about pollution of the earth, there is remarkably little concern about pollution of the fetal environment. Several recent studies revealed that more than 70 percent of pregnant women took two or more medications during their pregnancy. Yet it is well known that the fetus reacts differently to drugs than do children or adults. The tragedy of the thalidomide-induced abnormalities stands as mute but visible evidence of fetal vulnerability to seemingly harmless drugs for adults. A new and even more disastrous tragedy is anticipated with the growing use of heroin. Not only are the infants of addicted mothers born addicted, but a large percentage of them are seriously damaged.

There is little question that medication during the first trimester of pregnancy should be kept at an absolute minimum and self-medication during any part of the pregnancy should be avoided. Fortunately, the majority of drugs do not lead to fetal malformation, but unpredictable idiosyncrasies do exist. Large amounts of aspirin or phenobarbital have been known to cause neonatal hemorrhage; sulfanilamides, kernicterus; morphine, anoxia. Almost any drug may become a toxic agent to the vulnerable fetus. The potential for fetal damage is minimized by the cautious and judicious use of drugs and their general avoidance during pregnancy. This becomes yet another principle of prevention of retardation.

The complexities of our modern civilization have made preventable accidents a significant cause of serious brain injuries among all ages, but particularly of the young. Such injuries occurring early in life are often accompanied by retardation. One of the most common of accidents is the ingestion of toxic substances by young children. Their propensity to mouth, taste, and swallow things makes them specially vulnerable to the vast array of household substances that are available now in every home. Unfortunately, many of these substances are toxic, with some being so in small concentrations. These ingestions are completely preventable by the use of locked cabinets, sealed containers, and other simple precautions directed at keeping all such substances out of reach. Simple prevention is far better than attempts to cure. Physical injuries make up yet another major cause of brain injury. Their prevention is dependent on sound principles of child care. Special mention should be made of injury by fire. Extensive burns may cause a toxic encephalitis or death. The consequence of encephalitis among the very young is nearly always brain damage with possible retardation. Young children should never be left unattended, because of the potential hazard of fire in so many of our present-day homes.

The danger of radiation is truly a product of this century and, although its direct association with retardation has not been completely documented, there is enough evidence to demand our concern about and attention to this problem. Therapeutic radiation to the womb is damaging to the fetus throughout pregnancy. A diagnostic X-ray carries small hazard, yet caution should be displayed with elective X-ray studies, and the use of radioactive isotopes should be avoided during pregnancy if at all possible. The great unknown danger rests in any general increase in the levels of atmospheric radiation. There appears to be direct correlation between increased radiation exposure and increased fetal abnormalities through genetic mutation. This correlation suggests that any rise in the level of atmospheric radiation would lead to an increased number of damaged newborns among the general population. Any such increase would provide a new generation of retarded children whose presence could not be attributed directly to radiation except through scientific speculation. However, this speculation has a weight of substantial evidence to support it. Part of this speculation suggests that only minimal rises of radiation levels might serve to double the number of damaged newborns. All attempts, therefore, to control the release of any form of radiation into the atmosphere must be viewed as an important prevention of retardation.

The birth process heralds the start of life interacting with the world. The beginnings of this interaction can be quiet and uneventful or filled with the violence and fury of nature. Brain damage and retardation are among the products of the violence of birth. Good prenatal care equips the mother and fetus for this precarious moment. Good obstetrical care at birth reduces the potential for fetal-infant damage. Both good prenatal and obstetrical care are thus essential preventions of retardation.

RELATEDNESS

The infant's interaction with the world is dependent on his ability to relate. This ability emerges from the developmental processes of sensory-motor organization, individuation, separation, and adaptation. Any impairment of these processes demands that others compensate for the defects by the nature of the care rendered. Many of the principles of this care have continuing application to the retarded through much of their lives.

The primary objective of sensory-motor organization is the patterning of impulse. The retarded need help with this patterning and can benefit from routines at every stage of development. This need should, nevertheless, be recognized as a pathway for relatedness and not as an instrument by which the deficits within the sensory-motor system can be corrected. A number of procedures have been developed that try to compensate for primary neurological deficits by efforts directed at sensory-motor patterning. Regretfully, most of them substitute attempts at patterning impulses for the much more needed devotion to the relatedness of these damaged individuals. Initial efforts should be directed at facilitating the ordering of impulse relative to self and then extended to the objects and people within the environment. Attention must be paid to basic physiological rhythms of sleeping, eating, elimination, perception, and movement.

Sleep is an altered state of consciousness, just as is wakefulness. Many of the retarded demonstrate basic disturbances in the rhythms of their consciousness and require a sensitivity to these altered rhythms. It is difficult to obtain appropriate or sustained responses when general awareness is limited or momentarily inhibited. The infant will not feed properly, just as the young child will not follow commands or the older child respond to teaching, if their degree of consciousness is near to the state of sleep. The retarded often slip rapidly and at irregular time intervals from wakefulness to sleep and back to wakefulness. An awareness of this phenomenon permits more effective use of the best intervals for meaningful relatedness around such efforts as feeding, toileting, and instructing. It also leads toward better-designed efforts at encouraging more sustained involvement with activities. Formal teaching after a meal might better be replaced by a period of movement activities, or even a rest period. Yet so many classes for the retarded are conducted within the same model as the regular school, which has the children sitting down for learning exercises immediately after lunch. There may be heightened or prolonged periods of wakefulness or sleepiness. These, too, must be taken into account for the modification of schedules and the selection of types of activities. The appropriateness of the judgment and selection do much to help the retarded toward a better state of relatedness.

The rhythm of hunger, feeding, and satiation is variable but lends itself to being ordered. This rhythm is, however, linked to wakefulness, energy levels, and fatigability, as well as other facets of behavior. The ordering of eating occurs within the first year of life and responses become well established soon afterward, so that associated behavior is predictable. We quickly recognize our desire and need to eat, and how much. Our periods of rest and activity coincide with this recognition. This ability is not always well defined in the retarded, and helping them establish well-regulated patterns with all of these becomes another goal of their care. This goal requires an awareness of individual patterns and the introduction of routines that will modify but not conflict with the natural impulses. Successes with such routines lead to many more positive experiences through improved relatedness.

Good control of elimination depends upon the integration of impulses with acceptable rules of behavior. The child must not only synchronize sensations associated with evacuation and urination but must also coordinate various reflexes with each other in a time and place designated by others. The command of "go to the bathroom" is a complex one for any individual with disorganized impulses, poor capacity for synchronizing functions, and unrelated behavior. The instruction becomes a demand that cannot be responded to with ease. Even when understood, this command challenges the ability to synchronize impulse, reflex, function, and thought. It represents the relatedness of impulses, self to impulses, objects to impulses, and self to objects. It is no wonder that many retarded individuals have extensive problems with both bowel and bladder training. Yet socially determined attitudes demand and praise early achievements of control over bodily functions. They set the retarded aside as underachievers early in life. Many of these attitudes also detract from the more primary mission of helping the retarded come to an appropriate level of relatedness so that they themselves may achieve the integration of impulse, function, and behavior necessary for bowel and bladder control. Too frequently, the conflicts of human relationship of parent to child alters the circumstances, so that well-intended instructions go awry.

Once the complexities of impulse control are appreciated fully, procedures can be developed that respond to the needs of the retarded. Such procedures require routine, order, timing, and instructions geared to the developmental level. When impulses are disorganized, regular and repetitive routines are essential. When expected sequences and associations fail to appear, the order and timing of events become essential. When comprehension is limited by lack of relatedness, what is done and felt becomes more important than what is said. Thus toilet training becomes a function of relatedness—of the child to its own impulses and to its caring parents. Most retarded who have problems of bowel and bladder control do best with routines coinciding with the intake of food and drink. Toileting routines should be instituted to follow meals in order to recruit the most natural and common reflex associations between intake and output. The time interval of such efforts should be short, in order to simulate the rapidity of early responses. They must be repetitive for long periods of time in order to instruct by doing rather than saying.

Perception of impulse is critical to relatedness. A lack of awareness of self or objects other than the self eliminates responses that may be essential to existence and survival. Functions are not consummated. Behavior becomes meaningless. Communication is impossible. The retarded must be helped to escape the vacuums created by their defects of perception. They must be encouraged to develop their perceptive abilities through stimulation and exposure. They must be redirected into compensatory systems that link impulses in new ways. They must be aided by experimentation to find useful recruitments of their established modes of functioning. It must be recognized that perception stimulates function and functioning stimulates new perceptions. The young infant needs to be held, touched, tickled, grasped, stimulated by sounds and sights, and moved. All of these activities stimulate the formation within the infant of impulses that call for responses. The determination of these responses is part of early growing.

The greatest damage occurs when the infant is robbed of its birthright to the sensations of life and its discomforts. An infant left to its own resources quickly becomes preoccupied with itself rather than the world around it. An infant ignored for any protracted period fails to develop a discriminating awareness of its environment. And, finally, an infant who lacks the ability to discriminate fails to grow. Retardation becomes the significant by-product of the failures of perception. The child with defect has its own, built-in perceptual failures. The child without defect may be endowed with perceptual failures by lack of stimulation. Both may be offered some degree of relief by the stimulation of relatedness of the caring adult to the needs of the child.

The integration of perception by sensory-motor organization brings order, selection, priority, and sequence to the multitude of environmental stimuli. Early-established defects of the sensory-motor apparatus delay the appearance of order, hamper selectivity, preserve early priorities, and alter the sequence of perception. Retarded individuals perceive, but their perception may be changed in subtle ways. They may respond to many cues without discriminating which are the more important. They may structure a priority of responses that is inappropriate to their current situation. The retarded may be helped by a sensitivity to their perceptual difficulties. The number of stimuli to which they are exposed at any one time can be reduced. The infant can be offered many toys, but only one at a time. The young child can be given many instructions, but separately and distinct from each other. The older child can be taught many things, but within well-defined limits and with as few distractions as possible.

Movement provides new dimensions to perception and life. It permits and encourages change. It generates different stimuli from the same set of circumstances by altering existing combinations. It makes possible selections leading to priorities. Movement broadens the environment, attracting the individual toward the external world and away from the world within. Many retarded have motor deficits that impair their abilities to move toward relatedness. They need to be helped to overcome their deficits by being encouraged to move. The retarded infant tends to be placid and immobile or hyperactive but disorganized. Planned physical activity, within the limits of the capacity of the infant, becomes stimulating and organizing for both combinations. The retarded child is isolated from physical activities with chronological peers early in life and tends to withdraw from participation because of repeated failures. Yet such physical activity is a much needed stimulus to development and should not be permitted to disappear from the life-style of the retarded child. The same is true of the adolescent and adult.

Many programs for the retarded nevertheless make little or no provision for organized physical activities. They tend to protect the retarded from their own ineptness by a priority given to sedentary activities with emphasis on fine motor control, while the mastery of gross motor skills is left to chance. The best programs for the retarded place equal emphasis on both. The best institutional settings for the retarded incorporate adequate space for living with physical activity.

Any residual problems within sensory-motor organization slow the processes of individuation and separation, extending the period of attachment and dependency. The retarded young cling and react adversely to the unfamiliar. They are more likely to be made anxious by the introduction of new experiences and are reluctant to move into different situations. They become immobilized by strangeness. They tend to preserve their resources by limiting their contact with the world. They seek sameness as a relief from the anxiety generated by their disordered impulses, their poor self-image, and their failures in mastering the demands of their environment. Their capacity for relatedness to people becomes constricted, as do their emotional responses.

All of this places great demands on the caring adult. The more limited emotional responses to efforts in behalf of the retarded make relationships with them less rewarding. Expected feedback of interaction and feelings are weak or absent. Relatedness is minimal while need for relatedness is great. Only the efforts of the caring adult compensate for this disequilibrium. However, investment in seeking relatedness with the retarded has great returns in their progress with ability to control impulse, with growing self-esteem, with movement in a more meaningful way. Giving them this endowment of relatedness to emotions and people encourages them toward motivated interactions with others and sets the stage for the new experiences of learning, being taught, seeking relationships, and experimenting with new forms of adaptations to life.

So much of the behavior of the young is imitative. They imitate that which is close to them and what they themselves experience directly. Most of their responses are modeled after their own emotional interactions and reflect their needs. Weak interactions in their own affective existence promote weak responses to subsequent events. The retarded infant, left to its own resources for long intervals, tends to preserve its sense of isolation by not seeking much needed relationships in later life. The retarded child with more limited perceptions tends to respond to its environment as if there were fewer opportunities. The emotionally deprived relate to others with fewer emotions. These simple realities define the human and emotional needs of the retarded. They need more stimulation and more physical and emotional opportunities for interaction.

Often these needs exceed the capacities of any set of parents. Even the greatest devotion to these principles may fail to provide for the full range of needs. In many instances, it is far more appropriate to divide some of the responsibilities among several caring adults in order to maintain the quality of care without the danger of exhaustion in face of the protracted needs of the retarded. This division of labor and love has to be planned with care so as not to fragment experiences. Certainly the concept of the extended family may have great meaning. If every family and community pooled their imagination and resources the way could be paved for rewarding relationships and experiences for both the retarded and those devoted to their care. The retarded continue to provide the stimulus for many worthwhile efforts that bring many of us into closer relationship with each other. They need to benefit from this closeness as well.

CHAPTER IX

Later Interventions

Development creates demands that must be met if its progression is to be maintained. Responding to these demands is a primary task for the retarded, as well as for those who help them grow. Some of these demands are emotional, as with relatedness. Yet others are physical, intellectual, or social. Each changes with the stages of human development and the circumstances of life. Each is determined by biological need, maturational sequence, and social custom. The more effectively these demands are met, the more acceptable are the retarded to themselves and to family, peers, and community.

The physical aspects of life are intimately bound to daily routines. Eating, resting, moving, personal hygiene, playing, working—all lend themselves to routines. The earlier these routines become established with the retarded, the better it is for them. The best approaches link them to current levels of abilities and, by doing so, lead the retarded to their own attempts to achieve order. Most of these daily events are universal experiences known to all of us. They need only to be modified to the developmental level of the retarded infant or child in our attempts to communicate the value of the routines.

FEEDING

The earliest feeding patterns are irregular and blend with intervals of rest and sleep. It is unwise to permit retarded infants too great a range of variability, and a modified but definite schedule of feeding is best for them. Their sucking is usually poor and feeding periods may have to be extended slightly. Intervals between feedings should be regulated by judgment of food intake and weight gain. The changes in their pattern of feeding proceed more slowly, so that the three-meal-a-day schedule may not be achieved until the second or third year of life. Self-feeding is delayed. Their ability to coordinate the grasp reflex of the hand with the hand-to-mouth movements may be badly synchronized, making help with feeding necessary for a longer period of time. A good index of progress is the ability to grasp objects and let go of them in a purposeful manner. This level of reflex organization coincides with the beginning of experimentation with self-feeding. Proper encouragement of this experimentation is necessary. Parallel efforts of feeding and self-feeding should be extended over a long period in order to stabilize the pattern and stimulate learning by imitation. The consistency and order of foods may offer problems because of the persistence of the dominance of taste and smell within the hierarchy of the senses. A proper awareness of an earlier preference leads to a more skillful introduction of new foods by proper selection and timing. Sucking and swallowing reflexes may not be well coordinated, resulting in air-swallowing with eruction and regurgitation. Feedings may have to be slowed or modified to keep these to a minimum. Ultimately, such problems do subside. Sometimes the gastrocolic reflex stimulates a bowel movement during or immediately after feeding among the retarded young who are not trained. The persistence of this early reflex in so many of the retarded mandates their toileting immediately after food intake.

Progress with feeding leads to further efforts to help the retarded achieve early mastery of this essential behavior. Their preference for sameness can be recruited by routinizing time, place, and procedure for all meals. Plastic or other forms of unbreakable utensils should be used so that the retarded child can be involved with some of the aspects of preparation and serving of the food. As many meals as possible should be shared with them, so that the supporting elements of relationship through simultaneous eating is introduced. This stimulates eating by imitation—an important learning system for the retarded. The use of knife, fork, and spoon should be encouraged but some use of the fingers tolerated in order to encourage self-feeding habits as early as possible. Food should be selected and prepared in a manner facilitating easy handling of it. Once self-feeding is mastered, emphasis should be shifted to preparation and serving. Such training has great meaning since it links relationship and essential behavior for self-sufficiency early in the life-style of the retarded. It opens significant pathways for communication. Language is stimulated with the concrete representations and experiences of food preparation and intake. Such efforts represent one of the best pathways for strengthening the object-relatedness of retarded children. It is reflected in their subsequent recruitment of food and all that is associated with it for their spontaneous play. This kind of play should be encouraged and directed as a means of reinforcing the children's attempts to master these essential experiences. Play equipment for the slightly older retarded child should include cooking and eating utensils, as well as other toys permitting them to play house.

The importance of self-feeding needs to be reinforced at every stage of development. It remains a significant pathway for relatedness, communication of attitudes and values, and a means of training throughout the life of the retarded. The movement of the children into groupings in schools or training programs within the community or institutions provides many opportunities for the use of eating as a part of a system of peer or adult interaction. Meals can be recruited for such purposes as exposure to new environments, socialization activities, the reinforcement of habit formation, and work training. Food handling is probably the largest industry in the world and could and probably does place a large percentage of the mild and moderately retarded into productive adult roles. Many of our retarded can be prepared for a useful adult existence by early and proper training with their own eating habits and handling of food.

RESTING

Resting patterns among the retarded preserve many of the earliest rhythms of wake and sleep through long periods of their lives. Their lapses into inattentiveness, poor concentration, increasing errors of performance, weakened responsiveness, and episodic withdrawal can frequently be linked to their changing states of consciousness and need for more rest periods during the day. As infants, they demonstrate the extremes of prolonged sleep or excessive lapses into irritable states. As young children, their play and socialization is variable to a degree that often interferes with the success of their attempts. As older children, their ability to learn becomes hampered by some of the lapses. As adolescents and adults, their involvement with productive activities may be so variable that it becomes annoying to others who have to work with them.

Sensitivity to their distinctive rhythms permits approaches that make the most of peak periods of attentiveness and brings greater successes to efforts at modifying some of the rhythms. Daily schedules can be organized that respond to the individual's own pattern, while introducing changes. Activities can be reordered and given priorities that coincide with the fluctuating ability to respond. The infant can be involved with stimulating contacts when there is a tendency to prolonged sleep. The excessively irritable infant may require more frequent naps. The young child may have to be limited to shortened and well-chosen moments of social contact with peers. There may have to be planned variation of quiet play alternating with physically stimulating games. The older child may have to be taught early in the day and formal learning abandoned for the remainder of the same day. Physical activities can be substituted that reinforce the more sedentary formal learning periods. Adolescence is a stage of life that ordinarily involves spasmodic withdrawal. The retarded adolescent has this need as well but may require some direction with the timing and nature of the withdrawal. The adult seeks coffee breaks and other planned interruptions of work schedules. The retarded adult needs to be encouraged toward intervals that satisfy his special needs.

Special mention should be made of the judicious use of behavior-modifying drugs. A number of safe drugs have been developed that may improve attention span, degree of alertness, impulsiveness, control, and the general state of consciousness. Their effectiveness with the retarded has been demonstrated many times over. Their use must be correlated with a complete evaluation of the causes of the retardation and the nature of accompanying physical defects, as well as the specific objectives for their administration. The drugs include the amphetamines, some of the antihistamines, the ataractics, the anticonvulsants, and a scattering of other chemical agents. They need to be prescribed selectively and with appropriate medical supervision. Their proper application may result in changes of behavior that introduce successes in place of failures of performance. These successes can lead to more appropriate responses and greater acceptability within all levels of relationships. When behavior-modifying drugs are found to be effective, their use should be prolonged in order to stabilize the newly established and more desirable modes of functioning. So many of the retarded have biologically determined disorders of impulse. To ignore the possibilities of biochemical interventions in their behalf is to neglect a most important avenue of intervention.

MOVEMENT

The movement patterns of the retarded preserve many of the earlier styles of motor organization. Their awkwardness, posturing, ineptness, and clumsy responses are a direct reflection of inadequate developmental progression. As infants, there is obvious delay in the acquisition of basic motor skills. They sit, stand, walk, and talk late. As young children, these delays are accompanied by disturbances. Their gait may be wide-based and awkward. They may stumble and fall more than usual. They prefer flexed body positions. They shuffle, slouch, and move about in an ungainly manner. Gross motor coordination is poor. Fine motor coordination is nearly always disturbed. They have difficulty in picking up things, or they may be dropping them constantly. Their movement through space is disjointed and haphazard. As older children, their performance and competitive status with peers at play and in school are hampered by their poor capacity for well-synchronized, coordinated movements. As adolescents, they tend to be left behind and out of the group activities so intimately linked with expressive motor behavior—sports, dancing, arts and crafts, and other similar pursuits. As adults, the residue of their motor dysfunctions limits their competitive ability for jobs.

An awareness of the nature of some of these difficulties can lead to helpful interventions at each stage of life. Infants with obvious lags of motor development need to be touched, held, and moved more. This provides some stimulation to the receptor systems of the body and increases their awareness of self. Too often, there is a tendency to follow the lead of the infant. Placidity is met with decreased involvement. Hyperactivity is met with withdrawal. In actuality, the placidity of the retarded infant needs to be countered by extra stimulation, and the hyperactivity with soothing involvement. These efforts may not hasten the appearance of motor skills, but they do serve to improve the possibilities of better control over impulses, relatedness to self and others, and, ultimately, a better chance for achieving whatever the developmental potential may be.

Young retarded children need constant efforts directed at their movement activities. These efforts bring them into contact with objects and by so doing stimulate their perception of their world. Motivation for involvement comes from this perception. It should be remembered that the young child has a preference for sameness and is made anxious by the unfamiliar. Activities therefore have to be introduced under familiar circumstances or the surroundings made familiar before any exposure to new experiences. It should also be remembered that spatial organization is poor in the retarded young and there are persistent rostral and flexor dominances that play a role in the determination of their preferences. The use of walkers on wheels can be a productive form of stimulating interest in the environment when there is delayed locomotion. Furniture should be simple, sturdy, and designed low to the ground in order to give the children easily available support and objects which can be grasped. Rooms need not be too spacious, since large areas tend to produce anxiety. Push and pull toys help stimulate an interest and experimentation with movement. Floor areas should be kept reasonably clear to invite exploration and movement toward objects. Playpens are helpful aids, but their use should be limited because they tend to bound and constrict movement.

Searching by crawling needs to be encouraged, since it involves movement in a flexed position and puts the head forward, compared with walking, which puts the feet forward before all else. Crawling, as a rostrally determined movement, is more comfortable and less anxiety-provoking. Retarded infants and young children should be encouraged to crawl because it stimulates movement, leading to exploring the environment. Giving such preference to crawling will not interfere with later walking, nor will it be the cause of any unusual delay in the appearance of this motor skill.

Some movement activities have to be introduced cautiously. Swinging the retarded child through space can be very anxiety-provoking because of its problems with spatial perception. The use of swings should be delayed or offered with a sensitivity to the child's responses. Slides require a similar awareness on the part of the supervising adult. They move the body quickly through space and in unexpected positions. Both swings and slides are worthwhile pieces of equipment but require sensitive supervision and a knowledge of the difficulties they may present. Pedaling a tricycle offers many of the same spatial problems to the retarded, while adding a new one of coordination of flexor and extensor muscles for purposeful movement. Moreover, it involves the most caudal part of the body, which is the last to be synchronized within the patterns of mass body movement. It is no wonder that retarded children have real difficulties in learning to ride a tricycle early or the bicycle in later years. The skills involved with riding are much needed by the retarded, but their delay in acquiring them should be tolerated, as they are offered understanding and patience with their efforts with these movement activities.

The appearance of fine motor coordination is delayed in most of the retarded. The two outstanding areas are speech and writing. Apart from the capacity for thought and symbol formation, both can be viewed as activities of movement. Speech involves the movements of respiration and articulation for the production of sounds. Writing involves the coordination of visual motor pathways with the functioning of the arm, forearm, and hand. Both are complex tasks of synchronized movements. Very often their delayed appearance is the cause of considerable anxiety and the retarded child is pressured too soon into all kinds of remedial exercises.

Much of this early remediation may be inappropriate in timing because the readiness for fine motor functions has not yet been achieved. It is usually more appropriate to place initial emphasis on object-relatedness and correct symbol formation associated with the acquisition of general motor skills. These set the stage for the ultimate appearance of a better level of fine motor coordination. The child who breathes with a spontaneous, forceful rhythm will make the sounds of speech with greater ease. The child who can follow the arc of a ball thrown through space and catch it is more likely to be able to reproduce some of the arcs of the letters of the alphabet during attempts to write. Regretfully, retarded children turn away from sustained involvement with gross motor activities because of their failures, and we who care for them do the same because of our disappointment with their attempts. Supportive programs for deficits in speaking and writing should involve general physical activities such as rhythm exercises, noncompetitive games, ball-playing, swimming, dancing, and almost any kind of motor activity that brings together the movement of parts of the body in a rhythm of time and in harmony with space. Specific remediation becomes more effective against the background of these more generalized movement activities.

An important dimension of all movement is time. Rhythm, duration, sequence, progression, beginning, and ending are all time components of movement. The retarded have problems with all of these components, so that activities must be planned to encompass optimum timing. Attention span and concentration are variable. They repeat some sequences (perseverate), and omit others. Sometimes they run things together or correlate them inappropriately. They may have difficulty beginning a task or, if involved, they may be unable to end it. Awareness of these difficulties permits modification of schedules and planning of activities commensurate with ability. Shortened periods of involvement with varied tasks are tolerated best. Formal instruction periods need to be interrupted with periods of physical activities, and yet there should be some effort to achieve a continuity between them. Object and word recognition needs to be moved from the printed page into daily activities and back again to the printed page. Only by this kind of concrete representation and reinforcement can teaching efforts and learning experiences be made meaningful to the retarded.

Activity programs must mesh daily-living procedures with more formal teaching and learning. Many older children are taught reading, writing, and arithmetic, as well as home economics, shop, arts, and crafts in the classroom setting and then are left to their own resources or that of others to apply what has been taught. The break in continuity dissipates much of what may have been learned, because of difficulties with transposition. A continuity of teaching, learning, and living is basic for the older retarded child.

Adolescence is a time of life dominated by rapid and almost continuous movement. The forces of development are unleashed in order to prepare for the regulated, productive activities of adult existence. Involvement with self, others, experimentation, exploration, physical and social events, and the infinite variations of living require a heavy investment in movement and the pursuit of activity. Retardation has an inertia within it, setting the retarded individuals distinctly apart from peers during this stage of life. Their sense of inadequacy stops them from attempting to participate. Their failures curtail further experimentation. Their predilection for the familiar inhibits or distorts their explorations. Their problems of coordination set them aside within physical and social events. Often the result is isolation, leading to anxiety, withdrawal, and an overall suppression of activity levels.

Programming for retarded adolescents must compensate for this generalized state of physical and social inhibition. They need to be encouraged and supported in developing interests and involvement. Spectator sports lend themselves well to both. They permit varying levels of participation in both an active and passive manner, while maintaining social interaction. They offer the opportunity for identification with the activity and with all those who have a similar interest. A retarded adolescent boy may excel in his identification of the heroes of our national ball clubs, making his own ineptness with a ball more tolerable. A retarded adolescent girl may collect the memorabilia of a movie star, to the point of obsession, making her own awkwardness more acceptable. Both may attach themselves inordinately to the idols of the moment, giving themselves a social identification counteracting their sense of difference and isolation.

Special efforts need to be made to maintain their involvement with physical activities. Selection of these activities is most important to ensure that capacities are not exceeded and personal resources are not strained. Rhythm exercises are particularly helpful in establishing and preserving regularity of respiration, muscle tone, flexor and extensor balance, posture, and general physical well-being. Walking, the most natural of all exercises, can be recruited for many purposes. It can be used to extend the horizons of the retarded by introducing changes of environment and variations in social contacts. It can be incorporated into learning-teaching experiences. It lends itself to routine and repetition. It introduces patterns that can be reproduced spontaneously and easily by the retarded.

Simple running games like tag and different kinds of races help to develop motor skills and a sense of competitiveness. Hopscotch becomes an aid to balance and coordination. Bicycle riding extends motor activities and helps synchronize them with more rapid movement through space. Simple dancing routines stimulate the combination of rhythm and movement. Swimming exercises become an aid to breathing, balance, and coordinated body movements. Most of these lend themselves to group activities, permitting and encouraging social interaction with the opportunity for adequate supervision.

Adolescence is a moment of reaching out and experimenting with adult activities. This can be recruited for learning by imitation. The retarded need to be given the opportunities to parallel adult work and play experiences that recruit movement to these purposes. Household chores should be shared before being delegated. Work responsibilities require long periods of supervised apprenticeship. Tasks need to be simplified and broken down into their component parts. The more complicated motor skills may have to be introduced much later in the sequence of exposure. Patient efforts with this kind of apprenticeship-teaching may result in the acquisition of many socially productive skills, leading to some degree of independence and self-sufficiency in adult life.

SELF-CARE

Caring for one's self is a function of relatedness. The degree to which existence is determined by an awareness of self and others permits the varying acquisition of necessary controls and values involved with self-care. The retarded individual with limited capacities for relating is lacking not only in ability but also in motivation. Thus, as with all other interventions, primary attention must be given to the nature of relatedness and its disturbance, in order to help the retarded care for themselves. Efforts must be made as early as possible. Success with self-feeding leads to a better climate for approaching bowel training. Prompt attention to cleaning the young infant's skin initiates habit training with awareness by tactile stimulation. The natural searching activities linked to crawling motivate experimentation with all forms of motor control. The ordering of space and time through adherence to routines encourages an interest in self-control. The relationships bred by all of these early efforts of infant care culminate in a greater awareness of self, with an accompanying motivation for self-care.

Feeding is so intimately linked to survival that many of life's most significant messages are communicated through this act. "I am available. I respond. I satisfy. I frustrate. I help. I need. I accept. I love. I'm concerned." The "I" of the caring adult and the "I" of the retarded meet through the act of feeding. It breeds the earliest ingredients of relatedness and relationship. It encourages the retarded to become aware of their own sensations, needs, and variations of existence. It stimulates purposeful contact with responses directed at reinforcing the state of being. Not only is physical growth fostered, but so are awareness, contact, interaction, and motivation. Self-feeding becomes the cornerstone for learning about self-care.

Attention should be paid to self-feeding at each stage of life.

Essential reflexes may be stimulated and reinforced for utilization with more sophisticated functions. An early, well-developed grasp reflex that has been encouraged through clutching a bottle or food may be used later to button or unbutton a garment. A good sucking reflex may be the forerunner of better utilization of the muscles of articulation within developing speech. Feeding routines may serve as the prototype for other routines. Having the young child participate in some aspect of the preparation of food may encourage participation in other essential activities leading toward self-sufficiency. Having the older retarded preparing and serving food breeds relatedness and a sense of responsibility for self and others. The retarded should be moved toward self-feeding as early as possible.

Cleanliness has its roots in infant care. Many of the simple routines devoted to keeping an infant and young child clean serve also to stimulate an awareness of body surfaces and parts, as well as a relatedness to their general state of being. Retarded children start out in life with difficulties in their perception of themselves, so that the early efforts at maintaining a degree of cleanliness reinforce the essential recognition that establishes some of the motivation for acceptance of and participation in later routines for self-care. The infant who becomes accustomed to prolonged periods of wet and soiled diapers will have little reason to respond to toilet-training efforts or other routines directed at keeping the surfaces of the body clean and dry. Here again, repetition and sameness become the essential ingredients for communication of attitudes and habits. What is done and experienced provides the motivation for subsequent routines. The earliest systems for purveying the value of cleanliness exist within eating, elimination, resting, and movement. Attention to this detail sets the stage for all subsequent behavior to contain the values of cleanliness.

There is a need for continued reinforcement of this value

through most of life, since acceptability is linked to good habit formation and grooming. Bowel and bladder control represent critical areas of self-care for both. The earlier these are established, the easier is the retarded's lot within family and with peers. Regretfully, there are many barriers to the acquisition of the needed controls over these bodily functions. Both are caudally determined, so that the capacity for their achievement is delayed by the prolonged immaturity of the nervous system of the retarded. The neurologically damaged have difficulty in processing the sensations associated with these functions and synchronizing the motor impulses required for appropriate control. This immaturity and damage may be aggravated by further disturbance stemming from the emotional climate and confusion surrounding the attempts to communicate expectations. A good deal of sensitivity and awareness to capacity and readiness is essential to the success of training efforts.

Rarely can bowel training be achieved before gross motor control establishes walking independently as a way of life. The coordination required in walking seems to herald the maturing of the central nervous system to a level permitting the voluntary control of the sphincter muscles so necessary for management of bowel movements. This does not mean that no attempts at bowel training should be made prior to walking. It does suggest that such attempts may not be successful, so that disappointment is not experienced and disapproval of failure communicated in the efforts of bowel training.

Another indicator of readiness is predictable regularity. Many young children begin to demonstrate a pattern to their elimination. Motility of the lower bowel is stimulated by activity of the upper gastrointestinal tract by way of a gastrocolic reflex. An awareness of the interval between this stimulus and response permits toileting routines to be introduced with a better possibility of success. This kind of "catching" provides the opportunity for communicating purpose and approval while decreasing the sense of frustration with the effort. Regretfully, many retarded children are plagued by irregularity, hypermotility, and spasticity of their gastrointestinal tract. These manifest themselves in frequent, infrequent, or unpredictable bowel movements. Some allowance must be made for this. Persistent or recurrent constipation may require medical management with stool softeners, bulk laxatives, or intestinal relaxants. Episodic diarrhea may require yet other kinds of medical management. Either may require a delay in the introduction of bowel training.

Routine and sameness should be extended within bowel training long after it has been achieved in order to reinforce its significance. The retarded regress with ease through much of their young lives. Maintaining their essential patterns of control becomes supportive and helps them extend the experiences into other areas of self-care. The most important extension of the associations with bowel training are bladder control and general cleanliness. Many of the same forces are in operation with bladder function. Its control is delayed or subject to numerous variables, so that the routines of training need to be orderly and responsive to the capacities of the retarded. Here again, successes may be achieved by following some of the natural patterns of elimination of the individual child. Frequently medical assistance may be required because of poor bladder tone or variable sphincter control.

There are important distinctions to be made between the children who have never been dry and those who have episodic bouts of loss of bladder function. The absence of any evidence of transitory control may be an indication of severe immaturity or persistent defect, with a need for investigation or corrective intervention. Episodic control may reflect regression or the need for reinforcement of the child's own efforts. As with all developmental achievements, success breeds success and failure encourages additional failure. Appropriate timing and attitudes with training efforts can be reinforced by the use of medical procedures designed to complement them. There have been positive results reported with several medications that improve bladder and sphincter tone. The use of conditioning equipment has helped as well to pattern responses to impulse. However, the timing and attitudes of all these efforts do much to affect the relationship with the retarded and must be given the priority due them as attempts are made to establish control over bladder function. As with bowel control, it may too easily become a source of conflict within the parent-child relationship and be used as a nonverbal expression of general tension, anxiety, and even hostility.

It has already been indicated that attitudes toward cleanliness are determined to a great degree by what takes place around bowel and bladder training. So many of the values are communicated through the process of these early training efforts that they continue to dominate subsequent behavior. They remain as the basis for motivation by preserving and establishing a hierarchy of touch and smell sensations with responses conditioned by early childhood experiences. The older retarded child who has been subjected to long intervals of soiled and moist skin contacts at an earlier stage of life may have little motivation to wash the hands or face or pay any attention to foreign substances on any surface of the body. There may be an accompanying anesthesia to tactile sensations, so that little awareness exists of the soiled conditions. Such results may be countered by appropriate habit training but require prolonged efforts, with allowances made for easy regression to the earlier patterns. Thus a retarded child who has been trained to be clean under one set of circumstances may not preserve the same standards under another. The older retarded child must be encouraged gently, and with understanding, to extend what has been learned about cleanliness to new situations. Prolonged attention to such details is needed in this as well as other areas of habit training. The retarded adolescent often falls victim to the regressive tendencies of this stage of life and tends to be sloppy and inattentive to personal hygiene. Again, gentle persuasion may be needed in order to maintain some semblance of cleanliness. In adult life, there may be failure to use or project the learned values onto new social and work situations. Help may be needed to encourage the appropriate associations.

The saying "Clothing makes the person" is a reflection of the general awareness of clothes as an extension of the self-image. Our manner of dress announces who and what we are. It is also a pronouncement of what we think of ourselves. Nowhere can these truisms be better seen than among the retarded. There are always marked delays in getting retarded children to pay attention to the details of their clothing. Early in life, it is as if clothes have no relation to living. The retarded have little interest in them, and attempts to communicate their value are to no avail. There is delayed experimentation with taking things off and little effort to participate in being dressed. Not only do buttoning and unbuttoning defy the poor muscle coordination of the retarded, but there is little interest in this kind of exploratory activity. Retarded children will lose or abandon items as if they didn't exist. These early patterns may persist within the life-style of the individual, so continuing efforts must be made to reinforce both the self-image of the retarded and its association with clothes.

The earliest attempts should be directed at showing the functional purpose of clothes and the basic routines associated with them. They are put on and taken off. They are used for protection and warmth. They are changed. Clothes have different uses under similar conditions as well as separate occasions. All of this has to be communicated by what is done and then reinforced by some kind of constancy of approach. The same kind of clothes should be used for the same purpose in order to familiarize the child with their function. Color coding of clothes can sometimes be helpful. The same color spectrum can be used for certain items of apparel. These and similar efforts serve to strengthen and make significant the self through clothes. In later childhood, clothes may be used to strengthen the slowly emerging identity, while their care can become an instrument for communicating the need for order. By adolescence, they can strengthen the emerging sexual identity and offer a bridge to peer identification by appropriate selections. Attention to dress within adult life can help with self-esteem to some degree. Clothes should not be permitted to become a means of depersonalization. Too many of our institutional practices, by their devotion to nondescript and uniform dress, as well as uniform practices, rob the retarded of their limited opportunities to reach their own identity. The selection and attention given to clothes provides a valuable form of intervention in behalf of the retarded at all stages of their life.

SOCIALIZATION

The ability to interact with others serves as a general stimulus to development. Most retarded are deprived of this essential stimulation to a greater or lesser degree by the nature of their retardation, so providing appropriate opportunities for socialization should become a major intervention in their behalf. The early impairments of perceptions and response often lead to errors and failures in their attempts to interact with others. The caring parent must compensate for these by corrective and protective attitudes. Errors of omission must be helped by redefinition of objectives, repetition of opportunities, and support during the new attempts. Errors of commission should be aided by sensitive assessment of reasons for the errors, guidance in the corrective efforts, and redirection.

The prolonged dependency of the retarded places a heavy responsibility on the family, while locking much of the early socialization needs into the family interactions. During infancy and early childhood there may be a marked clinging and attachment to a single member within the family constellation. This involves the mother most frequently but is not limited to her. Such dependency does not have to be discouraged since it serves to reinforce the quality of relatedness. It does need some control with boundaries and limits, so that it does not consume or exhaust. It also provides the opportunity for communicating the essence and values of all relationships. The acceptance of these early dependency needs of the retarded gives them many of the basic ingredients for their earliest experimentations in socialization with others. If they have had a lot of physical contact, they will seek later relationships by physical contact. If there has been considerable emotional content, they will seek relationships reflecting the nature of the emotions. Thus the quality of the dependency influences the spontaneous efforts of the retarded child with others. Attention directed at the nature of the dependent relationship within the family will therefore serve to influence later attempts at socialization by the retarded child with peers and other adults.

Early efforts to move out of the family are cautious. They are based on the need for similarity and the opportunity for repetition of known experiences. These requirements introduce a kind of parallelism. The retarded child becomes accepting of situations resembling those that are known. There is a cautious acceptance of similar but new circumstances. With peers, there is parallel rather than integrated play. With adults, there tends to be a reduplication of the dependent behavior within the family, whatever it may have been.

These early efforts must be supervised closely so that known patterns of response can be adapted to the new and changing situations. Parallel or side-by-side play with other children should be encouraged. It should be remembered that young children know nothing of retardation. They select and respond by judging each other by equality of size, similarity of activities, and equivalent responses. They do not judge competence and ability to function until much later in childhood. This parallel existence permits some stimulation and learning by imitation. The placement of a moderately retarded child with slightly younger children often serves as an excellent initial exposure to socialization.

A regular nursery school setting is an excellent beginning for moving the retarded child out of the sometimes overprotective atmosphere of the family. It presents the opportunity for interaction with peers under the supervision of trained and motivated adults. The more severely handicapped young children may have to be grouped together for this early socialization effort, but such groupings can be organized in most urban settings. Indeed, many are already in existence through the efforts of parent organizations of retarded children, as well as other professionally based programs.

Since many young retarded children have noticeable disturbances of their coordination and movement, special attention needs to be directed to how early motor activities may inhibit first efforts at socialization. Spontaneous play and interaction should be encouraged. Emphasis should be placed on being and doing what comes naturally. This stimulates relatedness rather than success at doing. Once this interaction becomes well established and pleasant, experimentation with doing springs naturally from the comfort of the accepted relationships with peers and supervising adults. The activities flowing from this progression need to be closely observed and failures minimized by well-timed interruptions. Shorter intervals of involvement are needed by the retarded. Their brief attention span, distractibility, and easy frustration require more frequent pauses in their involvements with group activities. Appropriate interruptions serve to protect them from the consequences of their disabilities and permit them to return at another moment in their pursuit of involvement. This kind of planning of socialization efforts becomes more difficult as retarded children grow older. The discrepancies of their levels of performance become more evident, while competitiveness becomes more a part of the daily life of their peers. This begins to set them apart. Sometimes this separation is hastened by their placement in specialized programs. This segregation may be necessary to satisfy some of the particular needs of the retarded, as well as those of the community, but its too-early and almost universal application to children identified as retarded may rob many of them of much needed social experiences with peers. The academic goals of our educational system have mandated programs for the retarded not only in special classes but outside of the regular school plant. The results of this trend have been to increase the isolation already being experienced. Some of our retarded school-age children spend as much time being transported to and from specialized programs as they do within them. The consequence of this automotive isolation is to decrease general stimulation and socialization for the sake of particular needs.

It is very important to seek some kind of balance as attempts are made to structure the lives of the school-age retarded. Their special educational needs have to be responded to, while there are continuing efforts to sustain them within the milieu of their contemporaries. Educational goals have to be modified in recognition of their limitations. Above all, teaching and training techniques have to be altered to satisfy their requirements for relatedness and socialization.

Many retarded children find their limited resources consumed by the demands of the group experience. They may be excessively or inappropriately stimulated. Their rhythm of activity and rest may vary, one from the other and from day to day. Their attention span is changeable and often short. All of these factors require teaching programs that respect the need for variable involvement alternating with periods of disengagement. There must be a mixture of learning and teaching by saying, doing, and living with themselves, with their peers, and with their teachers. Periods of involvement should be short and clearly defined. Instruction should be concrete and well organized. No one activity should be permitted to dominate, while too many activities are to be avoided. No one relationship should be permitted to exclude the significance of others. The retarded need the protecting presence of each other, but they also require the stimulating presence of others. Too often their early grouping in special classes within regular school programs leads to a kind of internalized segregation, as the special schools for the retarded lead to their early isolation from the mainstream of their peers. Continuing efforts should be made toward their exposure to peers through planned and combined activities. Spectator roles can be as rewarding as participation in some instances, and the stimulation of peer identification in others.

It is during adolescence that the retarded reach a major crossroad of life. The more severely impaired become isolated by their defects. Many of them move into institutional settings for both protective and specialized care. The moderately retarded become overwhelmed by their inadequacies within the quickening tempo of a more competitive existence. Many require all kinds of specialized efforts to sustain them within the community with adequate opportunities for socialization. Family activities continue as a major source of social experiences. Regretfully, the fragmenting, changing nature of family life is making this less available. Where families are large and well established, grandparents and relatives should be recruited for as many different kinds of social experiences as possible. Family events, travel, visits, and work efforts should be used to provide the stimulation of different environments and people.

Supervised peer group activity becomes another important adjunct. Some retarded adolescents benefit from a peripheral existence within some of the organized group activities to be found in most communities. Such groups can be found within churches, community centers, and after-school programs. Common special interests may provide a vehicle for socialization experiences. Hobbies and other activity groups may provide a haven for a retarded adolescent. Camping experiences are usually well tolerated. The Boy Scout and Girl Scout movement and the 4-H clubs provide a philosophy and program capable of offering many sheltered experiences for the retarded. There is also a growing variety of special camps and supervised travel groups. Information concerning such programs can be obtained from the American Camping Association, the Association for the Help of Retarded Children, and local counseling services, travel agents, and directories. All such efforts are rewarding by their stimulating nature and the broadening of life-style.

Mildly retarded adolescents, plagued by their sense of inadequacy, often seek respite by unusual or intense identification within the grouping phenomena of this stage of life. They attempt to hide themselves within the current and fashionable group activities and interests. They are usually the avid followers of the styles and practices of the moment. This may take the form of attachment to modes of dress, behavior, or causes. However, their approaches to these are usually very concrete, so that their dress becomes overstyled, their activities exaggerated, and their interests seemingly unrelated to their resources. Their adaptive capacities make them peripheral members of the group, and sometimes they choose peripheral groups for their associations. They are then prey to the dangers of involvement in antisocial behavior of some of these peripheral groups. Adolescent gangs nearly always have some mildly retarded among their members and are unaware of their limited judgment. The nature of the gang activity may break down the poor controls of its retarded recruits and lead to some of the social disturbances that have been associated with the existence of such gangs.

Similarly, the adolescent pursuit of identity leads many of the mildly retarded into the exploration of activities they are ill equipped to handle. The adolescent stage is characterized by impulse giving way to action, and this takes place more readily within the safety of group-determined behavior. It thus becomes very important for the mildly retarded adolescent to be given the opportunity for constructive group experiences as early as possible in order to ensure appropriate attachments and identifications.

There are many examples of this going wrong in our contemporary society. The two prime instances can be seen within the movement toward acceptance of a drug culture and sexual freedom. Both have been adopted as causes of liberation by the young. Both have come to represent the arena for struggle for new values. Yet both are involved with impulsive behavior, the breakdown of impulse control, and the gratification of impulse through the concreteness of physical sensations. All of these represent serious problems for the young. It is no wonder that so many of our mildly retarded can be found preoccupied by these special interests of the times. They need to be helped to maintain reasonable boundaries and controls while they discover themselves and their innate resources for a constructive place within adult society.

This unusual overlay of their problems with those of the times places a distinct responsibility on the style-setters of the moment and those of us who are invested in helping the retarded to achieve their potential. The value of styles must be clearly weighed, along with their impact. The attraction of these styles to the young, as well as the retarded, should be bounded with limits so that experimentation is possible but not limitless.

The chronological movement into adulthood leaves many retarded stranded on the islands of their arrested development. The severely retarded with their multiple handicaps lack the resources for significant relatedness to others and must survive through the beneficence of those devoted to their care. The rewards of such investments of relationship with the severely handicapped can be seen in the maximum returns from minimum efforts. Sensitivity to their simplest needs results in the warmest of responses. The isolation of the severely retarded from the basic ingredients of socialization leads to their regression and the unleashing of the furies of raw impulse. Their separation from external stimulation causes them to be involved with self-stimulation, such as body-rocking, head-banging, masturbation, and self-mutilation. A minimum of effort directed at maintaining their contact with others reduces much of this self-destructive behavior.

Moderately retarded adults require support and direction, with efforts aimed at preserving their social ties within family and community. Their poor judgments and immaturity tend to disrupt relationships easily and they experience difficulties in creating new ones. Those requiring protective care within institutional settings need to have their opportunities for socialization both within the institution and the community. Their isolation within any particular setting is inhibiting as well as limiting. It narrows the horizons. It creates a quality of sameness that ultimately depresses and then regresses those exposed to this kind of life-style. It becomes far better to move the retarded back and forth from institution to community than to permit an unchanging existence in a single setting. Too frequently, visits with families are designed to take place within the setting for the retarded rather than the setting of the family, when the reverse would be much better. Such a reversal demands that we no longer place our institutions for the retarded out of community and out of reach of family, since both provide the essential ingredients for constructive socialization.

Mildly retarded adults need the supportive efforts of both family and community to be assured the opportunity of social interaction. They can usually make use of such opportunities within their own life-style and purpose. It is more our judgment of their efforts that exposes them to criticism, stimulates their anxiety, and causes them to withdraw from the nurturing process of their attempts to socialize. Their limited efforts must be respected and recognized for what they are. They must be encouraged by a tolerance of their slowness and by their incorporation within the variations of our social existence with each other. This requires an acceptance of the retarded as a variation of "normal." It implies our willingness to have them join our congregations, clubs, social activities, and work efforts. It means that we must struggle with ourselves to include rather than exclude the retarded from our midst.

PLAY

Play is a universal form of expressive behavior. It is an action or exercise by way of amusement or recreation. It represents movement within specified dimensions. It recruits motion. It stimulates perception. It brings relatedness into being in a pleasurable manner. It simulates all life experiences without making demands. It recruits fantasy in behalf of reality. It provides the opportunity for repetition, control, competition, and achievement. It permits identification with many different activities and successes within their pursuit. Play serves to divert, perform, define, emphasize, maneuver, and provoke. It stands as a human effort capable of bringing all aspects of living to every stage of life. The child can play at being a grownup. The adult can retrieve the essence of childhood through play.

For the retarded, play becomes a window on the world that must be pursued and that sometimes pursues. It provides access to experiences that ordinarily might not be available within the more limited resources of defect and disturbance. It is capable of making pleasurable events of challenging situations that may not be pleasurable by their nature. It supplies opportunities for developing and exercising many needed skills. Space and time can be reduced to units that can be mastered. Circumstances can be reproduced within acceptable dimensions. They can be ordered and structured. They can be controlled so that successes replace failures. They can be selected to coincide with the levels of individual achievement and be recruited for new experiences.

The infant's acceptance of play is established by its need for physical and emotional stimulation. This stimulation activates the transition of reflex to reactive responses. The sense of relatedness to self and others is helped into being. Impulse becomes channeled into purposeful activity, and the resulting movement opens the door to an expanding life. The retarded infant requires more of this kind of stimulation than do others, and play between adult and infant becomes an important vehicle for its achievement. Many retarded infants tend to be listless or inert, as do their older counterparts. Physical play with them offers the much needed movement they may be unable to initiate. Too often, their inertia is interpreted as unwillingness or lack of interest and they are left to their own devices. Sometimes their weak or poor responses serve to discourage the repeated efforts needed before appropriate reactions can be evoked. These infantile requirements for stimulation through pursuit, movement, contact, and interaction remain the cornerstone of all play activities throughout the life of the retarded.

The earliest play activities for retarded infants must reflect their need for physical stimulation. They should be picked up and held whenever practical. Their passivity should be transposed to active participation by repeated efforts. The simplest body movements involving flexion and extension of their extremities bring them to an awareness of these parts and their relation to each other. The retarded infant with a considerable lag in assuming the upright position needs to be helped to its achievement by appropriate moments of planned activity while being supported upright. The near receptors involved with movement, touching, tasting, and smelling have to be stimulated and synchronized before the far receptors of hearing and seeing lend themselves to developmental integration. This places a priority on intimate contact during all first play efforts. Early rostral dominance requires special attention to face-to-face contact between infant and adult. It is always best to have the retarded infant or child facing the adult during play activities. These early attempts at recruiting play as an intervention in behalf of the retarded must be directed at the synthesis of a self. For once they are helped to experience themselves, other kinds of experiences become more meaningful.

Movement, touching, hearing, and seeing become the basic ingredients of the play activities of young retarded children. Before they achieve their own mobility, toy mobiles should be placed in crib and playpen; cuddly dolls and stuffed animals offered as companions against loneliness; toy music boxes as well as music from radio and phonograph supplied as a rhythmical counterpart to their dysrhythm; and brightly colored objects and forms provided to introduce the dimensions of space to their limited perceptions. Once mobility is achieved by sitting, crawling, standing, and walking, toys that encourage this newly discovered mobility should be provided. Pull and push toys may serve to extend the meager horizon of limited perceptual abilities. Strollers and walkers that can be self-propelled may add new dimensions to movement. Simple toys with their own movement within their design may serve a similar purpose. The best of toys, however, are a poor substitute for the much needed continuing efforts to provide stimulation through human contact. Once the young retarded child achieves mobility, this mobility needs to be recruited for introducing the growing complexities of an enlarging world with the reassuring presence of a dependent relationship. Walking hand in hand should remain a principal play activity throughout the life of a retarded individual.

There are many toys and play equipment providing the basic and much needed perceptions of self and relationship to environment. The wagon, the wheelbarrow, and the tricycle offer opportunities to move and be moved. It should be remembered that most retarded children do not have well-organized spatial boundaries. Their movement will therefore tend to be faltering and sometimes disorganized. There will be a preference for staying close to the ground. They may bump into things. They may fall often. They may show an unaccountable hesitancy. They may prefer to experiment by pushing and pulling instead of riding. Their poor coordination makes all rapid movement a worthy achievement, pedaling a tricycle an outstanding accomplishment, and roller-skating a monumental success. Steps and jungle gym for climbing provide them with the opportunity to go up and down, as well as coordinating balance with movement of the upper and lower parts of the body. Slides offer additional sensations to the righting responses so necessary for maintaining the upright position. Swings provide the same kind of experiences but may evoke anxiety because of the changing direction of movement.

It should be noted that some retarded children enjoy moving through space with utter abandonment. This may be due to their total spatial disorganization. Such children must be supervised carefully during movement play, for they know no limits and may expose themselves to dangerous situations leading to injury. They may have to be given the opportunity for such activities within clearly defined boundaries of fenced-in playgrounds, backyards, or rooms. The sandbox and wading pool represent additional play equipment recruiting movement, coordination, and boundaries for activities devoted to experiencing the self in its many physical dimensions.

Toys that require coordination and manipulative skills should be introduced as early as possible, but with an awareness of the special limitations of each retarded child. Pounding sets can be offered early. They are attractive because they provide little room for error and, at their best, produce sounds through action. Nests of blocks, hollow blocks, crates, large cardboard cartons, and pots and pans are excellent introductions to the dimensions and ins and outs of space. As developing capabilities move the children toward more complex motor functions, small and large rubber balls can be rolled, pushed, thrown, and eventually caught. Balloons are attractive and easily managed. They can be used for teaching colors as a significant differentiation. Wooden trains, sturdy trucks, automobiles, and boat toys can bring the everyday world into the playroom of the child. With the appearance of further manipulative skills, large and preferably edible crayons, paints and easel, clay, scissors and paper, beads for stringing, wood, hammer, and nails, puzzles, and other readily available material can become instruments for stimulating function in relation to environment.

Now the functions of play need to be joined to relationship and behavior. Dolls, puppets, plastic figures of people and animals, and picture books can stimulate curiosity and the construction through play of the many situations of the life experience. They provide the opportunity for expression both by the child of his perceptions and confusions and by the adult playing with the child for directions and correction. This kind of play by the retarded child should be monitored by the supervising adult because it provides many opportunities for meaningful communication of ideas and attitudes. Too often the children are left completely to their own resources and their play becomes locked into their fantasies. The danger of unsupervised play for the retarded is its potential as a means of withdrawal from a painful reality. When this seems to be taking place, special efforts should be made to spend time with the child and other forms of activity interspersed with the play routine.

Television provides a visual, auditory, mechanical substitute for this kind of play. In many ways, this instrument has become a valuable adjunct for bringing both reality and fantasy into our homes and lives. Its widespread distribution has made it easily available, and in recent years it has variously entertained, educated, and trained our children. The scope of the television medium makes it an important new modality for stimulating our young into an awareness of their surrounding world. This value is even greater for the retarded, whose capacity to explore is limited by their disabilities. There is little question of its attractiveness to them.

It must nevertheless be recognized that watching television is a passive activity. It also offers a selective, flat, two-dimensional representation of experience. All of this places a limit on its value for helping retarded children develop. Since many retarded children suffer from impaired object-relatedness, heavy reliance on the electronic image robs the child of much needed human contact. The retarded need time and effort devoted to their development of human relationships. Television cannot be considered as a substitute for expressive play and its role in the life of our retarded young should be limited.

The extension of play from function and behavior into communication brings all objects within the realm of toys. Selective recruitment or substitution of simulated equipment makes play a learning and teaching experience. Percussion instruments lend themselves well to rhythmical expressions. Phonograph and records involve the retarded child in selection, preference, and a sense of participation with what is being presented. A variety of books offers similar opportunities, as well as a sharing of the effort to recognize images, whether they be pictures or words. Dolls, carriages, household equipment, garden tools, store equipment, and clothes all become agents of play, making reality acceptable and meaningful. Its meaning can be extended by well-timed supervision and recruited for day-by-day living with self and others.

Competition enters the life-style of the retarded with the passage of years and entry into peer grouping. Competitive play becomes a natural outgrowth of this new engagement. There is no way to avoid it, nor should it be avoided. Early play begins as a solitary activity tolerating the shadowy presence of the caring adult. It is replaced by parallel play as relatedness becomes better established. The awareness of self and others brings into existence cooperative play. The awakening to the differences amongst us stimulates selectivity and competition. All children must be exposed to this sequence if developmental progression is to be achieved. The retarded must be exposed gradually and in a manner designed to protect them from unfair demands on their limited capacities or repeated failures. Their first needs are in their competition with themselves and then with others. Manipulative toys and puzzles geared to their developmental skills can serve as an introduction. The varieties of available ball games provide simultaneous opportunities for solitary, parallel, cooperative, and competitive play. They lend themselves to continued involvement into adult life through spectator participation. They can become and remain meaningful vehicles for relatedness throughout the life of the retarded. There are many other games and sports serving similar goals. Ring tossing can lead to horseshoe pitching. The tricycle can lead to the bicycle, the scooter, and the sled. The punching bag can introduce boxing and wrestling, just as the wading pool can introduce swimming and boating. There are few reasons for excluding the retarded from any play or sport activity as long as their participation is based on their ability. Such participation assures them the same right to relationship by way of amusement and recreation that we would have for ourselves.

SCHOOL

School is defined as "a place, institution, or building where instruction is given." Its ancient roots are to be found in the Greek word *scholē*, or Latin *schola*, meaning leisure employed in learning. No longer does the concept of school include leisure or the implication of learning by choice. It has evolved into a twentieth-century institution of compulsory education with a liturgy devoted to the pursuit of academic achievement. Reading, writing, and arithmetic have become its altar and all who come must be judged before it. Schools have moved steadily away from the efforts of learning to the practices of teaching. They have become a social institution of the present, expressing more the needs of society. This transition has been progressive over the past hundred years. In the mid-nineteenth century, Joseph White, fourth secretary of the Massachusetts Board of Education, stated as follows:

> The children of the rich and poor, of the honored and the unknown, meet together on common ground. Their pursuit, their aims and aspirations are one. No distinctions find place, but such as talent and industry and good conduct creates. In the competitions, the defeats, and the successes of the schoolroom, they meet each other as they are to meet in the broader fields of life before them; they are taught to distinguish between the essential and true, and the fractious and false, in character and condition. . . . Thus, a vast and mutual benefit is the result. Thus, and only thus, can the rising generation be best prepared for the duties and responsibilities of citizenship in a free commonwealth. No foundation will be laid in

> our social life for the brazen walls of caste; and our political life, which is but the outgrowth of the social, will pulsate in harmony with it, and so be kept true to the grand ideals of the fathers and founders of the republic.

This aspiration of the past has become the reality of our present. The beginning of space exploration in the 1950s launched a demand for curriculum changes, with emphasis on more rigorous mathematics and science courses. The 1960s saw a shift to the "disadvantaged" student. No major school system is now without some special project for the disadvantaged. Educational innovation has become the byword of this movement. Much of our current attitude toward the present role of school is well stated within a report by the Committee for Economic Development:

> The well-being of individual citizens, the integrity of the nation's social institutions, the strength of the economy, and the long-term national security depend on the effectiveness of the schools. Unless schooling keeps pace with the large demands that will be made on it in the years ahead, the American people will not achieve their personal, community, and national goals. A free society must always depend on the capacity of its schools to provide the kind of education that produces rational, responsible, and effective citizens.

If these are the goals of our educational system, they have surely failed our retarded as well as other segments of the young. The search for teaching systems has consumed our slow learners and relegated children with defect or disturbance into specialized programs. Ability grouping has become a significant and almost universal educational technique. This quest for homogeneity within reasonable limits has led to an increasing incidence of educational failures and dropouts. It has moved some to suggest that ability grouping may represent selective deprivation. Many educational programs for the retarded reflect this quality of deprivation. They track the retarded from the moment of identification. Once so endowed, the retarded child can never lose this identity and must forever be so programmed within the school plant.

If there is any conflict produced by this identification, the resulting disturbance results in exclusion, institutionalization, or dropping out. Indeed, these are the fates of many children identified as retarded. Only the complacently retarded remain as suitable candidates for specialized school programs. And what becomes of these when the special programs come to their chronological end? Most school programs pursue the social and academic goals of the times. The very nature of the retarded defies both these goals. They are, by definition, poor candidates for the roles they are endowed with by the system as citizen supporters of the nation's social institutions and defenders of the economy and national security. It is no wonder that our school systems lose interest in the retarded as they become older. Their presence defies the social objectives of the schools and, in spite of their need for prolonged exposure to learning and teaching, the retarded are excluded by the paucity of programs for the adolescent and young adult.

Another significant deprivation and discrimination can be found within the concept of group teaching. The current practices of homogeneous grouping has evolved from the teaching of groups. This practice is predicated on the rationale of the social efficiency of the teacher and not the effectiveness of the teacher relative to learning by the student. The retarded, with their defects and disturbances affecting their learning ability, defy both the grouping and teaching practices of most of our current programs. And for good reason. Their readiness for formal teaching varies with the degree of their retardation. Their capacity for learning varies with the nature of their defect. Their success with the teaching varies with the extent of their relatedness to their teacher. Their comprehension of what is being taught varies with the concreteness of its presentation. All of these defy the accepted methodology of group instruction. The tasks of the most devoted and gifted teacher are made difficult and sometimes impossible to achieve under many of the present circumstances found within the special programs for the retarded.

The ability to learn should be viewed as a primary goal functioning from the very beginning of life. This capacity to function, combined with the experiences of living, leads to meaningful relatedness to objects and people. This combination results in the development of symbol and value systems permitting all forms of nonverbal and verbal communication to evolve. Appropriate identification of genetic equipment, degree of maturation, the realized capacity of function, and life history is vital to any definition of problems with learning. The levels of achievement become a reflection of these as well as of the teaching and social process.

There is a sequential appearance to disturbances of learning. Genetic and constitutional impairments may introduce disturbances of sensory-motor organization affecting the perceptual and cognitive processes so that there is an inability to function. There may also be disorders of the central nervous system, resulting in failures of integration of functions. This combination introduces defects of the basic equipment for learning. Appropriate object-relatedness fails to appear or is observably disturbed. Such afflicted children find it impossible to construct an integrated perception of themselves or their environment, nor can they respond adequately. They may fail to grasp the simplest fundamentals. They may not know which way is up or down. Laterality may never appear, robbing them of the ability to organize a horizontal. They may be unable to conceptualize the dimensions of space—height, width, length, mass, or volume. They may not be able to construct a whole from parts. Perceptions may be variable and confused.

The consequence of these disturbances to retarded children

is a pervasive anxiety over the lack of constancy to their existence. This inconstancy not only prevents learning from taking place but also interferes with their relationships with others —parents, siblings, peers, and teachers. Successful interventions are dependent on early and appropriate identification of the nature of these defects and the recruitment of compensatory mechanisms. This process must start as early as possible and makes child-rearing within the family the first and probably the most important "school" for the retarded.

Teacher training for this responsibility is found within one's own growth experiences, as is a sensitivity to the need of the retarded for meaningful relationship. All of us have mastered our developmental progression with varying degrees of success and have learned to live with the accompanying anxieties of the failures. This has bred within each of us a sensitivity to the nature of failure to function by our retarded offspring. Appropriate and compensatory responses by the caring adult can substitute success in place of failure, relatedness for non-relatedness, and relief for immobilizing anxiety. The certain, physical handling of the retarded child serves to introduce well-defined physical parameters to its existence. An awareness of the conditions that produce anxiety leads to their elimination by reordering the exposure and demand.

For example, permitting a longer developmental period of crawling may encourage better motor skills for the ultimate task of walking while relieving the accompanying anxieties of the upright position. This combination may stimulate a tendency for freer exploration later, with a richer object-relatedness. The placement of its chair within a room so that the young retarded child can follow visually the surrounding human activities is far more conducive to relatedness than periods of play with an elaborate array of dolls and toys. Or the correct placement of the same chair to eliminate the awareness of extraneous spaces and darkened corridors becomes another kind of compensatory judgment so necessary for relieving the anxieties of the young child's perceptual vagaries. This principle of selecting and focusing the perceptual exposure of the retarded child has many applications within all stages of training.

Readiness for learning is the cornerstone of all successful teaching. The correct assessment of this readiness makes the difference between success and failure with teaching efforts. Thus, knowing the child becomes a vital link to all educational procedures. Basic skills necessary for learning may be absent, defective, or disturbed. Nowhere better than within the intimacy of the family can these be known. Nowhere better can natural-skill teachers be found. The facade of cleanliness and dress is essential to acceptance by others. Such skills are produced by help with individual selection, repetition, imitation, and correction. These are most available within the intimacy of the family and home. The opposite takes place within the group. Grouping poses difficulties for selection. The value of repetition is diffused. There may be poor control over what is imitated and corrections may be variable and inconstant.

It should be recognized that an infinite variety of special-skill teachers is available within family and community, whereas a limited number of specialized teachers for the retarded are available within the programs for the retarded. Parental surrogates can be recruited for learning by experiences with feeding and self-care. Siblings, peers, or near peers can be used for the learning-teaching of movement, socialization, and play. A supervised teen-ager may be as effective as a sophisticated adult in communicating attitudes, values, and skills in these areas simply because of developmental proximity to the retarded or younger child.

The same may be true for transmitting some of the basic educational skills of writing, reading, and arithmetic. Our knowledge of the defects in these areas of learning suggests them to be multiply determined, with many different combinations of causality. Individualization of teaching efforts has become the principal instrumentation of all of our specialized programs for these disabilities. Here again, developmental proximity of the young to the retarded permits a natural sensitivity to some of their problems with learning. A nonretarded older sibling can become an effective teacher of basic educational skills within a proper family climate of mutual assistance. Similarly, a successful student can be recruited as a neophyte teacher.

This principle of mutual assistance through skill teaching can be extended within family and community even to our special programs for the retarded. Too infrequently are the skilled retarded used as teachers of the less skilled. Such matching of the partners within the learning-teaching system has been almost ignored as we have come to rely more and more on the specialized skill and training of the teachers of the retarded. This reliance has moved inexorably toward more complex and expensive procedures for identification without necessarily producing more effective means for intervention. It has led to the virtual abandonment of the apprenticeship system of training as an early-applied form of teaching. Yet the apprenticeship represents a valuable method of skill teaching, which can produce motivation for the acquisition of other learned abilities. It should be remembered that the service industries are the largest consumer of workers within our society and that the basic skills for work within these industries are acquired most readily within the home and by use of skill teaching and matched partners.

All these learning-teaching systems need to be utilized for the retarded and are as available to the family as they are to the professional and the specialized programs for the retarded. These make the schools-of-the-family important to every stage of development and provide teaching interventions that may be recruited more productively and economically outside specialized programs. Their recognition, as well as the needs of the retarded, places a limit on the delegation of the responsibilities for teaching and training to the professional. It creates a demand within the family for continued imagination and creativity. It represents a contribution of the retarded to their family through need.

Regular schooling has much to offer the retarded. Their readiness for this exposure is variable and related to their physical, intellectual, emotional, and social growth. The decision for their involvement with school rests with a careful assessment of needs related to growth. Not all the retarded should be moved into early schooling outside the family in order to compensate for their handicaps. Some need a longer period of intimate nurturing before they are able to benefit from the socialization and instruction of a school setting. The too-early movement into peer interaction and competition, along with separation from the familiar, may stimulate excessive anxiety, inhibiting learning ability. Appropriate decision-making may require consultation with others, trial and error of temporary placements, and a sensitivity to the general equilibrium of the child. The objectives of initial school placement may vary with specific needs. Particular defects such as blindness or deafness may mandate early involvement with specialized efforts directed at compensating for the pervasive impact of the defects. Disturbed interactions may mandate early interventions with corrective socialization attempts. Family decompensation in face of some of the stresses of caring for the severely disabled child may require early movement of the child into a nursery setting in order to obtain relief and to reestablish an appropriate climate for child-rearing. These and other reasons have led to the widespread use of nursery school experiences for helping the retarded.

These nursery schools are valuable, early extensions of the

home and family capable of providing many additional kinds of learning to the young. Fortunately, these schools have not succumbed too much to ability grouping and homogeneity within limits. This makes many of them available for the young retarded child who can be identified as in need of help with socialization for excessive dependency. Placement can be requested and achieved more readily by identifying the retardation as a form of immaturity. Differences of ability can be equated by departure from chronological placement procedures. The four-year-old retarded child with a 25 percent loss of functional ability can exist comfortably among average three-year-old children. The more physically deviant child is less likely to be acceptable to the regular nursery setting and may have to be placed immediately into specialized settings where available. This should be avoided as long as possible, providing the retarded child instead with a normalizing experience similar to the efforts within the family. This is not to suggest that the specialized nursery programs are without merit. But such early placement within them regretfully serves to identify and track the retarded child very early in life, and it is becoming increasingly difficult to move these children out of such tracking with our steady movement toward specialization. It is often better to delay the use of special placement in order to make the most of early normalizing experiences.

The specialized nursery programs have many advantages but are not without disadvantages. They do represent designs responding to needs, but they tend to group by selection and achieve segregation as much as the programs that group by exclusion. They tend to relieve the many of the responsibility of the few. As such, they participate in the drift toward conformity among the very young. They provide a single model of behavior when the young and the retarded need a less differentiated and more general model. They encourage imitation and accentuate defect as their point of reference. They motivate investment in the special when the retarded have already achieved it. These are some of the dangers of the specialized nursery programs. An awareness of these dangers permits a more judicious application of their particular benefits. Certainly some of the retarded with particular handicaps—such as some of the more severe physical disabilities—have a need for very special programs. Perhaps even these should coexist with other nursery programs in order to breach their isolating tendencies. However, their existence should be sought and known as a valuable resource for care of the young retarded child. Many of them provide essential supportive services to the families of the retarded, making the task of early child-rearing more acceptable and successful. The existence of such specialized programs within the community can be located through health and welfare agencies, counseling services, parent organizations, and professionals. Their help should be sought early because the seeking serves to define the needs, and with this definition come more appropriate interventions.

Regular school programs for the retarded have become very much part of every school system and vary with the local conditions, changing attitudes, and differing resources. It is beyond the scope of this kind of presentation of available interventions to deal with anything but some of the general problems of schooling for the retarded. Most of the existing programs have their roots within the trend toward special education that started in the latter part of the nineteenth century. These reflect the identification of the differences of children by intelligence tests and the related practices of teaching by ability-grouping and homogeneity within reasonable limits. The resolution of the educational needs of the retarded child is dependent on the nature of the specific defects and the quality of the learning disturbances. These can be and are quite varied, making identification procedures critical to the effectiveness of teaching.

The complexities of inability to function are compounded by fear of function. This may manifest itself very early through difficulties in starting school. Such children usually demonstrate an acute or chronic separation anxiety. They are unable to separate from the family and make a normal adjustment to the peer group. Many of these children adapt poorly to the group learning-teaching system and go on to demonstrate learning disabilities at all subsequent stages. Frequently they raise the question whether their learning disabilities are secondary to the separation anxiety or whether they are a basic inadequacy in the capacity to learn. However, the presence of this anxiety becomes a matter of concern within the teaching process and needs to be resolved. Teaching skills are made less important by the presence of this anxiety, which necessitates combined efforts of school and home in relieving the accompanying disturbances of learning. In recent years, a number of psychopharmacological agents have been demonstrated as effective aids for this kind of anxiety, and their use should be considered. Professional consultation must be sought when this problem has been identified.

Another type of malfunction is the inhibition of learning. This inhibition is related to the child's emotional development and may represent the repression of learning ability, accompanied by an unwillingness to learn. The normal emotional development becomes arrested by defect and disturbance, and neurotic adaptations of repression and suppression interfere with the ability to learn. This inhibitory process can be quite damaging. The potential exists. It is recognized and attempts are made to recruit the resources of the potential. Failure of these attempts breeds frustration for both child and teacher and behavioral disturbances become manifest within the learning-teaching system. Such disturbance usually leads to exclusion by identification so that the disturbed retarded child becomes separated from the regular school setting and is relegated and segregated into even more specialized programs or institutions. This sequence has become all too common a pattern within our overtaxed school system, which remains tied to teaching practices geared to ability and homogeneous grouping. The consequence of this social arrest is increasing numbers of more specialized and expensive programs, when its possible resolution may be the recruitment of other learning-teaching systems. When this hiatus has been reached, it becomes the responsibility of the parent and those professionals invested in providing individual care to offer different modalities of teaching the retarded child.

The use of tutorial and remedial techniques demands some critical assessment of educational goals. Remediation implies correction of defect. Yet some of the defects of the retarded are dissociated from educational needs and are related more to their physiological and psychological organization. Only too often efforts continue to be made to improve limited reading and writing abilities rather than to accept some of the limitations and turn toward the introduction of other, more appropriate skills. The concrete-thought organization of most retarded individuals serves to limit and place a ceiling on their levels of reading, writing, and arithmetic skills. Once this ceiling is reached, the most heroic tutorial effort yields limited returns. Persistence serves only to increase frustration and the anxiety of failure. This often destroys motivation for other kinds of learning by teaching. The retarded need careful assessment and early redirection as part of all tutorial efforts. Critical evaluations may even lead to the abandonment of formal educational objectives and the pursuit of vocational goals much earlier. Current educational practices have led to the artificial subdivisions of the retarded into educable, trainable, and nontrainable. These categories meet the needs of the special education system more than they do those of the retarded. They serve to track the retarded into such subdivisions for long periods of their life and fix unrealistic goals for many of them. Many educable retarded might do far better with early-imposed, vocationally oriented training programs. Malfunction can give way to fear of function can give way to the inhibition of function can give way to the outright refusal to function.

Refusal to function occurs as the retarded child grows older and efforts at learning have been frustrated by failure or participation in a nonrewarding process. Some children begin to feign illness or find reasons not to go to school. Such behavior should be viewed as an indicator of a decreasing return from existing efforts at education and again used as a moment for reassessment of directions and goals. The timing of educational and training interventions are paramount to their success, as is their selection. With some retarded, the degree of their disability mandates a sheltered life situation within the community or away from the community in some kind of institutional setting. Most of the retarded need to be moved out of the realm of the school and through the portals of work experience by vocational training, apprenticeships, on-the-job training, and sheltered workshops where learning becomes joined with working and living.

WORK

Level of education is being singled out as one of the most important indices for success in our contemporary industrial society. This judgment stems from the correlations of position and economic achievements within industry to the number of successfully completed school years. Such criteria serve society and its institutions as much as or more than they do the individual. They reinforce the concept of school as an instrument of society fulfilling its broad objectives. They do not reflect the more basic needs of the majority of people for surviving and living. They represent even less the needs of the retarded for a means of physical and social existence. School programs will have limited value and make incomplete contributions to the retarded as long as such criteria remain the basis for judgment of success. This serves to introduce the subject of appropriate management of the retarded as requiring early attention and high priority to training for work. Just as the school-of-the-family represents a cornerstone for educating the retarded, work-within-the-family becomes the base for training the retarded for their assumption of work responsibilities.

The family and home contain all the essential ingredients of vocational training, apprenticeship, on-the-job training, and sheltered workshops. These ingredients need to be recruited early, in a repetitive manner, and for extended periods of time, to make more effective later experiences outside the family and home. Such efforts may be more significant to the retarded than is formal education. Our present priorities have developed school with its emphasis on reading and writing as the principal instrument of teaching. It may well be that work should be the first order of teaching and training for the retarded. Their problems with impulse control, self, relationships, emotions, and thought organization lend themselves better to resolution through the conditions of work than through formal schooling. This would suggest that concepts of work should be introduced before those of formal schooling and begun early in childhood. Having the young retarded child participate in tasks of caring for the home provides experiences and attitudes essential to all kinds of work—mending clothes, cleaning, preparation of food, scheduling, shopping, maintenance, storing, filing, and repairing. The value systems of such activities are communicated best within a one-to-one relationship, as is correction of performance. It must, however, be remembered that the emotional climate is an important facet of relatedness and learning, so that patience and tolerance within such training efforts are most important. The recruitment of others for this purpose should be utilized as much as possible. A houseworker or homemaker can become a significant teacher to the retarded. A handy man, a baby-sitter, or an older sibling may expand objective experiences in a meaningful way. These and others should be recruited for the task of exposing the young retarded child to the concepts of living and working within the family.

The same principles need to be extended outside the home to the surrounding community. Early exposure to how people function and the concrete representations of their activities can do much to reinforce the object-relatedness of the retarded. Watching the baker make a loaf of bread makes the package of bread more significant. A visit to the local garage and seeing the repair of an automobile connects human effort to an inanimate but moving object. A visit to a local airport helps associate the noisy flying thing in the sky to more readily understood events on the ground. Objects become the product of action and people, and a concrete representation of work. Modern civilization tends to rob the young retarded of many essential bridges for association of human productivity with the daily products of life. Milk becomes the end point of a wax container, just as bread is that of a brightly colored plastic wrapper, because there are few opportunities to connect sources with human action and productivity. Supplying some correct associations through direct experiences establishes the necessary correlates for identifying work with self and as an objective of action.

The early introduction to this sequence may stimulate stronger motivations for later efforts of learning in other kinds of teaching situations. Too often, we become immobilized by the slowness of the retarded and fail to expose them to the sequences of experiences they cannot achieve themselves because of their poor association capacities. Or we depend on toys, play, or stylized representations of teaching models while failing to recognize the children's limited capacities to make the necessary transitions of the content of such activities to themselves and the real objects in their environment. It is within this frame of reference that early exposure to work becomes vital to the future of the retarded.

Another important association is the work of the significant adults in the life of the young retarded. There is a limit to their ability to comprehend the absence of those on whom they are dependent. This makes explanations of Daddy's or Mommy's working vague and often meaningless. Sometimes it may attach the anxiety of separation to work and anxiety may become equated with work in a dissociated manner. This possibility makes it important to expose the retarded child to the work experience of the parent. It accounts for separation, activity, productivity, and going with doing. It connects the world outside the home with the people within the home. It provides a model of work that is understood and accepted more readily. A carefully planned visit to the office, store, or factory of the working parent does much to lend substance to the time and space events involved in parent-child relationship. It not only accounts for coming and going, but also helps develop a meaningful association with work through its identifications with parental activities.

These patterns of connecting impulse to experience, to doing, to working, to learning, become a vital sequence in the ultimate achievement of self-sufficiency of the retarded. It must be repeated in each phase of their being taught. Formal schooling procedures need to be reinforced by experiences within the home, just as much as these school procedures need to be structured to reflect living requirements. The fabric of vocational training should be part of the formal schooling of the retarded from its very inception. It is no longer appropriate to teach the retarded child recognition of the letter C with the word *cow* and a picture of a cow. It becomes more effective to link the word *car* and a picture of a car to the identification and recognition exercises, because contacts with cows are negligible experiences in our contemporary life. In a similar vein, the discarded automobile tire becomes a more meaningful playground addition than the picturesque wagon wheel, as an abandoned automobile becomes a more attractive object of teaching and learning manipulative skills.

The same principles can be incorporated into the development of the language skills of speech, letter and word recognition, reading, and writing. The familiar must take precedence over the unfamiliar, just as doing must take precedence over saying. Actions speak more loudly to the retarded. Much of early learning is by imitation. School can become the first site of on-the-job, apprenticeship vocational training through introduction to tasks and language skills having bearing on work. Association of word recognition with daily tasks sets the stage for the recruitment of language as one of the instruments of doing. Every usable object can have its name attached to it by sound and sight techniques. This practice can be extended to their use and then to routines producing new learning situations. What has been done can be described by word, rhyme, story, and writing. The products of such activities can be saved, stored, and organized in a retrievable manner. In this way, action becomes wedded to objects and skills, and expressive behavior to work.

The act of teaching is a working and learning experience within itself. Rarely are the retarded recruited for their ability to teach other retarded. And yet such utilization of their potential provides another device of making school an on-the-job, apprenticeship vocational training ground. The communication of one learned task to another, no matter how simple, reinforces the ability to learn and communicate. It also builds self-esteem and motivation for further learning. Very few teachers remain satisfied with just being the same. School provides an unusually fertile ground for exposing the retarded to the rewards of teaching. But the practices of the school must include the early recruitment of the retarded child. Many imaginative procedures can be developed that permit the more advanced to demonstrate and help the less advanced to similar levels of achievement. The fact that they are not so far apart from each other sometimes eases the communication of values essential to learning.

Too often the basic objectives of school for the retarded remain locked into the models of nontrainable, trainable, and educable. This division into worst, better, and best links progress to success with the formal educational achievements of reading, writing, and arithmetic. Such linkage may account for the judgment of ability to read and write as the critical index of progress, as well as for the priority given to such teaching efforts within programs for the retarded. It may also account for the protracted emphasis on teaching reading and writing skills long after such goals become meaningless and other objectives should be substituted. The majority of the retarded have concrete thinking as their principal system of thought organization. This lends itself poorly to the abstractions of the higher levels of reading and mathematics. Their problems with impulse control and fine motor coordination serve them badly in writing.

On the other hand, their concrete thinking and need to pattern impulse increase their availability to vocational training if instituted early enough, before repeated failures with formal scholastic efforts reduce their motivation for learning. This constellation serves to reinforce the idea of early incorporation of vocation into the objectives of school programs for the retarded. Besides this, it suggests that teaching of the essentials of reading, writing, and arithmetic should be limited to the basic skills necessary for survival in society and then related to vocational efforts. This kind of transition would reduce the abstractions being offered within the teaching-learning efforts, increase the degree of success, and improve motivation. It is estimated that reading on a third-grade level will permit an individual to recognize directional signs, simple operational instructions, and other basic communications for daily living. Similar achievements of third-grade arithmetic concepts will permit a numerical value system for the exchange of money and other related efforts. Utilizing a simple typewriter can overcome most of the impulse and coordination problems of writing if these basic levels of reading and arithmetic are reached. Applied learning has much more meaning beyond these levels and ties further progress into the motivations for doing. This applied learning can be consummated best within a shift to emphasis on vocational training.

The types of vocational training made available to the retarded are of great importance. They must include choices and methods equaling their capacities and patterns of function. Fortunately an expanding body of knowledge correlating aptitudes with vocations has developed in recent years. Nearly all our programs have been strengthened by the growing presence of trained vocational guidance specialists capable of evaluating the resources of individuals, counseling, and serving as advisors on techniques of training. Their presence has helped to stimulate changes in existing programs as well as to provide the impetus for many new programs devoted primarily to vocational rehabilitation. Such efforts have been reinforced by the support of the President's Committee on Employment of the Handicapped. The combination of these programs with the governors' committees in the fifty states, and with local community activities, has resulted in a greater variety of attempts to integrate the retarded into the work force of the nation. These attempts vary with the local circumstances and resources and must be searched out. A good deal of the present efforts are centered around programs for the handicapped. These represent a healthy movement toward recognizing the retarded as being handicapped rather than inadequate.

Much of the responsibility for helping the retarded find their vocational niche nevertheless remains with the family and the local community. They require the continuing support of those on whom they have become dependent during their training period. They do not take movement from place to place easily or well. Transitions are difficult for them. Problems with space and time disrupt their ability to transpose acquired skills from one setting to another. The retarded are better off with on-the-job training and supportive attitudes maintaining them within familiar surroundings. Their tenuous relatedness makes the people with whom they work an important parameter of the working conditions. Many can be and are absorbed into family business ventures. More should be. A helpful device for providing useful work for a retarded member of a family can be found in the creation of a satellite work program with tasks related to ability.

The same principle can be applied to the local community once recognition is given to the common human purpose of mutual assistance. There are many simple responsibilities within every local community that can be delegated to the handicapped. There need be only motivation, imagination, and an acceptance of their presence. The families of the retarded can do much toward this by their own acceptance of their retarded offspring and the pursuit of the resources of the community. This has taken place more and more through the valiant efforts of voluntary organizations, which include the

American Association on Mental Deficiency, the Council for Exceptional Children, the Epilepsy Foundation of America, the National Association for Retarded Children, and the United Cerebral Palsy Association, among many others. Their promotional campaigns extending to many direct service programs have done much to provide opportunities for the retarded within the community, while expounding their cause.

A recent addition to the work concept for the retarded is the sheltered workshop within the community. This has come from the recognition of the need to provide them special opportunities for work. Their protection from the stresses of competitive existence has helped many to achieve more satisfying lives. This sheltering provides the device by which many can be aided with their own attempts at productive existence within the community while living with their families. Such programs also serve as places where vocational and on-the-job training are combined with work, while blending the efforts of family, community, and industry. Regretfully, too few of these programs exist, while the numbers who might benefit from this kind of effort are increasing.

The weaving together of community resources by the design of sheltered work programs may represent one of the more economical social means of helping the retarded while providing them with the human dignity of their birthright. Several countries have extended this sheltering concept to working communities devoted to the handicapped. Here working and living are made possible by extra supportive services provided by the government. This kind of subsidization is, in reality, no different from our established patterns of subsidizing agriculture and industry. Both are prompted by the recognition of responsibility by government for the survival of its citizens and for stimulating them into a productive role for the common good. The rapid industrialization of society was made possible by outright allocation of funds, tax benefits, and preferential treatment to the coal, oil, steel, banking, transportation, and communication industries. Now a rapid transition to a socially responsible industrial society demands a similar allocation of funds, tax benefits, and preferential treatment to industries of the handicapped. The acceptance of this new priority will serve to relieve the ever-growing burden of caring for the handicapped, the retarded, the disadvantaged, or whatever name we wish to give to this increasing group within society.

CHAPTER X

Special Interventions

DIAGNOSTIC PROCEDURES

The range of special interventions for the retarded extends to the limits of human experience and imagination because potential defects are as infinite as the variations of development, giving each of us our individuality. These defects need to be identified early for assessment of their role of impairing function, disturbing behavior, and disordering communication. This early identification permits a timing and priority for meaningful interventions. Impairments of perception like blindness or deafness require early and prolonged interventions. Muscle imbalances may be helped better by corrective measures imposed later, when a child's cooperation can be recruited.

Early identification places a high priority on the availability of competent diagnostic resources for the infant and young child. Fortunately there has been considerable progress in this area through the creation and funding of many centers and programs devoted to this objective. The majority of these centers have been located within universities and medical schools, with others at principal hospitals. Yet the earliest identification of retardation remains vested in parents and family physician. This alliance provides the necessary coalition of concern and knowledge, encouraging the initial identification and assessment of suspected developmental deviations. Usually this diagnostic team is able to recognize the majority of disturbances leading to retardation. This ability of the parent-physician team to make an early identification fixes the site of the first and most meaningful interventions within the home. The infant and young child with physical defects leading to arrested or disturbed functions require immediate help with relatedness to impulses, objects, persons, and emotions. This can be provided best within the parent-child relationship, making the recommendations of the family physician or pediatrician vital to these first attempts to overcome deficits.

Early diagnosis provides an extra dimension for the "do's" and "don'ts" of child-rearing. It also begins the essential process of adapting the parent to the special needs of the child. This adaptive process is a complex one. It combines physical with emotional responses. It contains many of the subtleties of the parents' reactions to themselves and others, as well as to their offspring. The delaying of diagnosis and recommendations for interventions may ease the anxiety and initial reaction that come with the discovery of defect, but it introduces a time lag for interventions directed at the correction of relatedness and may produce distortions of expectations. There are some circumstances that may warrant postponement of early diagnostic procedures for accurate identification. However, all such decisions require critical clinical judgment, making the presence and role of the family physician most significant.

The involvement and attitudes of the family physician during the infancy of retarded children represent important links to all interventions. Recognition of this linkage has resulted in many diverse efforts within training programs to sensitize the general practitioner and pediatrician to the special problems of retardation. Currently this program of sensitization has been extended by the efforts of the United States Department of Health, Education and Welfare in coordination with other governmental and voluntary agencies. These efforts attempt to coordinate communication and utilization of resources, as well as mobilizing support for related activities. Now the individual practitioner has many diagnostic resources at his command. Nearly all of the mental retardation centers provide a full range of evaluative procedures. They extend from laboratories capable of the most complex biochemical and chromosomal studies to clinical assessment of all kinds. Equally important, this growing emphasis on early diagnosis has been accompanied by an increasing number of services devoted to minimizing the physical, emotional, social, and intellectual disabilities of retardation.

Most forms of retardation are accompanied by some physical defect. These need to be searched for and corrected when possible. Any organ system of the body may be involved. Regretfully, the highest incidence occurs within the central nervous system, where identification of specific defect may be difficult and correction limited by the nature of the anatomy and physiology of this system. Yet, within these limitations, many habilitative procedures are available.

VISION

The eye, as the organ of seeing, represents our window to the world around us. Parts of the eye are direct extensions of the brain and may mirror the defects of the nervous system. Some disorder of the visual apparatus can be anticipated in a majority of the brain-damaged retarded. Disturbances of vision occur with enough frequency to warrant early assessment of sight and may range from total blindness to subtle impairment of perceptual abilities. These may include the problems of eye imbalance of strabismus, eye movement of nystagmus, and eye shape of myopia (nearsightedness), as well as other developmental variations. An alertness to the probability of such defects among the retarded permits careful assessment of their nature and well-timed interventions directed at correction or compensation.

The totally blind require highly specialized efforts, and their early referral and involvement may help child and family adapt better to the accompanying problems. There are government-sponsored programs in most communities, with all kinds of special subsidies for the care of the blind. Patient search for these resources will reveal some of the needed combinations of services. There are, as well, a number of excellent nongovernmental organizations offering vital services in this area. The American Foundation for the Blind (15 West Sixteenth Street, New York, New York 10011) goes so far as to provide word and board games, along with other kinds of educational equipment. Some communities have nursery schools and nearly all have classes for the blind within their regular schools. It is interesting to note that the defect of blindness eradicates all stigmata of retardation. The blind retarded are treated as handicapped and rarely exposed to some of the segregation practices reserved for those identified solely as retarded.

Many of the less severe visual disturbances can be helped to a considerable degree by appropriate interventions. Competent diagnosis of the nature and extent of the underlying defects is essential, as is the timing of the prescribed corrections. Elimination of a strabismus may have to be undertaken early in order to prevent disordered perception. A severe myopia may alter learning capacities. A congenital cataract may change early object-relatedness. Besides this, so many of these visual defects affect the developmental acquisition of binocular vision, which is an important milestone of maturation of visual perception. Thus early ophthalmological interventions may facilitate a more adequate developmental progression.

Recently considerable attention has been given to optometrics as a system of correcting visual functional imbalances, which has been extended to a more generalized management of the brain-damaged and retarded. Some caution needs to be shown with this and other similar generalizations. Many of the visual disturbances of the brain-damaged retarded are but a single aspect of a more diffuse damage of the central nervous system. Corrective efforts directed at the specific may not affect the more diffuse defect. Overinvestment in such corrective efforts in the hope of altering the broader disturbance becomes an impossible demand similar to the tail being expected to wag the dog. The finite limitations of this as well as other procedures need to be recognized in the attempts to help the retarded achieve their optimum.

HEARING

Impairment of hearing is another common type of deficit found among the retarded. Profound deafness may occur in association with severe damage of the central nervous system. It is not the deafness that causes developmental retardation, but the damaged nervous system. The deafness, however, may accentuate perceptual disorders and, by so doing, increase the degree of retardation. Early detection of loss of hearing therefore becomes an important part of diagnosis and treatment of retardation. This need poses problems of accuracy of observations and tests for hearing disorders. The young child does not lend itself readily to the cooperation required for the usual examinations.

Fortunately recent developments with skin psychogalvanic testing and other electronic procedures permit early and accurate assessment of hearing loss, as well as of alterations of hearing range. This kind of identification has led to more appropriate interventions minimizing the possible disturbances of relatedness occurring among some children with impaired hearing. Much of the knowledge derived from this early detection has been applied to electronic instruments for the improvement of hearing. The use of these hearing devices early in the life of the partially deaf retarded child may make a substantial difference. By their nature, these diagnostic and treatment procedures need to be relegated to the specialist. A good audiological evaluation performed early with detection of hearing loss may result in meaningful alterations of interactions with the retarded child. Inattentiveness as well as other behavioral manifestations can be responded to differently. Communication techniques can be modified to compensate for the hearing loss and special systems recruited. Nonverbal communication can be extended by attitude and by special speaking techniques.

Additional help for the deaf can be obtained from local organizations for them and by writing to the National Association of the Deaf, 814 Thayer Avenue, Silver Spring, Maryland 20910.

BALANCE

Attention should be paid to disturbances of balance associated with the vestibulary apparatus of the ear. The organ of hearing is linked structurally to an organ devoted to maintaining general spatial orientation known as the vestibulary apparatus. The closeness of the two to each other makes them vulnerable to simultaneous damage. Any kind of defect of the vestibulary apparatus is manifested by difficulties in assuming and maintaining the upright position, crawling, walking, and running. It may affect postural attitudes and body positions. Many of the retarded show evidence of some disturbance of vestibulary function by slow progression of movement skills within their developmental sequences. Much of this disturbance is also linked to more diffuse damage to the central nervous system, making careful neurophysiological assessment a necessary part of the management of the retarded.

THE FACE, MOUTH, AND NOSE

Developmental variations of the face, mouth, and nose occur with enough frequency among the retarded to warrant special mention. This area of the body has a complex derivation, with physical and psychological significance. It is closely linked to the respiratory and digestive systems and represents one of the earliest points of relatedness to self and environment through the functions of breathing, eating, and communication. It is a highly visible area and attracts the concern of all of us. Many of the profoundly retarded demonstrate anatomical variations of the face and asymmetry of its formation. Not much can be done for the gross abnormalities, but there are some developmental disturbances warranting correction because of their effect on vital functions. Chief among these are cleft lips and palates, branchial cysts, and abnormalities of jaws and teeth. Many are correctable through plastic and oral surgery.

The timing and nature of the corrections are important because of the impact of such procedures on emerging functions of this area and on emotional development. Each child needs to be assessed individually in order to determine the necessary priorities. This assessment requires the blending of the skills of several professional disciplines and has resulted in the emergence of clinical teams at medical centers devoted to such reparative efforts. The highly specialized circumstances surrounding these corrective procedures warrant the consultation with these clinical teams when they are available.

The dental requirements of the retarded are numerous. The immaturities and developmental vulnerability of the retarded lead to a greater potential for all kinds of disturbances of their teeth and jaws. Interventions are difficult because of their lack of comprehension of dental procedures, as well as a higher level of anxiety and fear of any kind of oral assault. Some dentists and oral surgeons have developed specialized approaches to the problem. One of the common procedures for rehabilitative work in the mouth is the use of general anesthesia. This permits the most effective conditions for rapid completion of work while eliminating much of the awareness of the retarded of any associated physical and psychological discomforts. The use of general anesthesia is a safe and humane way to circumvent some of the difficulties of the complex and protracted orthodontic corrections.

In addition, the young retarded are excessively involved with the oral manipulations of finger-sucking, which leave their mark on jaw and teeth formations. This warrants careful evaluation of the need and timing for corrective interventions and the possibility of their delay instead of imposing a demand for cooperation that cannot be readily achieved.

THE NERVOUS SYSTEM

Minimal damage of the nervous system may have far-reaching consequences because of its primary functions as a message and control center. Its progression toward maturity is the slowest of all parts of the body and coincides with general physical maturity. This slow rate keeps the nervous system vulnerable to damage and the effects of this damage potentially diffusable within the progression of development. In order to limit or compensate for neurological damage, early and well-determined judgments of all perceptual and motor functions have to be made, rendering the special diagnostic and therapeutic skills of the neurologist and psychologist particularly important.

There are many neurological techniques available now. Progress in engineering and electronics has provided the electroencephalograph (EEG) for study of brain function. Focal damage can be identified with its use. There are also other complex diagnostic instruments and procedures available. This growing ability to identify the nature of nervous system damage has encouraged a number of special interventions. One of the outstanding contributions to the care of the retarded coming from the field of neurology has been the use of anticonvulsant medications. The concept of protecting and isolating the epileptic retarded within residential colonies disappeared with the introduction of these anticonvulsants. Equally important has been the extension of the successes with these drugs to behavioral modification. Today's use of anticonvulsants has been augmented by a full range of tranquilizers, stimulants, sedatives, and antidepressants. Their judicious application to the retarded has facilitated the control of disordered impulse, the relief of disorganizing anxiety, and the integration of functions into more meaningful and useful behavior.

THE NEUROMUSCULAR SYSTEM

The ability to move easily and well is an essential skill, and yet so many of the retarded are handicapped by their neuromuscular disturbances. The early disruption of the delicate balance between flexor and extensor muscles causes both mild and severe disabilities of the musculoskeletal system. Deformities may result from some of these imbalances, sometimes causing handicap. Fortunately an elaborate array of nonsurgical and surgical procedures is available, so that most of the progressive muscular disabilities can be attenuated and many of the deformities minimized. These procedures are highly specialized for the most part and require the particular skills of the orthopedist and rehabilitation expert. Their special interventions should be applied early where possible because of the importance of locomotion in stimulating contact and experiences with the surrounding world.

THE METABOLIC AND ENDOCRINE SYSTEMS

The discovery of the effects of vitamin deficiencies, enzymatic disorders, and hormonal imbalances during the early part of the twentieth century stimulated a new attitude as well as an optimism toward the treatment of retardation. Substitution and replacement therapies have been in vogue ever since the first chemical deficiencies were described. There is little question of the efficacy of these biochemical agents when specific disturbance has been demonstrated or is suspected. But there has been a tendency to endow these biochemical agents with magical and curative properties they do not possess. They can never stimulate developmental progression beyond the biological resources of the individual. Rarely can they compensate for the effects of biochemical deprivation at an earlier stage of development. They can only arrest further damage and permit the recruitment of existing physiological systems. The current vogue of massive saturation dosages of vitamins attempts to overcome the limits imposed by nature on all biological systems. These limits account for the unsatisfactory results and the many failures of the megavitamin therapies. They also explain past disenchantments with thyroid, pituitary, adrenal, and other hormonal replacement therapies. These limits do nevertheless define the requirements for early identification and appropriate timing of all interventions. They do reinforce the need for integrated treatments.

A special experience has emerged within the treatment of PKU. In this condition, by-products of the enzymatic disorder have been identified with the retardation so that special diets have been developed to minimize their production and effects. There have been some successes with this approach and current research is attempting to extend the concept of nutritional control to other metabolic disturbances accompanied by retardation.

THE CARDIOVASCULAR SYSTEM

Apart from the congenital defects that may be present with a higher incidence of occurrence among the retarded, the general equilibrium of their heart and blood vessel system may be less stabile. They may demonstrate greater or lesser tolerance of heat or cold. They may sweat more profusely or not at all. Their heart rate may vary under the same or different conditions. It is necessary to be aware of this potential lability so that appropriate adjustments in activities and schedules can be made and reactions to variable responses kept in their proper dimensions.

THE GASTROINTESTINAL SYSTEM

The same kind of variability is seen frequently in patterns of eating, digestion, and elimination. The early developmental histories of the retarded are replete with evidence of functional disturbances of the gastrointestinal tract. The retarded have a much higher incidence of infantile colic, malabsorption syndromes, constipation, soiling, and diarrhea. These malfunctions are not necessarily outright disturbances. More often they represent the difficulty of establishing balance and control over physiological functions. Their presence mandates extra attention and tolerance. Colic and indigestion may require careful feeding and the use of medication. Recurrent or chronic constipation may need the use of the lubricant type of laxatives. Diarrhea may require special diets. An alertness to the greater frequency of occurrence of these functional disturbances permits earlier and more appropriate interventions and better attitudes toward some of the resulting problems.

THE GENITOURINARY SYSTEM

Disturbances of bladder control may occur at every stage of life and for many different reasons. Causes must be defined as part of intervention. Congenital defects of the genitourinary system account for a large number of the instances of wetting, of incontinence, or enuresis. A common anatomical defect is spina bifida, which is a developmental abnormality of the end of the spine affecting the nerve supply to the bladder, and to the lower extremities in the more severe forms. This kind of congenital abnormality requires careful evaluation and many of the more severe forms may be corrected by appropriate surgical procedures.

The milder forms of congenital abnormalities, along with other neurological disturbances of sphincter function, may require special training before adequate control can be established. Treatment with drugs such as imipramide derivatives (Tofranil) have been successful with the enuretic, as has been the use of a conditioning apparatus known as the Enuretone. This device consists of a bed pad that closes an electric circuit when wet. The circuit turns on a light and rings a bell, waking the enuretic at the moment of wetting. The sequence of immediate arousal is designed to condition and reinforce appropriate response to bladder and sphincter sensations. This approach has been successful with many enuretics. However, the subtle interlocking of emotional factors with enuresis requires careful and sensitive application of this approach so that attempts at helping the emergence of control do not become displaced into a power struggle with the caring parent.

Another common problem of enuresis is its reappearance with emotional stress and associated tensions. The psychological aspects of genitourinary function makes the system vulnerable to physiological responses in the form of regressions to earlier stages of organization. The retarded demonstrate their persistent immaturity by the ease with which they regress to enuresis. Its reappearance should prompt an immediate assessment of the life circumstances in order to identify new stresses and resolve associated conflicts. Sometimes psychological help is required before the enuresis can be overcome.

SEX

The sexual problems of the retarded are as complex as our own. They contain all of the dimensions of the self, the relationship of the self to others, and the values of society as they apply to sexual behavior. The associated problems are merely heightened and made more visible within sexual functioning, attitudes, and judgments by the presence of retardation. They emerge as difficulties through our concern or lack of concern, our prejudices, and our distorted perceptions of sexual activities. Only too often we apply special standards to the retarded while excluding others from these standards. This dissociation becomes a destructive force to those identified as retarded. It increases their vulnerability to our prejudices. It places our personal and social needs over theirs. It permits us to project our sexual anxieties onto them so that our own weaknesses and preoccupations are not so apparent.

Fear of pregnancy for the young adult woman judged retarded is a common concern. Yet more than a quarter of a million out-of-wedlock children are born each year in the United States within our nonretarded population without any great hue and cry. This and other fears have resulted in the indiscriminate application of sterilization procedures to those identified as retarded while assuring all others the right of their own sexual behavior or indiscretions. More than twenty states within the United States still have sterilization laws applicable to the retarded alone. As recently as the 1950s, at least one state practiced compulsory castration of the retarded. These and other practices serve to highlight the need for thoughtful and sensitive responses to the sexual problems of all, as well as the retarded.

The earliest form of identifiable sexual behavior is the self-stimulation of masturbation. The immature nearly always use this kind of activity to obtain relief from their physical tensions. Those who remain immature or are deprived of relationships, for whatever reasons, continue the practice of masturbation. The retarded are plagued by their immaturity and isolation, making their masturbatory activity a common and sometimes very noticeable part of their daily behavior. In some instances their poorly patterned nerve impulses become channeled into the rhythmical activities associated with masturbation, and among the more severely regressed, compulsive masturbatory activity may emerge as a serious problem. These retarded may be helped considerably by the use of pharmacological agents. There are many different tranquilizers that serve to dampen the impulse, relieve the tensions, and calm the anxieties associated with this kind of compulsive activity. The amphetamines are helpful in augmenting the effectiveness of some of the tranquilizers.

However, it is necessary to recognize the need for prevention and relief of excessive physical and emotional tensions as a primary approach in helping the retarded with their problems of masturbation. Adequate physical activities programs will do much to help them release their motor impulses into these more socially acceptable behaviors while helping breach the sense of isolation that surrounds them. So many of such planned activities are rhythmical in nature that they serve to channel excessive impulses away from the more regressive behavior of masturbation, while helping to synchronize and integrate new patterns of motoric release. Almost any kind of isolation will stimulate regression and the appearance of more masturbatory activity. This mandates special attention for social activities of all kinds as another form of prevention. Yet, despite all such efforts, a greater amount of masturbatory activity can be anticipated because of the immaturity of retardation and allowances must be made for it.

Many sexual dysfunctions plague the retarded as they strive for their maturity. Often they remain arrested at earlier stages of psychosexual development so that the determination of sexual identity does not keep pace with their physical growth. Their needs remain those of the immature. They want to be comforted, held, touched, and soothed as much as or more than they seek gratification for physical, sexual drives. Many of their sexual needs remain undifferentiated. Some of their efforts to resolve the problems of their sexual identity are confused and lacking in discrimination. They may hold a hand or sit on someone's lap for the closeness that it represents without thought of the consequences. Even the selection of the hand and lap may show the same confusion and poor discrimination. Much of their behavior is imitative and repetitious. All of these characteristics must be understood within the attempts to help the retarded achieve their sexual maturity.

Family life represents the best milieu for the transmission of the essential values of psychosexual identity. All the ingredients of male, female, and relationship are present. They are readily visible and available to the young and immature. They can be communicated by being and doing. They can be reinforced by the normal repetition of daily family living. They should be recruited with purpose in the cause of helping retarded offspring achieve their own identity. The relationships within the family to which they are exposed will do much to help determine the pathways for their future. However, the immature may still come to adolescence and adulthood with lessons poorly learned and themselves poorly differentiated so that supervision and value judgment must be extended to them for longer periods of time. Supervised peer groups become important transitional activities that need to be sought out. Simple, direct representations of the facts of life must be offered as the occasions present themselves through events. And finally, some experimentation must be tolerated so that their progression toward maturity can take place.

The sexual dysfunctions of the retarded are the same as for all of us, but the incidence of their occurrence may be greater because of preserved immaturities. Poor psychosexual differentiation may result in an increase of homosexual experimentation during adolescence. Such experimentation does not mean an increased incidence of homosexuality among retarded adults. Appropriate personal guidance is necessary when such behavior comes to light. Immaturity breeds impotence and frigidity within adult sexual existence. Such problems are common among the retarded adults. They, too, require special evaluation and interventions. It is not accidental that the fertility rate among the retarded is lower than among the general population.

Special mention should be made of contraception, abortion, and sterilization. Recent years have witnessed tremendous progress in the field of contraception. Pregnancies need no longer be the end product of sexual activity, because of the availability of contraceptives. The presence of contraceptives has challenged many of the established attitudes of our society and resulted in changing values. However, the prevention of pregnancy among the retarded has long been an acceptable medical goal and the advances in contraceptive methods have lent themselves to this goal.

The two recent contributions of the greatest importance have been the use of hormones (the Pill) and intrauterine devices (IUD). Both have proven to be highly effective and easy to apply. Neither are permanent procedures, as is sterilization. By far the most applicable to the needs of the retarded is the IUD. Its insertion into the opening of the uterus is a simple medical procedure and its effectiveness is assured without subsequent efforts by the wearer. Its continued use may be subject to modification with appropriate consultation and judgment of all concerned. The Pill has proven to be equally useful, but its effectiveness is subject to the vagaries of breaks in the routine of administration. It requires constant supervision, which may pose other problems of communication and relationship with the retarded. In some instances, this interaction may be desirable, making the Pill the contraceptive of choice. Consideration should be given to the special circumstances and needs of each individual situation.

The growing trend of legalizing abortions has added yet another dimension to the care of the retarded. Its acceptance as a method for interrupting undesirable pregnancies provides the opportunity for careful assessment of the merits and disadvantages of each pregnancy. Both the rights of the retarded and the social values of society can be considered within the decision-making process. The newer techniques of therapeutic abortions have made them relatively safe procedures, so that judgments of their value are more closely related to need. This medical progress has created a demand for clarification and agreement of our indications for these procedures for all, but especially for the retarded.

Medical progress with contraception and abortion challenges the persistence of the generalized application of sterilization procedures to the retarded. Such procedures do have meaning in particular situations. There are special medical indications for their use. These indications exist unrelated to the issue of retardation. They are based on physical and emotional needs that are the same for all of us. These include the health and well-being of the individual, the danger and probability of damage during conception, and predictable defect. The concept of protection by sterilization is destructive. It destroys both the sterilized and the sterilizer. It robs each of his rights to relatedness and his responsibilities to the other for meaning and fulfillment. Compulsory sterilization laws have not altered the incidence of retardation nor have they eased the task of caring for the retarded. They have contributed to the depersonalization and institutionalization of so many of our attitudes and procedures.

Sterilization, when indicated for medical reasons, can be a relatively simple surgical procedure. The principle is the same in both male and female. The availability of the sperm or ovum to the process of fertilization is interrupted. In the male, the tube (the vas deferens) conveying the sperm from the testicle to the outside is interrupted by being cut or tied. In the female, the tube (the Fallopian tube) conveying the egg (ovum) from the ovary to the uterus is interrupted by being cut or tied. The ease with which these procedures can be performed may partially account for their ready recruitment for the complex sexual problems of the retarded. Sterilization can also be accomplished by removing the testicles in the male or the ovaries and/or uterus in the female. These procedures have been used but are rarely justifiable except in very special situations.

There has been a growing interest in sex education as a

means of helping our young and immature achieve their sexual maturity. These attempts are necessary and often useful, but some of their limitations with the retarded have to be recognized. The life values contained within their sexual existence have to be experienced and learned and can be taught to them only with difficulty. Their acquisition of a physical and emotional self-image is very much slowed, so that they demonstrate many problems in applying what is taught to them by educational techniques. They also do much better with concrete representations of subject matter, while most of our sex education programs are presented by means of generalizations and abstractions. Despite these handicaps, more educational efforts of this kind need to be woven into the fabric of training of the retarded.

PHARMACOTHERAPY

The last two decades have seen the widespread utilization of all kinds of drugs for the management and treatment of the retarded. Some of these have been most helpful and others less than good. Aiding a child to tolerate frustration and the anxiety of failure by prescribing an appropriate tranquilizer represents sound treatment, just as does the use of stimulants for increasing attention span and ability to concentrate. Many retarded suffer from the inhibitory process accompanying depressions, and relief from this inhibition by use of antidepressant medication will improve their general state of well-being as well as their capacity to function. Yet others are plagued by disturbances of their basic biological rhythms of eating, elimination, movement, and resting, and improvement of these rhythms by the appropriate prescription of drugs is very much indicated. But these chemical agents cannot alter the defects; they can only compensate for them. They cannot provide missing functions; they can only facilitate existing ones. They cannot alter behavior; they can only modify established patterns. They cannot substitute for appropriate communication nor the fulfillment of significant relationships.

BEHAVIOR-MODIFICATION THERAPY

This form of therapy has attracted many adherents in recent years. Behavior modification assumes that behavior is modifiable to some degree even among the more severely retarded. It emphasizes that significant variables controlling behavior can be found within the environment and that these variables can be altered to facilitate change of responses. It offers that procedures may be found for the development of desired behavior that is absent, for strengthening desired behavior that is weakly present, and for eliminating or reducing the strength of undesired behavior. Its techniques are based on concepts from a variety of learning theories and on behavior principles and experiments concerning stimulus-response relationships. The models of operant conditioning, classical conditioning, and social learning (imitation) are fundamental parts of all procedures. They rely heavily on the relationships between changes in the environment and changes in responses. The environment is manipulated by the therapist to provide meaningful and differential responses to given stimuli. Most behavior is assumed to be learned and emerges as adequate or inadequate, appropriate or inappropriate, and adaptive or maladaptive. The focus of the behavior modification efforts is directed at the overt behavior that is causing difficulty or concern. The major strategy becomes one of teaching alternative ways of behaving. No attempt is made to alter all disturbing behavior. Attention is given only to those types of behavior that functionally interfere with the attainment of educational and vocational goals deemed feasible and desirable.

This approach incorporates the attitude that lesser undesirable behaviors frequently lose their visibility or negative social value as other behavior patterns emerge that make the retarded more generally acceptable in a variety of settings. Problem behavior is considered not to be symptomatic of internal events such as dysfunctions of the nervous system, conflicts, poor self-concepts, or learning disabilities, nor is it viewed as the product of low intelligence. Present behavior is considered the end result of thousands of previous experiences and controlled by present stimulus conditions. It is learned and not symptomatic.

The behavioral therapist engages in a behavioral analysis with the objective of reaching a set of speculations concerning the conditions under which certain behavior results. Treatment strategy is based on a specification of problem behavior representing behavioral deficits or excesses within given environmental situations. Information is gathered only in relation to those behaviors judged to be relevant to treatment goals. This information serves the formulation of specific program goals relative to those behaviors that require developing, strengthening, elimination, or alteration and the definition of specific treatment strategies. The treatment techniques seek to modify the relationship between behavior and the stimulus events that control the behavior; the discriminative stimuli that determine the time or place in which the behavior will result in suitable reinforcement; or the reinforcing events that maintain or otherwise control the rate of occurrence of the behavior. Reinforcement may be positive or negative. The strength of behavior is measured in terms of the rate or frequency of occurrence within a specified set of conditions and time. Other components are the magnitude and promptness of responses and the occasion for their occurrence.

The attractiveness of this therapeutic approach stems as much from its concise theoretical formulation as our concern for the high incidence of occurrence of behavioral aberrations among the retarded. In actual practice, there is little question that results have been obtained representing positive behavioral modification. The question that remains unanswered is whether any similar investment of human resources, relatedness, and attention might not achieve the same, different, or better results. For it is impossible to provide an adequate behavioral modification program without a considerable body of personnel willing to devote their energies to nurturing care, demands of relationships, and devotion to helping the retarded achieve new and better levels of functioning. Within this context, behavioral modification has the same limitations as all other therapeutic efforts. As it is related to other useful procedures in behalf of the retarded, its theoretical formulation tends to deny the multidetermined nature of human behavior and should be applied with recognition given to its limitations so that other meaningful efforts are not excluded.

MUSIC AND DANCE THERAPIES

Music and dance are a universal presence. Both have emerged as types of expressive behavior that are immediately recognizable by all without regard to nature, form, content, or style. They have existed throughout human history. They evoke responses in young and old. They have become a significant part of the ceremony of living, and part of the expected stimuli of life. Not to have them available represents a deprivation of an essential component of existence. This universality raises the question of whether music and dance should be considered as forms of therapy or as therapeutic, as is nurturing care and meaningful relatedness.

The nature of music and dance contains some of the possible explanations for their significance. Both represent the recruitment and organization of impulse. Both represent stimuli and responses intertwined and inseparable. Both express the rhythm and juxtaposition of variations of time and space. These are the fundamental ingredients of life and make up some of the essence of existence, maturation, and growth. They help us confirm our existence by becoming expressions of our being. They provide substance and dimensions to our life. Thus both music and dance have some of the essential components of organized human functions leading to meaningful behavior and communication. This parallel makes each a useful instrument for helping us achieve our own organization.

The rhythms of the sounds of music and the movements of dance evoke responses from the earliest stages of life. They appear to be acceptable stimuli with little or no conditioning necessary and quickly emerge as a form of desired stimulation. The young and the immature demonstrate an overinvolvement with these rhythms, as if they are coming to some kind of organization of their own impulses by way of the rhythms of the music and dance. This makes both useful intermediaries for stimulating the retarded to an awareness and organization of their own impulses, while encouraging them to an awareness of things around them. The therapeutic benefits of this blending of the external and internal environments are obvious.

The planned recruitment of music and dance for the specific objectives of facilitating awareness, responsiveness, relatedness, and organized behavior has emerged from this as a form of therapy and they have become meaningful adjuncts to programs for the retarded. Regretfully, they are not utilized as widely as they might be. Too often they are used intermittently as entertainment rather than being a part of the therapeutic programming. In this electronic age, where all kinds of music can be reproduced at will, rarely is it used as a form of stimulation to breach the isolation of the profoundly retarded in our institutions. We pipe in music to our homes and places of work, while the silence of our residences for the retarded remains deafening. We watch our children learn their word symbols through the musical jingles of radio and television advertising but rarely use the combination of music and rhythm to purposefully help our handicapped learn. There are many constructive applications of music possible within the living and the teaching programs for the retarded.

Dance therapy offers additional dimensions because it recruits movement in a purposeful and organizing manner. Not only does it stimulate awareness and response, but it helps bring partial awareness closer to complete awareness of self and others. It has emerged as a very useful means of stimulating body image, expressive behavior, and communication. It lends itself well to the coordination of basic motor rhythms involved with the flexor and extensor muscle balance, so that it can be used in rehabilitation efforts for the neurologically handicapped. The hearing, seeing, and doing of the dance has many applications within our efforts to help the retarded.

LANGUAGE AND SPEECH

Intelligence has been defined as the capacity for understanding and for other forms of adaptive behavior. In turn, retardation has come to be identified with the impairment of intelligence. Much of what has already been described has dealt extensively with the developmental circumstances altering this capacity to understand and adapt while leading to disturbed communication. Efforts directed at minimizing such disorders represent important special interventions in behalf of the retarded.

Arrests and deviations of language and speech are common within all human development. The retarded have a higher incidence of these variations, and particular attention needs to be paid to their appearance and possible remediation. The language of most retarded individuals preserves the dominant characteristics of early thought organization. The word symbols are sparse and tend to represent objects that have been perceived directly. The use of these word symbols is concrete and there are few abstractions. There is considerable experimentation with sounds and imitations. Selections and presentations are egocentric in that they express personal need above all else. They tend to be undifferentiated. They are colored with the magical creations of the inner perceptions of fantasy by the special uses of language. They are constricted by a limited awareness of the surrounding realities, are victimized by disordered impulses, and are bound by response to what is. To the retarded, a rose is their rose, is all roses, is many different roses, is a rose is a rose, is a rose.

The language needs of the retarded are determined by their nature. They must be exposed to their world in a manner designed to help them become part of it. If we fail to help them acquire the necessary experiences of living among us, they become locked into their egocentricity, their infantile omnipotence, and magical thinking. They tend to remain immature and become sacrificed to dreams. Their perceptions of reality get to be limited, imitative, and repetitious. They become creatures of impulse doomed to respond concretely to the more limited stimuli coming from within themselves rather than the exciting variety from the world around them. Our retarded need to be approached in response to where they are rather than where we are or where we think they should be. Their egocentricity recruits what we offer them in an undifferentiated manner. Everything blends with their fantasy, limiting and altering content. They must be exposed to their world simply and concretely. Otherwise they reduce our symbols and abstractions to absurdities that plague them and us. They cannot be stimulated beyond the point of their own tolerance because then they become victimized by their disordered impulses. They must be helped to achieve a maturity of thinking by an exposure to all dimensions of human experience so that the world becomes their rose, their flower, their oyster, and not just a rose.

Speech can be viewed as the expressive behavior that communicates the thoughts, symbols, and feelings of language. This makes speech a motoric activity that can and does recruit movement of all kinds for expression. Evolution has determined the movements of respiration to be the principal system of speech (verbal), but not to the exclusion of other kinds of movement. The most effective form of speech can be found within the expression of emotions (nonverbal) by way of general body and facial movements. This affective behavior is one of the most important determinants of the meaning within attempts to communicate. The more immature, including the retarded, remain more dependent on these nonverbal forms of communication during much of their lives. What is done becomes far more important than what is said, making the doing significant for the saying. The most important part of all speech help for the retarded is invested in their relatedness combined with their doing.

The first gasping breath and cry of the newborn infant locks respiration to relatedness and motoric expression, and makes the sounds of respiration the significant sounds of human language. The *a*nxieties, *e*motions, *i*mpulses, *o*rder, and *u*niversal qualities of life are projected forever through the modulations of respiration, making vowel sounds—*a, e, i, o, u*—common to all language and speech patterns. Difficulties with these vowel sounds portend serious problems within the basic neurological organization. The infant who cries poorly at birth may express itself poorly in later life. Severely brain-damaged infants have weak or disorganized cries. This manifest weakness and disorganization may persist within the subsequent speech patterns in the form of irregularities of rhythm, repetitions, and variations in starting and stopping. Such problems require careful total assessment of neurological organization so that multiple approaches can be developed for their remediation. Many of the basic approaches to the development of speech combine object-relatedness and expressive motor behavior. This ties together the rhythm of body and breathing movements, sound imitations, and the use of speech with all human experiences.

An ancient Egyptian king ordered a group of Hebrew infants born into slavery to be reared in absolute silence in order to demonstrate the deification of the Egyptian language and tongue. He predicted that these infants would speak the Egyptian language as they developed their ability to communicate. Unfortunately the experiment proved to be a disaster. All the infants died without developing speech, proving only that an essential nurturing ingredient for life exists within the stimulation of communication.

The retarded prove this human truism many times over. They need to be spoken to before they themselves can speak. As with all the young, they need to be given an identity by name and relationship within the family. They need to be helped to imitate the sounds of speech by hearing these sounds relative to themselves and the objects of their world. They need to be encouraged to discover themselves through all kinds of expressive motor behavior. They must be spoken to and with even before they are able to respond in kind. Their concrete response to stimulation assigns a priority to what is being done. They cannot be expected to respond to distant perceptions because there is a priority given to proximity. The mother calling the child from another room is not as significant as the sounds of play in which the child is involved. Face-to-face verbal expressions are the most meaningful and guide the slowly developing children toward their recruitment of speech for communication. Until this motivation emerges, special remediation efforts offer poor returns.

The infinite variations of speech stem from the production of consonant sounds. These appear in a definite progression suggesting their relation to development and the acquisition of motor skills. The babbling of infants contains the initial experimentations of modifying the basic vowel sounds by controlled use of the muscles of the larynx, throat, tongue, cheeks, and lips. This experimentation is closely associated with the expressive behavior of eating, crying, smiling, and other affective states. The *m* sound of *ma* incorporates many of the same muscle movements of the smile. There are other similar parallels within infant experiences that make the early affective relationships important to the initial modifications of sound. The heavy reliance on imitative behavior is another early determinant of speech. Thus the use of speech within the procedures for infant care becomes an important aspect of child-rearing, providing many opportunities to the parents of retarded children for making useful contributions to evolving speech patterns.

Remedial speech programs cannot substitute for these initial efforts, nor can they compensate for any deficiencies in the primary relatedness of the young child. They can and do make valuable contributions in the identification of the nature of established speech disorders and provide many useful techniques for corrective interventions. Appropriate timing of these interventions is of the greatest importance. Intervention too early introduces the stress of demand for performance when the essential developmental ingredients for meaningful speech are not present. Intervention too late many alter the circumstances for effective remediation. Experienced speech therapists become important adjuncts to programs for the retarded by their ability to diagnose and intervene at the appropriate time.

READING, WRITING, AND ARITHMETIC

Reading and writing abilities are end points of expressive behavior. They not only represent the organization of perceptual-motor skills but also reflect the total developmental progression of object-relatedness, emotional and environmental experiences, and language formation. The complex determination of these abilities provides the explanation of why so many individuals display deficits and disturbances in them. The retarded by their very nature can be expected to demonstrate a high degree of disorder within these abilities. Most have extensive problems with their visual-motor organization, fine and gross motor coordination, and integrative functions. Often their object-relatedness is subtly impaired, their emotional and environmental experiences are limited, and their thought process remains locked within the earlier stages of concreteness and inadequacy of symbolic representations. These deficits make reading and writing difficult skills to acquire for the retarded. Yet a primary emphasis within all programs in their behalf remains vested in trying to give them these skills. Our failures often result in more heroic efforts or the assumption that these efforts have been attempted too late. Recently there has been a movement toward early interventions through readiness programs, based on the assumption of need for stimulating potential for reading and writing. It is conceivable that these efforts will create their own disturbances, as has been experienced already within some of the Head Start programs where premature advances were discovered to handicap subsequent learning.

Some consideration should be given to the possibilities of late introduction of the retarded to the teaching and learning of reading and writing. This would permit them to approach the demands of these skills at a more appropriate developmental moment when their perceptual-motor system is stabilized, fine and gross motor coordination is established, relatedness and experiences are more meaningful, and needed thought processes more evolved. The retarded are recognized for their deficiencies, but efforts in their behalf sometimes ignore the existence of these deficiencies. This is particularly true in many of the approaches to their training with priority given to teaching writing and reading as if such skills will compensate for their more general retardation. It should be recognized that the achievement of third-grade reading and writing skills permits basic survival within our complex industrial society through recognition of directional signs and the majority of simple written instructions. The achievement of fifth-grade reading and writing skills permits independent coexistence with all of us.

A high percentage of the retarded have numerous difficulties with their visual-motor-perceptual organization that handicap them in recognizing the letters of the alphabet and the sequence of these letters into words. The earliest organization of this perceptual system is in vertical alignment, while many of the symbols and sequence of letters and words are horizontally aligned. The persistence of the vertical dominance as an immaturity of the perceptual organization will limit the ability and speed of recognition of letters and words and sometimes confuse their perception. Ordinarily the progression from the vertical to the horizontal gestalt takes place between five and eight years of age, coinciding with the state of reading readiness. The delay of this progression among the retarded may account for some of their confusion at early demand for letter and word recognition and compound their apparent degree of retardation. The persistence of this and other forms of visual-motor immaturities (rotations, reversals, angulations, foreground-background and spatial distortions, and so on) may make it impossible for the retarded to learn letter and word recognition through visual presentation techniques. They may not be able to recognize or differentiate the printed word. They may have to be taught by phonic (hearing combined with seeing) or by tactile and kinesthetic techniques (touch combined with seeing and hearing by the use of wood, felt, and sandpaper letters). But most of all, they require an appropriate timing to their introduction to the tasks.

Here again, the remedial expert can be invaluable through

the skills of special identifications and interventions. These specialists exist within most communities. They can be found through the local school systems and the many diagnostic and treatment centers for the young. Individual tutorial help under their guidance is an important instrument for training the retarded and may offer better results than prolonged efforts with group instruction. The direct interaction of the tutorial relationship permits immediate recognition of error with correction at the moment of commission. This concrete interchange more accurately approaches the level of thought organization of the retarded and recruits the one-to-one relationship for the needed communication of the symbols, responses, and ideas of reading and writing.

There are many different methods for teaching the intricate processes of reading. Not one of them seems to have universal application, supporting the assumption that reading disabilities are multidetermined and may be the end result of defects in teaching, deficiencies in cognitive stimulation and motivation, and sensory and intellectual deficiencies. The most popular and relatively effective technique of teaching reading is the sight-word method. This emphasizes the importance of content and meaning in reading instructions. The alternative systems include many linguistic and phonic methods grouped together as decoding approaches. These include phonic systems wherein sounds are keyed to specific colors, programmed linguistic workbooks, and the Initial Teaching Alphabet of forty-four symbols that provides a correspondence between sound and printed symbol. The decoding methods involve teaching the child to relate sound to symbol with comprehension following automatically as the child reads the word. Many special programs for the retarded emphasize a multisensory approach stressing the use of several senses, such as auditory, visual, tactile, and kinesthetic in the teaching and learning process.

Also, a number of test batteries have been devised to assist in the construction of psychoeducational profiles for curriculum planning and for the selection of remedial teaching methods. These include the Frostig Developmental Test of Visual Perception, the Illinois Test of Psycholinguistic Abilities, the Wepman Test of Auditory Discrimination, and the Wechsler Intelligence Scale for Children. More and more, teaching of retarded readers is being based on accurate appraisal of specific difficulties, with careful analysis of skills and abilities required to complete the accompanying tasks. Emphasis is shifting to the development of functions and performance with repetition of instruction, reinforcement, and review, while controlling hyperactivity and distractibility.

Specialized techniques include programmed instruction, behavior modification, and perceptual-motor training. Programmed instruction involves specific and clearly defined goals, the analysis of a task into simple components progressing from the most simple to the more complex, and the use of appropriate teaching strategies to meet these goals. Behavior modification employs basic principles of good teaching, giving a meaningful reward, and providing an appropriate degree of teacher control and classroom structure. Perceptual motor training is an essential prerequisite for reading remediation. An application of this approach can be found in the Optometric Extension Program, which emphasizes the role of adequate visual-perceptual development as a basis for cognition and reading and includes a systematic program of perceptual training techniques. Another type of training program involves motor activities, based on the assumption that neurological organization can be altered through physical activities. The Delacato program attempts to achieve neurological reorganization, culminating in cortical dominance, by motor activities, including creeping, crawling, sleeping in a particular position, and preventing the use of the preferred eye, among other planned movements. Many questions have been raised concerning the claimed effectiveness of this program, as well as its diffuse application to so many problems of human development. The relationship between motor and perceptual training and reading has not been established, nor has been the ability to teach perception.

There are many instructional programs and materials having application to the retarded. Descriptions of these are available in a number of handbooks and listings of teaching aids and activities, games, and materials useful for readiness and perceptual training. These can be found in the extensive body of literature on special education. Their use requires careful selection and sensitive assessment of their appropriateness to the particular needs of each child.

The skill of writing links the complexities of perceptual organization with the gross and fine motor achievements of muscle coordination. This combination produces many difficulties with writing for the retarded. They are handicapped in recreating the products of their poorly organized perceptions. These difficulties must be respected within their failures of performance. They require much longer intervals of training, with expectations geared to an awareness of their inadequacies. The early introduction and training in the use of a typewriter becomes a helpful adjunct in overcoming some of their deficiencies in motor coordination. The more profoundly retarded may never come to a level of organization of reading and writing and should be helped with their general rather than specific communicative skills.

The complexities of our society make arithmetic processes and the ability to handle money a more important skill than reading and writing. Most retarded individuals exhibit pronounced defects in their everyday arithmetic dealings and need special efforts to give them some basic skills with handling numbers and concepts. Approaches should be geared to an awareness of their perceptual difficulties in recognizing numbers, their concrete thought organization, and their inability to conceptualize the abstract representation of objects by way of a numerical figure. Serialization and sequence can be handled if there is number recognition. Attempts to move beyond this ordering process to addition and subtraction nearly always runs into the problem of limited abstract thinking, so that the concept is learned by rote and not really comprehended. Rarely is there any major success with efforts that go beyond this point of arithmetical processes.

Arithmetic instructions should be correlated to a step-by-step exposure to numbers representing objects, quantities of objects, and their relationship to different objects. This concrete formulation permits the comprehension of numbers as relevant to many different things, so that the serialization of objects can be used to teach the simple principles of addition and subtraction. Once this level of understanding is achieved, the transition to handling money can be made and some kind of comparative value system encouraged. Too often, major efforts are directed at the complexities of multiplication, division, and fractions as principles of arithmetic without the sound development of the principle of numbers.

PSYCHOTHERAPY

The professional community's practice of discriminating against the retarded has been as extensive as that found in society at large. Too often, the retarded are identified, labeled, and excluded. The exclusion takes the form of keeping them out or expelling them, or of offering programs with special or limited goals. These attitudes assume that the retarded have meager resources requiring such defined objectives or are not able to benefit from the broader aspirations of the available programs. Both approaches fail to recognize the arrests or deviations of developmental progression of the retarded as nothing more than severer forms of developmental disturbances of physical and emotional growth, of intelligence, and of social adjustment. This failure becomes a destructive process to professional and retarded alike. It limits and stunts each by distorting and narrowing objectives, introducing conformity, and inhibiting the humanistic goals that stimulate a dedication to good clinical services for all.

The current utilization of psychiatric services in behalf of the retarded often demonstrates many of the subtleties of these discriminatory practices. Not only is psychiatric consultation sought infrequently but the psychiatric discipline tends to discourage such consultations by its unwillingness to offer treatment services to the retarded and their families. Yet the inherent disturbances of retardation make autism, impulse disorders, depression, symbiosis, anxiety, and maladaptive defenses common problems in the retarded while introducing many disharmonies of relationship within their families. The very nature of retardation mandates a greater utilization of psychiatric judgments and techniques. The rewards of such investments are relief of some of the anxiety and turmoil of inner conflicts, some amelioration of the havoc of developmental arrests, possible decrease of regressive behavior, and the adjustment of essential relationships. These are the ingredients of all psychotherapeutic programs and are needed for the achievement of developmental potential.

Primary disturbances of object-relatedness introduce autistic qualities into the lives of the retarded. They acquire a poor awareness of the world around them and respond more to the stimuli from within themselves. This egocentricity interrupts and distorts their perception of events. It is accompanied by a variability of their performance, so that the constancy of their experiences is weak or lacking, adding further distortions. These special characteristics of autistic behavior have to be identified and interrupted to minimize their devastating impact on early relationships. Regretfully, the profoundly retarded are plagued by these circumstances through most of their existence. Psychiatric techniques are particularly suited for diagnosing and managing the ravages of some of these primary disturbances in object-relatedness. The resulting problems require programs of total intervention, involving combined efforts with other professional disciplines—counseling of families, guidance of child care personnel, consultation with nursery and special education professionals, and periodic readjustment of treatment objectives. In addition to fulfilling a diagnostic, consultative role, the psychiatrist may sometimes be of additional help by direct efforts at relieving some of the conflicts of autistic thinking, of confusions of fantasy and reality, and of the problems of relationships. These objectives remain as relevant treatment goals throughout much of the life of the retarded individual because of the persistence of some of these early disturbances.

All kinds of impulse disorders occur with great frequency. Some are neurologically determined, while many others represent the general lack of organization plaguing the retarded. The resulting variations of perception, behavior, relatedness, and communication need constant identification, with corrections directed at the emerging concepts of self and the acquisition of values from experiences. Awareness of these behaviors and relationships are parts of all programs for the retarded. However, the special efforts of a psychotherapeutic program may add additional dimensions through its supportive and directive nature.

Some depression appears to be significant part of the life-style of all retarded individuals. The immature manifest this depression through a general state of inhibition that interferes with their ability to recruit function for needed behavior and communication. Recognition of the impact of this inhibitory state and helping the retarded individual come to grips with some of its reactive processes can become another part of the psychotherapeutic efforts. Such treatment relationships breach the isolation of autistic thinking, bring order to the inner world of disorganized impulse, and replace the loneliness and inhibition of depression with the stimulation of meaningful treatment contacts.

The universal psychological demand of growing is individuation and separation. Maturation requires the destruction of the old and the creation of and devotion to the new. Anxiety and depression are bred from the potential loss of the known while conflict is generated between the past and future worlds of maturational existence. Here again, planned psychotherapeutic interventions seve to relieve some of the conflicts and pain of this inner plight and lead to an easier coming of age. These conflicts of individuation and separation are intense among the retarded. They are exaggerated by their own developmental problems and by the dependency that their retardation breeds within themselves and encourages others to impose upon them. Few parents or their surrogates can avoid falling prey to making their retarded offspring dependent upon them. A good psychotherapeutic relationship can offer the dependent, immature, or retarded child the opportunity to gain insights into dependency patterns and to experiment with new models of relationship more suitable to current and future needs. This objective of helping individuation and separation is a cornerstone of all treatment and makes psychiatric procedures valuable adjuncts to the many programs for the retarded viewed as therapeutic. Proper utilization of these procedures serves to minimize the distortions and maladaptations to the demands of survival.

An underlying principle of psychotherapy is the application of the knowledge of the dynamics of personality development within a relationship designed to be therapeutic. The interchanges encourage and stimulate the spontaneous expression of attitudes, thoughts, and feelings significant to the patient. They permit the emerging relationship to serve as the catalyst for reactions reflecting some of the inner conflicts while maintaining the boundaries of these reactions. Expressive behavior becomes an important part of the interactions and, with the appropriate responses of the therapist, awareness and insights may emerge that are useful within other more significant relationships. Thought and behavior linked to the inner life of fantasy can be identified and separated from the realities of existence. This kind of reality testing is an important part of psychotherapy with the retarded. Their preservation of earlier forms of thought organization tends to victimize them as they struggle for their identity and relatedness. Frequently they are unaware of this process within themselves and need the opportunity to examine what they are doing with an accepting, nonjudgmental relationship.

There are different forms of expressive behavior. The earliest are nonverbal, followed by activities containing symbolic representations as occurring within play and speech. These permit the recruitment of what is done or said and what takes place for communication of thoughts and feelings. An awareness of their content encourages appropriate responses without the distortions of involved emotional relationships. These different interactions permit the experiencing of emotions under different circumstances so that they need not remain locked to a single response. In this way, a therapeutic relationship can become a learning situation encouraging new modalities of reacting to a given set of emotions or experiences. The catalytic nature of psychotherapy emerges within the changing responses.

The same principles are recruitable in different ways. They can be used within peer interactions of group therapy, within the relationships of family therapy, and within counseling of parents. They may aid the structuring of activities deemed to be therapeutic and stimulate programs responsive to developmental needs. But as with all forms of interventions, the limitations must be recognized as well. Psychotherapy cannot be viewed as a means of overcoming basic deficiencies. It can only minimize distortions. It cannot become a singular effort to the exclusion of other necessary interventions. It must take its place as one of many techniques for helping the retarded.

PARENT COUNSELING

New parents have limited or no experience with child-rearing and undergo varying reactions to the discovery of retardation and the problems of its subsequent management. They are exposed to its many complexities within parent-child, parent-parent, and parent-society relationships, making diagnosis, planning, and support the essential components of counseling. The initial responses of parents are concern, confusion, and the search for cause and cure. The adjustment to the presence of the retardation lies within these responses. The parents are mobilized into action. Consultation is sought and identification becomes possible. Simultaneously, thoughts and feelings are experienced, beginning the gradual process of acclimating to the variations that the retarded bring to the lives of those who care for them. Sometimes these reactions are viewed as disturbance and may not be recruited in a constructive manner by making the concern and confusion a cause as well as an effect. Skillful evaluation and blending facts with understanding and support permit the parents to adjust to the deviations of their offspring as well as their own turmoil. Good counseling sets the stage for problem-solving based on recognition and response to need. It serves to minimize confusion or harmful denial. It breaks through the sense of difference engendered by retardation and limits the accompanying sense of isolation.

Many different professionals are able to fulfill the demands of counseling. Usually the physician is the first to be cast in this role, as the children show developmental lags. By training the physician is devoted most to diagnosis and treatment of physical defect. This does equip the majority of them for the initial responsibilities of identification. However, difficulties with diagnosis, the uncertainties of prognosis, and the limitations of medical treatment restrict the effectiveness of physician within the role of counselor and may even lead to some dissatisfaction with them within long-term management. Many doctors are themselves aware of their own limitations and have come to depend on others to assume the responsibilities for counseling the families of the retarded. The public health nurse, social worker, psychologist, and educator have added their skills to the counseling role. But, as with the physician, they may each fall prey to their own background and orientation. The nurse may tend to emphasize the relief of pain; the social worker may tend to emphasize the understanding of interactions; the psychologist may provide insights to inner turmoil; and the educator may become strongly motivated to train, teach, and correct. Each of these are necessary dimensions but should not exclude the others.

A positive trend within recent years has been the integration of all of these professionals and their points of view into clinical teams at centers devoted to the diagnosis, treatment, and management of retardation. The nature of the disturbances requires a holistic approach, and these clinical teams are more likely to reflect this.

Each developmental stage introduces new circumstances and demands shifting objectives for counseling. The diagnosis of defect and disturbance with attention to the physical and the relatedness must receive priority during infancy. The profoundly retarded continue to require these priorities during most of their lives. Developmental progression brings a new order to parent-child and parent-parent relationship as the emotional climate of the family becomes more significant to the growth of children. Retardation may introduce alterations of attitudes and judgment having significance within child-rearing practices and family equilibrium. Helping to identify and correct some of these alterations eases the weighty responsibilities of parenting the retarded and maintains some of the boundaries for the family. The continuing growth of the children moves them into the community and into a greater visibility. This leads to a shift of emphasis to parent-society relationships, making important the social interactions between people and the institutions of society. The complexities of these processes introduce an infinite variety of problems, rendering counseling as complex as the problems themselves while establishing the parents of the retarded as knowledgeable and themselves capable of fulfilling the counseling role to each other and to the institutions of society.

There is no singular technique or simple formula for counseling the parents of retarded children. Attention must be paid to the needs of the child as well as other members of the family. The immaturity of the retarded makes them vulnerable to everything and makes more situations stressful. Counseling serves to minimize some of these stresses while decreasing the vulnerability of all to the inadequate intelligence of others, their inappropriate emotional reactions, and their lack of social awareness to the problems of retardation.

PARENT ORGANIZATIONS

Parent groups dedicated to the cause of the retarded are a phenomenon of the last twenty-five years and may reflect the industrialization of retardation as much as many other practices. The appearance of these groups was in response to many things. There was an acute lack of community services for retarded children. There was and is a growing popular concern about the deplorable conditions in many state institutions. There was a need for a lobbying force for potential state and federal funding of programs. Also, parents of retarded children had a sense of being neglected by professionals. Some of this sense is rooted within efforts designated as therapeutic. Primary attention is directed at accepting the concept of retardation and then alleviating the accompanying depressive reaction. Clinical findings masking ignorance are designated as confidential and withheld. Some of the unpleasant realities of the concept of retardation have been avoided by interminable referrals. Professional omnipotence within unilateral decision-making procedures has been fostered at the expense of parents. These practices have led to parental disenchantment with existing services and their investment in other strategies in behalf of those designated as retarded. Other factors that have stimulated the organization of parent groups included the growing trend toward organizations of all kinds, a long-established preference for voluntary rather than governmental programs in the health and welfare fields, and a strong humanitarian and philanthropic attitude within the general population.

The earliest local organizations appeared in the 1930s around such issues as school placement and state residential institutions. The American Association on Mental Deficiency began to host members of parent groups at its annual conventions during the 1940s, leading to the founding of the National Association of Parents and Friends of Retarded Children in 1950. By 1951 there were 125 member organizations, with approximately 13,000 active members. In 1952 the current name of National Association for Retarded Children (NARC) was adopted. By 1969 NARC had 1,370 member organizations with approximately 200,000 members. Most of these member organizations have preserved their autonomy in response to their dedication to local needs while participating in the development of a common national policy. Advisory boards or panels are used to recruit the assistance of professionals while preserving the policy-making and management functions of the organizations for its members. There is a heavy reliance on committee functions with major subdivisions directed at residential, education, day care, and rehabilitation services.

These associations were started by parents as compared with the initiation by professional groups of most other health-oriented agencies. They encouraged member participation and multiple rather than single goals, including health as but one of many needs. They represented mutual aid by persons with common problems. They emphasized self-help and parent-members' shared leadership responsibility. They encouraged social action and have done away with the mask of confidentiality. Their object is to recruit themselves and others to the cause of helping those identified as retarded. A discomforting fact is the socioeconomic composition of these organizations. They are primarily middle-class, whereas the majority of retarded persons come from poverty areas. This discrepancy suggests the existence of many reasons for involvement with the stated objectives of the organizations. It can be recognized that they serve some personal reasons, as well as others. They do recruit individuals and much needed support for programs for the retarded. Also, they more distinctly represent the consumer point of view. However, they involve the parents with the direct responsibility for care of the handicapped. They stimulate activity in place of passivity, hopefulness instead of doom, and communal efforts in place of institutional practices. These organizations have created public awareness and improved understanding, experimentation with new approaches, public pressure on government agencies on behalf of the retarded, and specialized services that would not otherwise be available. They have resulted in all kinds of novel and much needed programs that have normalized some of the approaches to the problems of retardation. These include counseling, halfway residences, short-term residential care or respite services, sheltered workshops, vacation programs, leisure-time clubs, training of parents in residential settings, trusteeships, "watchdog" committees on local services, and preschool and day-school programs, among many others.

This involvement of parents in behalf of the welfare of their offspring represents a significant force in dispelling their impotence generated by the concept of retardation. Inherent to this conceptualization of handicap is the designation of the parent as cause and the professional as cure. This separatism is far removed from the reality and may represent a reversal of roles. It has been often stated that backward countries do not identify their retarded population and that their agrarian economy is better able to assimilate this group. It is also possible that they lack the institutional practices and professional body to create a retarded population by identification and exclusion. The essence of involvement with parent organization is giving the parents the curative role and thus allowing parents to become activists, diagnosticians of the retarding effects of some of our institutional practices, and accepting of their children's handicaps without guilt or fear of their consequences.

Information concerning local groups can be obtained easily from the many facilities providing services to the severely handicapped, or directly from the National Association for Retarded Children, 2709 Avenue E East, Arlington, Texas 76010.

COMMUNITY RESOURCES AND PROGRAMS

Many diverse programs have come into existence in response to needs and by legislative mandates. At present, the diversity and complexity of the resources within the community are so great that any attempt to describe them can only make reference to many of them as an indication of patterns and trends. However, a general awareness of what may be available and of their possibilities can be helpful.

The activities of the federal government in behalf of the handicapped, including the retarded, has accelerated dramatically within the last decade. The staff of the Secretary's Committee on Mental Retardation, U.S. Department of Health, Education and Welfare, Washington, D.C. 20201, serves as a focal point for information on all aspects of the department's mental retardation program. The President's Committee on Mental Retardation, Washington, D.C. 20201, was established through the efforts of the late President Kennedy and continues to advise and assist the President on all matters pertaining to mental retardation. The PCMR has a major responsibility for evaluating national, state, and local efforts and for helping coordinate federal activities. It is also involved with facilitating communication between federal, state, and local agencies, as well as informing the public and mobilizing support for related activities. The President's Committee on Employment of the Handicapped, Washington, D.C. 20210, has similar responsibilities with impact on programs for the retarded.

An examination of the activities of the Congress of the United States serves to highlight some of the current trends in behalf of the retarded while giving information for specific help. The Mental Retardation Facilities and Services Amendments of 1966 funded construction of additional mental retardation research centers and university-affiliated facilities for demonstration programs and training of personnel. These facilities now provide multiple diagnostic services and have many different kinds of service projects available. Although far from adequate for the numbers of handicapped requiring their services, these centers are able to handle a sizable group of the retarded requiring special help.

Some of the recent changes in the Social Security laws are important to the retarded and other handicapped individuals. Now benefits are paid to the disabled child of a retired, deceased, or disabled worker if the disability began before age twenty-two instead of eighteen. The amount a Social Security recipient, including a childhood disability recipient, may earn without loss of benefits was raised from $1,600 to $2,100 annually. These and other changes are indicators of significant benefits that are available to the handicapped and their families for their care through Social Security. Similar provisions for the retarded exist within the governmental structure of many other countries as well.

A recent development in the distribution of medical care in the United States has been Medicare and Medicaid. These provide government-financed medical services. Hospital and medical insurance coverage is being extended to Social Security disability beneficiaries and will provide coverage for some 260,000 childhood disability recipients between the ages of eighteen and sixty-five, including some 179,000 who have been diagnosed as mentally retarded. This Medicare coverage begins only after the recipient has received regular disability payments for twenty-four consecutive months. Also, inpatient care in mental institutions for Medicaid-eligible children under twenty-one years of age is now being made available, providing they are involved in an active treatment program. The results of this extension of medical services are yet to be felt. They should, however, provide much needed interventions, and their availability should do much to improve the care of the retarded within their communities and some of the institutions devoted to their care.

By 1974 existing state-operated programs of Old Age Assistance, Aid to the Blind, and Aid to the Permanently and Totally

Disabled will be replaced by a single federally financed and administered program of cash assistance to needy aged, blind, and disabled citizens. Such individuals with no other source of support are guaranteed a monthly income of $130 for an individual and $195 for a couple. The first $20 of Social Security benefits or any other income each month will be disregarded in determining benefits under the program. An additional disregard of $65 of earned income plus one-half of all earnings above that amount will be allowed in order to encourage recipients to work, when possible. The current definition of disability as applicable to these benefits is "inability to engage in any substantial gainful activity by reason of any medically determined physical or mental impairment which . . . can be expected to last for a continuous period of not less than twelve months (or, in the case of a child under the age of eighteen, if he suffers from any medically determinable physical or mental impairment of comparable severity)." One important new feature is that needy children of all ages will be eligible for benefits, although the resources of the parents will be considered in determining eligibility of an applicant under twenty-one years of age. Individuals residing in public institutions are not eligible for this assistance. Here again, this basic assurance of financial support of the permanently disabled makes possible constructive planning for their care.

Other legislative changes are assuring the inclusion of the retarded in more general programs. Intermediate care benefits have been extended to the mentally retarded in institutions provided that the primary purpose of the institution is the provision of health or rehabilitative services to retarded individuals. Special preference in bidding on government contracts to workshops for the severely handicapped has been extended to include the retarded as well as the blind. Not less than 10 percent of Headstart enrollment opportunities now must be made available to handicapped children in response to the general practice of excluding handicapped children in the past. There is a new program of Small Business Administration loans and loan guarantees for handicapped individuals and public and private organizations operating in their interest. These and similar enactments indicate a growing and much desired trend to assure the inclusion of the handicapped within existing programs. For it is only by such assurance that their place within the community can be preserved and their rights to an equal opportunity be guaranteed. Those of us committed to helping the retarded must utilize these resources within the development of supportive community programs in their behalf.

Traditionally, state governments have assumed the major responsibility of residential care facilities for the retarded. This pattern had many reasons for coming into existence, but a singular result was a general trend to separate the retarded from the communities of their origins. Nearly all of our institutions for residential care have been located unrelated to the needs of their residents until quite recently. Most often, they were placed in removed areas, ostensibly to protect their vulnerable inhabitants while actually eliminating them from visibility and isolating them among strangers. In many instances, artificial communities were constructed that were incapable of their own economic or social survival, thus creating their own particular demand for growth by acquiring more retarded individuals. The result of this process has been large state institutions devoted equally to the thousands needing care and the other thousands whose livelihoods depended on rendering the care. Both groups not only became dependent on each other but emerged as dependent on the institutional practices to which they were related by diagnosis or job. This unnatural relationship served to depersonalize producer and consumer and make a commodity out of the retarded individual requiring the supportive effort of residential care.

The depersonalization of the producer was shown in the

ever-expanding size of some of the institutions for the care of the retarded; the use of architectural designs that denied the individuality of their residents; the application of mass-production technology to management; and personnel practices that made everyone replaceable and impersonal. The depersonalization of the consumer emerged within the dissociation of the general public from the life-style of the retarded and the institutions devoted to their care; the ignorance and detachment from the problems of retardation; and the practice of abandonment of retarded individuals to institutional care. But most important was the depersonalization of the individuals, who became labeled as retarded as a result of their combination of defect and immaturity. They could be given less rather than more. They could be isolated and moved about according to the needs of others. They could be pushed into a subculture known as mental retardation.

Fortunately for all, this trend is slowly reversing as the result of the combined efforts of producer, consumer, and commodity. Government agencies on all levels and professionals devoted to the care of the retarded have begun to respond to the demands of the general public and to the needs of its retarded members. Large institutions are no longer in vogue, although they are still the major resource for residential care of the retarded. Fewer individuals are being relegated to them. Priorities have been shifting to supportive services for the families of the retarded, community-based programs, the relocation of residential care facilities within the communities of origin, building designs and locations reflecting living rather than existing, and ancillary programs encouraging productive and social coexistence. State governmental agencies are beginning to devote more of their resources to the support of diversified programs rather than the singular responsibility of residential care. In conjunction with local communities, they are developing resources for the diagnosis and treatment of defects, for special education and vocational training, for socially productive lives for the handicapped, and for varied living arrangements.

This change in orientation is progressing at different rates and taking many forms within each state and country. It has resulted in a burgeoning of designs of programs responding to local circumstances. It is beyond the scope of this presentation to describe all of these different variations. However, their appearance represents a healthy transition toward the "normalization" of designs and projects in behalf of the retarded. They include such diversified efforts as small residential facilities for the profoundly retarded in close proximity to the diagnostic and treatment resources of hospitals, residences attached to special schools and rehabilitation centers, sheltered workshops, foster-care services, preventative child welfare programs, special adoption services for hard-to-place physically and mentally handicapped youngsters, foster grandparent programs, preschool nurseries for the handicapped child, group residences and halfway homes for the retarded adolescent and adult, leisure activities programs, travel and camping experiences, and many others. These efforts are beginning to extend through the entire range of current social experiences, bringing the retarded back into the mainstream of the life process where they belong by reason of their developmental needs for relatedness, stimulation, and productive existence.

These programs are sparsely distributed as yet and are not readily available to the numbers requiring them. In many areas they need to be formulated, designed, and developed. They all require the support and cooperation of the families of the retarded, their parent organizations, and the state and local officials who are able to provide the necessary governmental aid. Those that do exist can be found through local organizations in behalf of the disabled, the voluntary agencies within the communities, and the various governmental agencies that have the delegated responsibilities for helping the retarded and their families.

RESIDENTIAL CARE

Some of the special characteristics of retardation and family life-styles make residential care a necessary intervention. The effects of certain types of developmental defects are so profound that they cannot be managed within the community except at great expense to the handicapped and their families. Our transition to an urban society has further compounded the problem by decreasing the space and circumstances for coexistence with defect. Economic and social changes have moved the majority of adults, both male and female, out of the home and into the working community. Few families can survive without accepting this movement. These and other combinations of events—the single-parent family, poverty amid plenty, population mobility, changing cultural values—have all contributed to the need for residential facilities. They are required equally by our physically handicapped, who are unable to meet the demands for survival in a complicated society; by our emotionally handicapped, who cannot handle the stresses of coexistence with others; by our socially disabled, who have difficulties with the commonly derived values of society; and by our intellectually retarded, who cannot master easily the complexities of modern-day living.

The decision to seek residential care is a highly individualized one. There can be few generalizations. In the majority of instances, this decision is reached through necessity. The critical issue is whose necessity. Wherever possible, it should be determined in response to the needs of the individual requiring the residential care. When the severely handicapped can be helped to survive and exist less painfully in a residential facility designed for their appropriate care, there should be little question about such utilization. Most of the profoundly retarded have major physical defects that need constant attention and disrupt individual attempts to help them exist. Their residential care within settings designed to minister to their special requirements becomes a humane resolution of the problem of their survival. Such facilities require appropriate medical and nursing services. However, the plight of any of the profoundly retarded is great, and so they cannot be abandoned to impersonal care, and require the liaison of devotion of family and community with the professional devotion of the caring personnel. Out of this union comes the moral climate for dedication to the higher purposes of life and respect for each other's existence.

For most other retarded individuals, the decision of placement emerges out of the combination of their needs with the needs of others. A substantial number require order, a protected and structured existence, special training and education, and supportive services that are unavailable to them outside a well-organized residential facility. These can also benefit from a planned exposure to the social process of supervised group living. The utilization of the residential facility with these objectives becomes therapeutic and habilitative.

Regretfully, too large a group of handicapped individuals is referred to residential facilities because of the inadequacies of community resources and the inability of their families to provide the necessary supportive efforts for their proper development without supplemental aid. It is this group to which our community programs must respond. It makes up the largest segment of the population identified as retarded. It represents the group that benefits least from residential care and diverts many facilities from carrying out their objectives because of overcrowding and diversion to tasks and responsibilities that can be better met by others within the community.

Residential care should be recognized as serving multiple

purposes. The profoundly retarded often require long-term, chronic residential care. The mildly and moderately retarded require intermediate long- and short-term residential care. The mildly retarded often have a need for intermittent short-term residential care. Only in recent years has the concept of intermittent short-term care become recognized as a valuable adjunct to the management of the retarded, and a device for giving special experiences to them and aid to their families. It can be built into vacation programs, respite services, leisure-time clubs, and training of parents and children in residential settings. The concepts of stimulation and relief from stresses can be served simultaneously by short periods of separation, making intermittent care away from family and community an effective means of helping the retarded move toward independent existence. Supervised travel and camping groups lend themselves well to short-term care. There is a directory of camps for the handicapped available from the American Camping Association. Additional information about camping and residential facilities can be obtained from the National Association for Retarded Children. There is an annual Directory for Exceptional Children published by Porter Sargent that lists most of the public and private facilities.

Another aspect of residential care exists within programs of foster homes and halfway residences. These programs not only provide resources for housing the retarded within their communities but also permit their therapeutic recruitment for the necessary process of individuation and separation from the dependent child-parent relationships that come with developmental defect and immaturities. It becomes apparent that identification of the particular needs of each retarded individual should serve as the basis for the decision for residential care.

LEGAL RIGHTS

The identification of a segment of the population as retarded has created a multitude of legal issues for this group, as well as for society. It has introduced the questions of competence, responsibility, and special rights. The complex problems of competency extend into every area of living—consent for sterilization, the right to surrender a child for adoption, to sue or be sued, to enter into a contractual agreement, to make a will, to hold a driver's license, to vote, the validity of marriages and the grounds for divorce, and many others.

It has also extended to special treatment under criminal law. An outstanding example of this can be found within the State of Maryland's Defective Delinquency law. In 1951 Maryland's State Legislature passed a law defining a defective delinquent as "an individual who by the demonstration of persistent aggravated antisocial or criminal behavior, evidences a propensity towards criminal activity, and who is found to have either such intellectual deficiency or emotional unbalance or both, as to clearly demonstrate an actual danger to society so as to require confinement and treatment, when appropriate, as may make it reasonably safe for society to terminate the confinement and treatment." This was followed in 1955 by the establishment of an institution devoted solely to treating "this disease" created by law—the Patuxent Institution in Jessup, Maryland. It introduced the concept of indeterminate sentences and mandatory rehabilitation of defect within a penal system. The procedure under this law involved being convicted and sentenced in the usual way, followed by an examination to determine whether or not the individual could be diagnosed as a defective delinquent. Obviously, the designation of an offender as defective is extremely arbitrary. Defective in what? Intelligence? Nurturing? Emotional growth? Physical endowment? Social values?

These same questions plague our entire judicial procedure relative to pleas of insanity and have led to the current proposal for revision of the federal criminal code by President Nixon, calling for the abolition of the insanity defense. This proposal would provide that mental disease or defect does not constitute a defense against federal crimes unless the defendent "lacked the state of mind required as an element of the offense charged." The state of mind required is defined as criminal intent and allows for professional testimony on the alleged offender's capability to exercise that intent.

The original criteria for a criminal defense by reason of insanity evolved from the M'Naughten rule propounded in the British House of Lords in 1843. This rule provided that a defendant had to be suffering from disease of the mind so as not to know the nature and quality of the involved act or the wrongdoing. A recent American Law Institute's revision of this concept proposed: "A person is not responsible for criminal conduct if at the time of such conduct, as a result of mental disease or defect, he lacked substantial capacity either to appreciate the wrongfulness of his conduct or to conform his conduct to the requirements of law."

The mentally handicapped have been plagued as well as aided by the special legal categorization of their defects. They have been subjected to trial and judgment without benefit of jury, indeterminate sentencing, indefinite detention for therapeutic purposes without assurance of treatment, and other forms of denial of due process. However, the most far-reaching consequence of this separatism rooted in the protection of the rights of British Lords of the nineteenth century has been the development of a two-class legal system extending into every facet of jurisprudence. In today's society, the judgment of retardation may evoke discrimination as well as sympathetic consideration. It may deprive the already deprived. It establishes an ill-defined set of criteria for classifying individuals in the eyes of the law, while permitting their exclusion from the protection of the main body of the law. Within this context, the defective delinquent came into being, as did special laws for sterilization of the retarded, as well as other questionable practices. Decision-making has come to be equated with such judgments as the source, nature, and degree of retardation, with social class serving often to distort the decisions. To be judged handicapped by retardation is one thing. To be judged as defective, poor, and of a minority population group invariably leads to exclusion from the community in some form of institutional setting with a grave prognosis warranting minimal efforts at rehabilitation.

The impairment of ability and capacity to adapt to the demands of society among the retarded places them at a disadvantage within such a climate of jurisprudence. This requires a protective attitude by those devoted to their care. The infant-child's right to the nurturing climate of family must be preserved. This raises questions concerning the constant assaults on our public assistance programs. In 1972, 15,071,000 individuals were recipients of $19,097,688,000. This represented an annual expenditure of $1,270 per individual. Aid to families with dependent children involved more than two-thirds of this public assistance, with 10.9 million in this category, of which 7.9 million were children. Aid to the permanently and totally disabled involved an additional 1.1 million, with aid to the blind totaling another 81,000. Old-age assistance was given to another 2 million. (The source of this information is the Social and Rehabilitation Service, H.E.W., as reported in *The New York Times*, January 7, 1973.) These figures on public assistance suggest a need to reinforce the ancillary and supportive services for caring for children within their families and communities while recruiting and strengthening the family courts in a guardianship role. These figures also support the concept of developing a child advocacy program as a primary prevention of disability among children.

Special mention needs to be made of child abuse and the rights of children to be protected from severe physical and emotional damage. In a growing climate of violence of all kinds, only recently has our society become aware of a major violence against its helpless and dependent young. The reporting system coming from recent legislation on child abuse has revealed the frightening disclosure of thousands of children who are being seriously damaged each year. Yet relatively little constructive action has been taken to protect them from this abuse. These battered children require an effective guardianship program wherever they reside. Their needs are often recognized and then ignored. The retarded infant-child is specially prone to abuse and battering. Their defective response system makes their behavior difficult to interpret and their care easily frustrating. These become the ingredients of a breakdown in relationships between them and their caring adults and contributes to their vulnerability to further damage.

The issues of protective care of the young retarded are many and complex. They involve the very complicated social and legal structure for care of dependent children within their families as well as child-caring facilities. All of the associated problems are compounded by their developmental retardation. So many of the laws concerning the accompanying practices have emerged in response to protecting the rights and values of family, and yet the need to protect the children has become an overriding concern in this day of fragmenting families and fluid community structure. The number of children being abandoned or excluded from their families, partially or completely, appears to be increasing. This raises many legal questions concerning their care within foster homes and child-caring facilities and challenges some of our practices of preserving family ties in the face of partial abandonment. It poses problems relative to our adoption procedures and increases the number of hard-to-place children. The identification of young children as retarded handicaps them further when they are surrendered for adoption. They are placed in a special class and often relegated to the more impersonal care of the institutional setting. They tend to become permanent wards of the state and subjected to a system of care that breeds a sense of impermanence. Within this context, one wonders whether the concept of retardation becomes punitive, since it tends to deprive those who are so identified of the intimate, nurturing relationship they so desperately need during their early formative years.

There are special problems surrounding the profoundly retarded who require the institutional setting to meet their severe degree of handicap and particular defects. Only too often they are placed in "special" settings for the purposes of management and treatment and then deprived of their basic rights by the inadequacies of funding and programs. This pattern of segregation of the retarded into special and often depriving settings raises the question of the validity of their existence. Perhaps the needs of the profoundly retarded might be better met if they were interspersed with all other chronically handicapped individuals. However, the existing pattern of their care within institutions for the retarded requires that their rights to adequate treatment be protected. In recent years, a number of legal actions with the objective of achieving this have been launched by parent and civil rights groups. These legal maneuvers have served to highlight many of the issues of social attitudes toward the retarded, as well as the adequacies of our approaches to their problems. These actions must be continued in order to recruit the existing judicial apparatus for the resolution of the difficulties posed by their handicaps.

This kind of recruitment raises additional questions of the existence and role of parent groups, watchdog committees, citizens' task forces, citizen participation within governmental departments, patient or resident participation in programs, boards of visitors, citizen boards of appeals for grievances, the use of volunteers, and others. It challenges many long-established practices and creates new problems relative to intake, management, and discharge policies, which always have been within the province of the professional responsibility. The legal issues of medical responsibility and confidentiality of clinical records are extensive. The resolution of the many conflicts posed by this changing pattern of community to institution may depend ultimately on legal actions within our court system.

The nature of our social organization moves the child out of the family and into the school for a major portion of his young life. Many of the same problems are reproduced within this institutional setting for those identified as retarded. Their encapsulation within special programs has led to some deprivation as well as exclusionary practices. Many educational programs for the retarded are inadequate for the numbers so identified. This leads to their exclusion from the benefits of training and education within our school systems. It has been estimated that as many as half a million children in our country are excluded from school each day because they are unable to benefit from the existing programs. These exclusionary practices represent a parallel to some of the uses of residential institutions for the retarded. Here again, the rights to education and training may be violated and legal actions may have to be taken to assure a basic privilege of citizenship—the right to education.

Adolescence—that transitional period between the dependent state of childhood and the independent state of adulthood—is always prolonged for the retarded. This prolongation magnifies all of the expected difficulties of this stage of life and brings many retarded adolescents to the attention of our courts. The rate of delinquency peaks at the age of seventeen years—halfway between the end of compulsory education at sixteen years and acceptance within the labor force at eighteen years, when industry feels comfortable with the presence of the "young adult." Retarded adolescents lose out at both ends. Many are permitted to drop out or be withdrawn from school before the age of sixteen years because they "cannot benefit" from the existing educational program. Many others are not acceptable within industry because they are prejudged as incompetent. This exclusion makes them vulnerable to the many social phenomena of adolescence which are sometimes viewed as predelinquent or semidelinquent by others. They tend to be followers in the experimentations with living and, because of their immaturities and poor judgments, tend to be the more visible and the ones most likely to be caught. Careful assessment of their needs becomes as important as judgment of their actions when confronted with their violation of the laws of the land. They do not need any special body of regulations so much as acceptance of their handicaps. Their legal defense must rest with those who recognize their needs and with a continuing assault on the lack of training and work experiences available to them.

For the retarded the right to work is an area in which they have been long discriminated against. It is here that the judgment of their competence and responsibility has led to major discriminatory practices. This kind of exclusion has resulted in the exaggeration of their dependent status. Only in recent years have their rights to equal opportunity been acknowledged and begun to be protected by legislative action and by work programs designed to fit their special abilities. Legal actions to assure them to their right to work may be necessary as attempts are made to reduce the population of our institutions. These are some of the social legal questions requiring our attention.

There are many individual legal issues relative to the retarded that vary with their circumstances and those of their families. These cannot be dealt with in any general form. They can best be responded to by expert legal advice. The associations for retarded children can frequently recommend competent sources of help and counsel on the structure of wills and the establishing of trusts and guardianships. The legal aid societies can often provide special counsel for a variety of these and other problems. Also, many of our voluntary and governmental agencies are able to offer expert advice on the many legal procedures involving their own special areas of competence.

The range of the problems of legal rights of the retarded is as broad as the body of laws that governs us. As with the other aspects of their needs, the special nature of their legal problems evolves from society's concept of retardation. If we do away with this obsolete concept, the retarded's needs become the same as everyone else's—the right to exist, to grow, to achieve one's potential, and to have equal opportunity.

Selected Bibliography

HISTORICAL PERSPECTIVES

Personality in the Making: The Midcentury White House Conference on Children and Youth. Helen Leland Witmer and Ruth Kotinsky, eds. New York: Harper & Brothers, 1952.

Action for Mental Health: Final Report of the Joint Commission on Mental Illness and Health. New York: Basic Books, 1961.

Centuries of Childhood: A Social History of Family Life. Philippe Ariès. New York: Alfred A. Knopf, 1962.

Message from the President of the United States Relative to Mental Illness and Mental Retardation. House of Representatives, 88th Cong., lst sess., document no. 58. February 5, 1963.

The President's Panel on Mental Retardation. Report of the Task Force on Law. January 1963.

SELECTED BIBLIOGRAPHY

A History of the Care and Study of the Mentally Retarded. Leo Kanner, M.D. Springfield: Charles C. Thomas, 1964.

The Child and the Republic: The Dawn of Modern American Child Nurture. Bernard Wishy. Philadelphia: University of Pennsylvania Press, 1968.

The Irony of Early School Reform. Michael B. Katz. Cambridge: Harvard University Press, 1968.

Innovation in Education: New Directions for the American School. The Research and Policy Committee of the Committee for Economic Development, July 1968.

Crisis in Child Mental Health: Challenge for the 1970's. Report of the Joint Commission on Mental Health of Children. New York: Harper & Row, 1969.

Children and Youth in America: A Documentary History. Robert H. Bremner, ed. Cambridge: Harvard University Press, 1970.

Children and Mental Health Centers: Programs, Problems, Prospects. Raymond M. Glasscote et al. Washington, D.C.: Joint Information Service of the American Psychiatric Association and the National Association for Mental Health, 1972.

Children's Rights: Towards the Liberation of the Child. Paul Adams et al. London: Panther Books, 1972.

The Rights of Children: Emergent Concepts in Law and Society. Albert E. Wilkerson, ed. Philadelphia: Temple University Press, 1973.

DEVELOPMENT

Introductory Lectures on Psychoanalysis. Sigmund Freud. London: Allen & Unwin, 1922.

The Trauma of Birth. Otto Rank. New York: Harcourt, Brace and Co., 1929.

Developmental Diagnosis: Normal and Abnormal Child Development. Arnold L. Gesell, M.D., and Catherine S. Amatruda, M.D. New York: Paul B. Hoeber, 1941.

Infant and Child in the Culture of Today. Arnold L. Gesell and Frances L. Ilg. New York: Harper & Brothers, 1943.

Infancy and Human Growth. Arnold L. Gesell. New York: Harper & Brothers, 1946.

The First Five Years of Life. Arnold L. Gesell. New York: Harper & Brothers, 1948.

The Image and Appearance of the Human Body. Paul Schilder, M.D. New York: International Universities Press, 1950.

SELECTED BIBLIOGRAPHY

Trauma, Growth and Personality. Phyllis Greenacre. New York: W. W. Norton, 1952.

The Origins of Intelligence in Children. Jean Piaget. New York: International Universities Press, 1952.

The Construction of Reality in the Child. Jean Piaget. New York: Basic Books, 1954.

The Growth of Logical Thinking from Child to Adolescence. Bäubel Inhelder and Jean Piaget. New York: Basic Books, 1958.

Education and Physical Growth. J. M. Tanner, M.D., D.Sc. New York: International Universities Press, 1961.

Prenatal Influences. Ashley Montagu, Ph.D. Springfield, Illinois: Charles C. Thomas, 1962.

Cerebral Function in Infancy and Childhood. Albrecht Peiper, M.D. New York: Consultants Bureau, 1963.

Modern Perspectives in Child Development. Albert J. Solnit and Sally A. Provence, eds. New York: International Universities Press, 1963.

Contributions to Developmental Neuropsychiatry. Paul Schilder, M.D. (Lauretta Bender, M.D., ed.) New York: International Universities Press, 1964.

Intelligence and Affectivity in Early Childhood: An Experimental Study of Jean Piaget's Object Concept and Object Relations. Thérèse Gouin Decarie. New York: International Universities Press, 1965.

The First Year of Life: A Psychoanalytic Study of Normal and Deviant Development of Object Relations. René A. Spitz. New York: International Universities Press, 1965.

Maternal Care and Mental Health. John Bowlby. *Deprivation of Maternal Care: A Reassessment of Its Effects.* Mary D. Ainsworth et al. New York: Schocken Books, 1966.

Behavior in Infancy and Early Childhood: A Book of Readings. Yvonne Brackbill and George G. Thompson, eds. New York: The Free Press, 1967.

Theories of Child Development. Alfred L. Baldwin. New York: John Wiley & Sons, 1967.

Early Child Care: The New Perspectives. Caroline A. Chandler, Reginald S. Lourie, and Anne De Huff Peters. (Laura L. Dittmann, ed.) New York: Atherton Press, 1968.

On Human Symbiosis and the Vicissitudes of Individuation. Vol. 1, *Infantile Psychosis.* Margaret S. Mahler, M.D., in collaboration with Manuel Furer, M.D. New York: International Universities Press, 1968.

Malnutrition, Learning and Behavior. N. S. Scrimshaw and E. Gordon, eds. Cambridge: M.I.T. Press, 1968.

SELECTED BIBLIOGRAPHY

Disadvantaged Children: Health, Nutrition and School Failure, Herbert G. Birch, M.D., Ph.D., and Joan Dye Gussow. New York: Grune & Stratton, 1970.

RETARDATION

A Manual on Terminology and Classification in Mental Retardation: A Monograph Supplement to the American Journal of Mental Deficiency (2nd ed.), 1961.

The Mentally Disabled and the Law: The Report of the American Bar Foundation on the Rights of the Mentally Ill. Frank T. Lindman and Donald McIntyre, Jr., eds. Chicago: The University of Chicago Press, 1961.

Caring for Your Disabled Child. Benjamin Spock, M.D., and Marion O. Lerrigo, Ph.D. New York: The Macmillan Company, 1965.

International Classification of Disease (8th ed.). World Health Organization, 1965.

Mental Deficiency: The Changing Outlook (rev. ed.). Ann M. Clarke and A. D. B. Clarke, eds. New York: The Free Press, 1965.

Mental Retardation: A Handbook for the Primary Physician. Report of the American Medical Association Conference on Mental Retardation, Chicago, 1964. Chicago: American Medical Association, 1965.

Teaching the Troubled Child. George T. Donahue, Ed.D., and Sol Nichtern, M.D. New York: The Free Press, 1965.

Prevention and Treatment of Mental Retardation. Irving Philips, ed. New York: Basic Books, 1966.

Early Childhood Autism: Clinical, Educational and Social Aspects. J. K. Wing, ed. London: Pergamon Press, 1966.

Mental Impairment and Legal Incompetency. Richard C. Allan, Elyce Zenoff Ferster, and Henry Weihofen. Englewood Cliffs, N.J.: Prentice-Hall, 1968.

Mental Retardation: An Annual Review. Vols. I–IV. Joseph Wortis, M.D., ed. New York: Grune & Stratton, 1969–1972.

Psychiatric Approaches to Mental Retardation. Frank J Menolascino, ed. New York: Basic Books, 1970.

The Mentally Retarded Child and His Faily: A Multidisciplinary Handbook. Richard Koch, M.D., and James C. Dobson, Ph.D., eds. New York: Brunner/Mazel, 1971.

Behavior Modification in Mental Retardation. William J. Gardner. Chicago: Aldine, 1971.

SELECTED BIBLIOGRAPHY

Mental Retardation Publications of the Department of Health, Education, and Welfare, U.S. Department of Health, Education and Welfare, May 1971.

Standards for Residential Facilities for the Mentally Retarded. Joint Commission on Accreditation of Hospitals, 1971.

Mental Retardation and Its Social Dimensions. Margaret Adams. New York: Columbia University Press, 1971.

"Classification of Mental Retardation." Supplement to the *American Journal of Psychiatry*, vol. 128, no. 11, May 1972.

92nd Congress: Federal Legislation Affecting the Mentally Retarded and Other Handicapped Persons. National Association of Coordinators of State Programs for the Mentally Retarded, Inc., February 1973.

Human Sexuality and the Mentally Retarded, Felix F. de la Cruz and Gerald D. La Veck, eds. New York: Brunner/Mazel, 1973.

Mental Retardation and Developmental Disabilities: An Annual Review. Vol. V, J. Wortis, M.D., ed. New York: Brunner/Mazel, 1973.

Standards for Community Agencies Serving Persons with Mental Retardation and Other Developmental Disabilities. Accreditation Council for Facilities for the Mentally Retarded, Joint Commission on Accreditation of Hospitals. Chicago: Joint Commission on Accreditation of Hospitals, 1973.

Manual on Terminology and Classification in Mental Retardation (rev. ed.). Herbert J. Grossman, M.D., ed. The American Association on Mental Deficiency, 1973.

Biographical Note

Sol Nichtern, a prominent child psychiatrist and former pediatrician, has devoted thirty years of his professional life to the care of children and their families. He is a graduate of New York University and earned his medical degree from the Chicago Medical School. He received his psychiatric training at Bellevue Psychiatric Hospital, New York, where he became the psychiatrist-in-charge of the internationally renowned in-patient services for children. Dr. Nichtern has invested much of his career in research, training, and the development of programs for children as well as the private practice of child and adolescent psychiatry. He is the former Clinical and Re search Director of the League School for Seriously Emotionally Dis turbed Children, Brooklyn, New York, and the Nassau Center for Emotionally Disturbed Children, Woodbury, New York. He designed the Elmont School District's "teacher-mom" program for the care of emotionally disturbed children, which received the Silver Mental Health Achievement Award of the American Psychiatric Association. Dr. Nichtern is also a former President of the New York Council on Child Psychiatry and former Director of Child and Adolescent Psychiatry of Hillside Hospital, New York, where he developed a training program in child psychiatry. He is presently Director of Psychiatric Services of the Jewish Child Care Association of New York, Assistant Clinical Professor of Psychiatry at the New York Medical College, and Special Instructor in Child Psychiatry at the Mount Sinai Hospital Services–City Hospital Center at Elmhurst, New York. Dr. Nichtern has published numerous professional papers, coauthored the book *Teaching the Troubled Child*, edited the book *Mental Health Services for Adolescence*, and is currently working on a textbook in child psychiatry.

Index

Index

Index

Index

development

personality development
(Erikson)

— —

brain, nervous
system
blindness
retardation — —

psych.
child psych
(devel.)
psychoanalysis
— —
learning
language
(thought)
Intelligence
+
biology
physiology
emotions